Author

Your

Life

Become the Hero of Your Story

David McCrae

Cover Design: Paulo Duelli
Paperback ISBN: 9781726624268
1st Edition, December 2018

To Laura,

Our stories are not written for us, they are written by us. I hope this book helps you write your story.

Author Your Life

David

In memory of my dad, Jim McCrae, whose end was my beginning.

21/07/1939 - 24/07/2015

This book is dedicated to my stepdad, Andrew Owen, who passed during its writing.

31/08/1950 - 12/11/2017

Notes on Good Reading

In this book I have prided myself on showcasing the science and research behind the points I'm making. This is one of the foundational principles behind my work. I hold a science degree and I understand how to interpret academic material and present it in a non-academic manner.

I believe this makes me stand out from others in the personal development industry but this by no means makes me a "guru". Science is fallible, just like everything else in life, and it has shortcomings. Below I've listed three of the major pitfalls of research findings and why you should approach this book, just like any other, with a sceptical mind and thoughtful consideration.

1: Correlation Does Not Equal Causation

If you have ever read a newspaper, magazine, online article or blog, you have definitely been suckered by this one. Have you ever seen a title such as:

"Eating Bacon Linked to Heart Disease"
"Children Born in September get the Best Grades"
"Self-Harmers Shown to Have Higher Social Media Use"

Such titles show correlation, not causation. Correlation simply means seeing a relationship between two variables. If you examine all the variables in the world, you can find a correlation for *anything*. For example:

- "Increase in Ice Cream Sales is Associated with a Rise in Shark Attacks"
- "A Reduction in the Number of Pirates is Linked to Rise in Global Temperature"
- "Eating Less Margarine can Reduce Your Chance of Divorce (if you live in Maine)"

The reason why you can create such ridiculous associations is because correlational studies do not control the variables, they only observe them. Therefore, they can't say for sure that one variable causes the other. For example eating bacon may well cause heart disease, but it might actually be the eggs that someone eats it with, or the bread, or the tomato ketchup.

You can only imply causation if you do a controlled experiment, where you manipulate a particular variable whilst trying to keep other variables consistent. If you standardise the diets of two groups of people, where you make them eat exactly the same meals, but one group eats twice as much bacon, then you can start to measure whether bacon causes heart disease.

If a study doesn't tell you how they controlled the variables, then you can assume that it was a correlational study, not a causational study, and whatever findings they report should be taken with a pinch of salt.

In this book you will find both correlational and causational studies. Correlational studies are useful, and they further inform the progress of science, but they cannot prove anything.

2: Relative Change vs. Absolute Change

Imagine two foreman in different departments of a business. At the end of the month, they each report to their regional manager how much they've increased production since last month.

The first foreman says: "Since last month, production has increased by 100%".

"What?" The regional manager snarls. "100%? Get the hell out of my office?"

The second foreman enters the office and reports: "Since last month, production has increased by 1%"

"Excellent," the regional manager responds, "keep up the good work."

Why did the regional manager react in this way?

They were annoyed at the first foreman because the previous month he had produced one widget. This had increased by 100% this month to two.

They were pleased with the second foreman because the previous month they had produced a 1,000,000 widgets. This had increased by 1%, meaning an extra 10,000 widgets had been produced this month.

This is the distinction between *relative* and *absolute* change. Relatively speaking, the first foreman had doubled his production. But in absolute terms he had only produced one extra widget.

Relative change can be reported to make the effect of something seem larger than it is. Beware whenever you hear relative terms such as "higher/lower", "faster/slower", "longer/shorter". Do these terms represent significant absolute change, or minuscule relative change? With small numbers, percentage changes seem more impressive. For this reason, always take large percentage changes with a pinch of salt.

In fact, it is smaller percentage changes that can bring more cause for optimism, as they can actually represent good absolute changes. For example, if the second foreman in our scenario was to increase production by "only" 10%, then they would be producing 100,000 extra widgets in absolute terms.

In this book I will report both percentage changes and absolute changes, but a percentage change doesn't necessarily mean that we can get excited about the findings.

3: Averages Create Mediocre Results

You are sitting in a bar with fifty other people. The door opens and in walks Bill Gates. What is the average net worth of each person in the bar?

It's over $1 billion each.

Averages are skewed even by variables less extreme than Bill Gates. Let's imagine you test a drug on eight people to improve the symptoms of a medical condition. After a six week treatment, you measure the change in the severity of their symptoms.

Person 1: 5% worse
Person 2: 10% worse
Person 3: 15% worse
Person 4: 20% worse
Person 5: 15% better
Person 6: 25% better

Person 7: 25% better

Person 8: 30% better

What is the average effect of this drug? On average, patients in this trial report a 5.6% improvement in symptoms. Sounds good right?

Not when you look at the individual results it doesn't. Four participants — half of the group — got *worse* after the six weeks of treatment. But that inconvenient truth gets hidden in the averaging.

Most studies will report an average result. When you are measuring multiple participants, you have to make sense of the results somehow. Unfortunately, averaging is not a foolproof way of doing so.

In this book I will report averages. Averages can be useful to get a broad overview of a concept, but sometimes important information can get lost as a result.

Be Your Own Scientist

As you read this book, be mindful of the limitations of science. Learn to scrutinise the findings that are presented to you. Every time I make reference to the work or research of someone else, I will indicate so with a number in brackets (#). You can then turn to the back of the book and find the book, research journal, website or video I retrieved that information from in the Endnotes section.

When you encounter a finding that interests you, I would encourage you to find the source material and investigate further yourself. Don't take my word for it or anyone else's word for it. Do the research yourself and form your own conclusions.

Remember also where the biases in data reporting come from…it's the scientists themselves. The data doesn't lie but the interpretation of it can be altered. Scientists want to secure future research grants and validate their own work and beliefs. They want the outcomes of their research to be positive. There are safeguards in the scientific process to protect against the bias, but always keep in mind that you can never eradicate it completely.

I'm not sitting on my high horse and pointing at the bias of scientists, because I too am biased. In this book I will present to you the research that supports my beliefs and arguments. I won't be telling you about the research that contradicts my points or doesn't fully support them. This is not because I want to deliberately lie to you, it's because I honestly believe in the results I report to you. Yet just because I believe it, doesn't mean it's true.

You will not agree with everything I say in this book and you will find contradicting opinions amongst scientists. You have to find your own truth and that is really what this entire book is all about.

Contents

Section 1: The Story

*"There is no greater agony than bearing an untold story inside you." - **Maya Angelou***

Will you write the story, or will you let the story write you? It's time to Author Your Life.

This book is going to help you to become the hero of your story. To live from your best self day-to-day. To live the life you were born to live.

Too many people nowadays are living a life they are unhappy with. One in four people experience a mental illness (1). One in two people are unhappy with the work they do (2). One in two marriages end in divorce (3). These statistics are alarming, and I think we can do better than this.

However, where can we turn for help?

Our education system focuses on pumping us full of knowledge, not developing our character.

Our economy focuses on making profit, not making people.

Our social networks are built around projecting the ideal self, not exploring the true self.

We find ourselves at a time where people are investing more time and money searching for who they are. Trying to find their "passion". Seeking friends and lovers that "get" them. They spend months at a time travelling; they invest thousands reading books, attending workshops and embarking on retreats; they bounce from job to job; they find and lose religion. Sound familiar?

As individuals and communities, we are seeking a shift. People are recognising that our current stories have some flawed scripts and characters in them.

Industries are thriving on our unhappiness: Fashion, Beauty, Fitness and Pharmaceuticals make billions off us trying to change ourselves.

False idols are held up as a standard of living we should adhere to. Our magazines, television screens and social media feeds are plastered with role models of limited or even questionable character.

We have been inducted with a narrow definition of success: to acquire and achieve. But are these acquisitions meaningful and are these achievements fulfilling?

A movement of change is stirring. A new narrative is developing.

Many people are looking in the mirror, and saying "is this it?".

They are harvesting the democratisation of information to take education into their own hands. They are applying new filters to cut through the dross and find what's real. People are consciously working on themselves and striving to be better.

The leaders and bosses of tomorrow are offering the opportunity to grow yourself as well as their bank accounts. There is a calling to enter jobs that are more autonomous, offering more opportunity for expression and personalisation.

We are also starting to connect to each other in new and powerful ways. The world is now interconnected in a way like never before and we can find people like us anywhere in the world. More and more people are leveraging this connection not to serve their own vanity, but to educate and serve others.

For too long now we have hidden ourselves away, tried to be something we're not, and shouldered our challenges alone. This is no longer the way you have to live your life. You have permission now to choose your own story.

If you are frustrated, resentful and unhappy with the story you've been living to up until this point, then know that you are not alone. For too long I let my story be written for me. I spent the first portion of my life trying to be something I wasn't. I tried to find happiness and fulfilment in external sources but there was a hole in me that none of these things could fill.

At age twenty-two, I sat with my dad during the last sixty minutes of his fight with cancer. Death strips away the filters. I saw life stark and clear.

I saw I had it all wrong and started again. I took up the pen and started writing a new script for my life. This new script changed everything for me. It banished the demons of mental health issues. It helped me become a #1 bestselling author, run highly acclaimed seminars and launch a podcast that at the time of writing has listeners in over twenty-five countries. It helped me find true love with an amazing lady for the very first time in my life.

I want you to realise that it is possible to write a new script for yourself. You and me are different people but there is no difference in our capacity to change. There is nothing special about me that means I can change and you can't.

I took no drugs or medication. There was no magic hack or secret strategy. I wasn't loaded with money nor did I hold a privileged last name. I'm not blessed with some genetic predisposition or talent. There was little about my circumstances or resources that allowed me to change. It was what I learned and how I applied it. This book, and your change, is all about learning and application.

You can learn how to create a life with more joy, more meaning and more love. The concepts and strategies outlined in this book will help you become happy, motivated and confident. That is not my exaggerated sales pitch. It is not even my sales pitch. In this book I share the research of experts, and my own modest adaptations and applications, that has demonstrated time and time again that you can create these outcomes for yourself.

In this book you will learn how to Author Your Life, and become the hero of your story. This new narrative is based on three key principles: Consciousness, Calling and Connection. When you live life with these three principles in harmony, you enter a special state of living called Fulfilment. This is where you are "filled-full". There is nothing missing or broken.

That's what it means to Author Your Life. Pick up your pen, and let's get writing.

Chapter 1: Your Story So Far

"We get to choose what play we're in and what part we'll play." - Derek Rydall.

Let's take some time to examine where you are right now. To understand the blank pages in front of you, you must first understand the chapters that have already been written.

It all starts with our education. We are a product of the narratives we have been exposed to and lived so far in our lives. Our education system did not teach us to be human beings; it taught us to be human doings. We were filled with knowledge and graded based on how well we could regurgitate that knowledge. We did not have to understand that knowledge; resonate with it; or apply it; as long as we could reproduce it on a line of paper.

We were taught that knowledge is king; that pieces of paper in your hand or letters after your name would keep you right in life. Now, however, the value of those pieces of paper and letters is getting slowly diluted and all higher education promises now is crippling debt.

What went wrong was that our modern (and I use the term "modern" loosely, given how little it has changed in the last century) education system never grasped the difference between knowledge and wisdom. We were taught how to store and replicate, not how to learn and grow. So we now see a generation of people filled with more knowledge than ever, but less idea of who they are and what they want to do in life. I graduated from university with a large cohort of intelligent, skilled and hard-working individuals, but very few of them have used that degree to author their lives. Some moved back to live with their parents; some have bounced from job to job; some have gone travelling; some have been prescribed anti-depressants. We were taught how to succeed in education: we weren't taught how to succeed in life.

Our society has only really been shown one path to succeed. It involves extracting as much as you can out of education, getting yourself the best job you can, and earning as much money as you can. This has continued to mould us as human doings, rather than human beings. The first question we ask when we meet someone new is "what do you do?", and a job title is the expected response.

Additionally, it is not considered to be a prerequisite to do a job that you love. A job is often just seen as something that you need to put up with, a necessary evil. We are not encouraged to find a job that is an extension of our natural expression. We are expected to devote the majority of our lives to our work but we are not expected to enjoy it. Therefore, many of us find ourselves in the middle of a horror story, stuck in a rat race we can't get out of.

There is something inherently unhappy in swathes of our society, but rather than confront it, we put on the masks. Indeed we pretend that things are better than ever. We project what a great time we're having in the bars and clubs of the world. We advertise the postcard lifestyle on our social media pages. Our weddings are getting increasingly lavish.

But the memory of the conversation in those bars and clubs is hazy. How often do these nights produce arguments and crying rather than joy and connection? We have thousands of "followers" but how many people truly care for us? Why does the expensive wedding not equal a long and happy marriage? (1)

Quite simply, if we have lost connection with ourselves, how can we expect to experience connection with other people? There's no point starting the party when you are missing a part of you. There's no point having the selfie without the self-awareness. There's no point saying the "I do" when you don't have the "I am".

So we find ourselves in an existence where we aren't really conscious of who we are, don't have much of a calling to engage in our work, and don't really feel connected to others. Not a nice story to be a part of. Is this your story?

Thankfully, this story is changing from current affairs to historical documentary. People are beginning to change the script for their lives and the lives of others.

There is more than one place to educate ourselves and more than one way to do it. There are a number of companies, institutions and projects who pride themselves on doing things differently; to provide not just the raw knowledge but to instruct in its application. There are teachers, mentors and experts who are empowering people to find and express their true selves. Furthermore, with the democratisation of information online, you can also embark on this journey entirely by yourself.

There is more than one way to earn a living and plenty of ways to enjoy doing it. Progressive companies are throwing out the script for how workers are expected to contribute, placing emphasis on the individual's unique insight, rather than the company's broad perspective. There is a wave of innovation and entrepreneurship, where you can create what you are truly fascinated with and inspired by. The opportunities for self-employment and flexible working give you executive control over how and when you wish work to factor into your life.

There are more ways to connect than ever before. Technology can be blamed for impacting our relationships but it can also be credited with increasing our scope for them. Technology can help us find new social groups in the same city. Technology can bring together like-minded individuals from dozens of countries in one place. Technology allows us to speak to our friend halfway across the world.

If you want to change the narrative of your life, the possibilities are more numerous and grander than at any other point in our history. However, you are going to have to work for it.

You might want to change but the desire to change is not enough. Surveys suggest that as many as 90% of people would like to write a book, but they don't. (2) Over 50% of people want to start a business, but don't. (3) About 40% of people make New Years resolutions but only half stay committed beyond January. (4)

Have you said you were going to lose weight but didn't? Have you said you were going to quit smoking but didn't? Have you said you were going to quit your job but didn't? Have you said you were going to complete a qualification but didn't? Have you said you were going to stop dating the same type of scoundrel but didn't? Have you said you were going to settle down with someone but didn't?

The desire to change is vital but is also insufficient by itself. People fail to change because they do not shift their mindset and they do not follow a framework. A certain mindset caused you to put on weight and until you change that you will never lose it. A certain mindset caused you to date the wrong type and until you change that you will continue to settle for them. A certain framework is required to write a book, without it, you will never string the words together. A certain framework is required to start a business, without it, you will never make a sustainable profit.

I know because you're reading this that you want to change...but why haven't you done so yet?

There are three likely reasons: you haven't changed your state of mind (Consciousness), you haven't connected with your "why" (Calling) and you haven't found mentors and inspirational peers (Connection).

Because of this, you continue to bang your head against the same challenges and obstacles. Fear and doubt paralyse you. Low self-esteem and confidence taunt you. Failure and setbacks frustrate and demotivate you. Loneliness and helplessness grip you.

If you want to write a new script, you need a new approach. Anyone who wants to change must first understand themselves and in particular their mind. This is what takes executive control over our lives. Despite our education system's emphasis on knowledge, most people know precious little about what runs their life day to day.

When you are able to control your mind, you will elevate your Consciousness. There are three steps required to make this happen. You must first Understand who you are and how your mind works; then you must Unlock your unused capability; then you Unleash the full potential stored within.

Anyone who wants to change must also find their true purpose. We all have a mission in life: there was something we were born to achieve. Until we identify that, we will forever be wandering in circles.

There is a reason that you are on this Earth. This is your Calling. To answer your Calling, you must first connect with your Purpose, your "why" for being here; then you must develop your Proficiency which gives you the key ingredients for any form of success you aspire to; then you must learn how to maximise your Performance so that you can create the work you are meant to do.

It is important to remember that we don't experience our stories in a silo. There are other characters in our narrative. How you interact and bond with these characters is key to creating a noticeable change in your life. The real extent of your change will be marked by how much that change spreads to others around you.

Change without Connection feels hollow. To develop Connection, you must first Integrate with others, recognising how we learn from and are modelled by the people around us; next you must learn how to Influence others, to be able to interact confidently and deeply; finally you will find the deepest levels of connection when you find ways to Impact others.

I discovered these answers at the side of my father's deathbed. In our final conversation, I hit upon three truths of life. It was these three truths that allowed me to make my change and Author my Life. These three truths have evolved into what you will read in this book. In the next chapter, I will share this evolution with you.

Chapter 2: My Story So Far

"In the depths of winter, I finally learned that within me there lay an invincible summer." - **Albert Camus**

In sixty minutes, my life changed forever. At age twenty-two, my dad lost his fight with cancer. I was fortunate enough to spend the last sixty minutes of his life by his bedside. This gave me the opportunity to have a final conversation with Dad: the most important conversation I will ever have. If events had transpired differently, I might never have had that opportunity. I doubt I would be sitting here writing this book without those sixty minutes.

When I arrived at Dad's hospice room just after 4pm, on Friday 24th of July, 2015, I could see the immediacy of what was about to happen. Dad had been holding on for me. I had the frightening realisation that this was going to be the last time I would speak with my dad.

I didn't have a script for this situation…who does? So as I sat down by Dad's bedside, I admit I was rambling. The first thing I wanted to tell Dad was that I was going to be all right. I started talking about my flat, my job, my girlfriend. I said they were all fine. This was superficial nonsense really. Anything you can find on a Facebook profile is not what you should be speaking about in your final conversation with a loved one.

What did I want to say to Dad? What did I really want to tell him? What did I want him to know before he left this Earth?

It was then that I hit upon three of the most important things I will ever say, one after the other:

"I'm grateful for the fantastic job you did of raising me; I'm incredibly proud to be your son; I love you Dad."

There was an impactful silence after I said those words. I had just said the words "I love you" to Dad for the first time.

Realising this, I rambled some more. I said I hoped he had always known that I had loved him, that I showed my love through everything I said and everything I did.

Dad had listened patiently through all my rambling and as I finally finished, he turned his head towards me and said:

"You should still say it, David."

I have never forgot that. Dad was still teaching me, even with the final words of his life.

Our final rites as father and son were complete. From here Dad soon lost consciousness. Myself and other members of the family gathered round and stayed with him until he took his last breath. Dad was declared dead just after 5pm, sixty minutes after I arrived.

One-by-one the family members left to find space for their grief. I was the last to leave. As I too was about to leave, I stood at the doorway of that hospice room and looked back at Dad, lying in his deathbed. In that moment, I had a profound realisation.

I realised that one day that was going to be me. One day we will all be lying in our deathbeds and when we're there, we will look back and judge the quality of our life. Was it the story we wanted to be a part of? Were we the protagonist we wanted to be?

At that moment, standing in that doorway, I realised a chapter of my life had just ended: the chapter with my dad in it. A new chapter of my life had just started. The chapters without Dad. There were blank pages ahead and I could choose to write whatever script I wanted for myself on those pages.

Up until that point, I hadn't liked the way my life had been going. I had struggled with depression and an eating disorder. I was only dabbling in pursuing my dream of being a full-time author. I hadn't been able to hold down any romantic relationship.

I wasn't living a life that was fully or truly me. I had been trying to be something I wasn't: The Party Animal; The Player; Mr. Cool; Mr. Muscles. I had been living in fear. Fear of being who I really was. Fear of pursuing the mission I was put on this Earth to accomplish. Fear of intimacy with others. I had put on masks and built up walls around myself.

So I started a reconstruction process. I threw away my Playstation; stopped drinking alcohol; threw away earrings, bracelets, rings and other countless pieces of bling as well as stupid, trashy clothes. I distanced myself from my group of friends, which was painful but necessary. I had to separate myself from the old David, the false David.

I started to practice yoga; meditate regularly; plug myself in constantly to personal development podcasts and read self-help books. I started to invest in one relationship that really meant something, my new girlfriend, who had been an amazing support during my time of sorrow and grief.

I started to pursue a goal of helping others by using my experiences and expanding knowledge to educate and inspire. I had just graduated with a degree in psychology and had experienced mental illness so, with this in mind, I decided to be a life coach, specialising in mental health.

I made all these changes…and nothing happened.

I still felt in fear; still felt trapped; still felt insecure; still felt too attached to my old way of living. Coaching clients didn't come. I launched an online course and it bombed. On more than one occasion I found myself crying into my girlfriend's shoulder, despairing that I wasn't changing and I wasn't helping others to change.

Change is a difficult process; you will spend some time in the valley before you start to ascend the slopes. The gradient does change eventually and sometimes there will be a friendly tour guide there to give you a little push up.

I was lucky enough to find a friendly tour guide. At the end of April 2016, nine months after my dad's passing, I attended Brendon Burchard's *Experts Academy* Seminar. I travelled for twenty-seven hours from my home country of Scotland to San Jose, California to attend this four-day seminar on thought-leadership and creating a business from sharing your message. The phrase "life-changing" is thrown around a lot nowadays but this is exactly what it was for me.

I couldn't believe how much someone standing on stage and speaking could influence you. The event gave me so much belief and confidence in myself as a person and the message I had to share with the world. I was so filled with hope and emotion on the last day that I cried.

It was here that I realised that I wanted to be a speaker. Brendon had stood on stage and changed my life in those four days and I wanted to be able to do that for other people. One day I wanted to inspire someone the way Brendon inspired me.

On my return from California, that is what I set out to do. I started to speak at groups and workshops. I hosted my first event, a small two-hour workshop to begin with. A couple of months later, I took the plunge and hosted my first full-day seminar.

Twenty-one people had enough faith in me to buy a ticket for the event. As I stood on stage delivering the content, I felt incredible alignment with myself and what I was doing. I knew that this was my mission in life and something I had to keep doing. The feedback from the students was fantastic, with some of them saying it was the best personal development seminar they had ever been to! This confirmed for me that I had found something within that I could use to serve others.

Another vital insight came out of *Experts Academy*. During the group activities across the days, we were asked to create an imaginary product — such as a book, course or workshop — and work out how we would structure and market it. In these activities I started to create a book. It was based on the story of losing my dad, what I learned from the experience, and how I was making changes in my life.

The feedback I heard during these sessions was amazing. People told me what an inspiring story it was and some gave me their emails so that I could send them the book when it was finished. This response was so encouraging and really helped fortify the growing belief that I had something of value to share with the world. This seminar was the birth of *The Last 60 Minutes*: my debut self-help book.

I gathered my thoughts and reflections and a couple months later I started the book. I completed it within a month. The message flowed from me as if guided by something beyond myself. I knew this book had power and meaning within it. I released it a few months later in January 2017, a resource to help people make their change at the beginning of the year.

Within a week, *The Last 60 Minutes* hit the #1 spot on Amazon in the Death and Grief category. This was obviously an incredible personal achievement, but what this really showed to me was that people resonated with this message and it was helping people in their lives. I got the opportunity to speak about the book on BBC radio. I received beautiful messages and reviews: readers reconnecting with their estranged fathers; people staying up until the early hours of the morning to finish reading it; one review even starts "this book changed my life".

Things started to take off with the publication of the book. I was invited to speak in more places and I had more feedback on what I was speaking about. As I shared the story more, I started to recognise some common patterns.

Firstly, it was a story that many people were relating to, far more than I had anticipated. My story is nothing special. I'm not the only child to have lost a parent. I'm not the only person to have lost a loved one to cancer. One in two people will contract a form of cancer during their lives (1), so everyone has been exposed to cancer in some degree. What surprised me was I was hearing two common responses among people with whom I shared my story.

The first was someone who would say: "David, I lost my…(loved one). Just like you I was able to speak to them one last time and it is something I have treasured ever since."

The second was someone who would say: "David, I lost my…(loved one). Unlike you I never had that final conversation with them and I have regretted it ever since."

What was clear to me was that people were going through the same experience but having different interpretations of it. What affected them wasn't the experience, it was the story that was connected to the experience. For one person their loved one's death was a story of closure, fondness and nostalgia. For the other, their loved one's death was a story of conflict, separation and regret.

Of course there was a key distinction between the two: whether they had the opportunity for those last words. However, I spotted another distinction. It was the story connected to the experience. Why was I up on stage sharing my experience and they were sitting in the audience listening to it? I realised it wasn't the experience that mattered, it was the decision you made after the experience. What story did you continue to tell yourself after the experience?

Why didn't I descend into grief and regret? I was perfectly entitled to; no one would've faulted me. I realised it all came from a decision.

When I stood at that doorway and looked back at Dad, I made a decision about what story I was going to tell myself when I walked out that door. This wasn't going to be a story that haunted me for the rest of my life. It was going to be a story that motivated me for the rest of my life.

One day, during my morning meditation, a phrase came to me: "Author Your Life." It was not a new phrase, I had seen plenty of quotes cards and blog posts on being "The author of your life." This, however, was different. "Author" was not a noun, it was a verb. It was something you did. It was something you needed to consciously create for yourself.

The word "author" has held significance for me from an early age. I have wanted to be an author since the age of five and fulfilled that desire at age twenty when I self-published my first novel during my time at university. As I explored personal development, I was also fascinated to find out that the root of the word "authentic" was "author". This was a concept I had mentioned briefly in *The Last 60 Minutes* but didn't quite put the two together fully at that time.

If I could sum up the changes I have experienced since Dad's death, it would be using the word "authentic". I feel I am finally being who I really am and doing what I am really supposed to do. I realised that morning that the link between these two words was not an accident.

I recognised that we are all the author of our lives: we all have the choice about what story we want to be a part of. However, I recognised that many people in the world aren't exercising that power. They are not turning the noun into the verb. That was what I had done at that doorway in that hospice room. For twenty-two years I had been the author of my life but I hadn't been writing the story I wanted to be a part of. It took the impetus of Dad's death to change that. At that doorway I made the decision to Author my Life and that's when everything changed.

At my next full-day seminar, I introduced the concept of Author Your Life to my students. I walked them through the components of Author Your Life and they loved it. I realised I had stumbled upon something and I started to grow and evolve it. I created the Author Your Life Community on Facebook, which now has hundreds of members. I launched the Author Your Life Podcast, which has listeners in over twenty-five countries. I planned the inaugural Author Your Life Summit, my first multi-day event. And, of course, I realised I needed to bring it all together in a book.

In this book you will learn how to turn the noun into the verb. If we don't take charge of our lives and force a change, that same chapter rewrites itself again and again in different contexts. Whether that story be bereavement, mental illness, abuse, redundancy, bankruptcy, discrimination, or divorce, too many people are the victims of their stories, not the heroes.

Now the thing about heroes, is that they are not heroes due to an absence of challenging circumstances, they are heroes because of them. Harry Potter was an orphan who was raised by his miserable aunt and uncle. Frodo Baggins had the fate of Middle Earth thrust upon him. Daenerys Targaryen was hunted and betrayed because of the crimes of her parent. These characters are not heroes to us despite their struggles but because of them.

What our heroes were able to do was to use their past to drive and motivate their future. Nelson Mandela emerged from prison after twenty-seven years ready to lead his country to freedom. Oprah Winfrey promised she would never be a victim again after being molested as a child and created the highest-ranked talk show of all time. Stephen Hawking did not let amyotrophic lateral sclerosis stop him from becoming one of the greatest physicists and cosmologists of all time.

That is the essence of a hero; the ability to turn pain into gain and to turn a mess into a message. This is the journey I want to take you through in this book. To show you how you write your own story; how you become the hero you are meant to be; how to Author Your Life. In the next chapter we will breakdown the process by which you achieve this.

Chapter 3: Becoming The Author

"However difficult life might seem, there is always something you can do and succeed at." - **Stephen Hawking**

In the last 60 minutes, I learned three truths of Gratitude, Identity and Love. These truths came from three key statements I said to Dad: *"I'm grateful for the fantastic job you did of raising me; I'm incredibly proud to be your son; I love you Dad."* These truths were powerful. They changed me. They have changed other people. But there is more to them.

As I started to develop myself more on the foundation of these truths and as I started to teach others about them, I noticed an evolution of the truths. I eluded to this briefly in the last chapter but will expand upon it here.

My message of Gratitude was all about finding joy and positivity in our existence. I spoke of the power of gratitude to change our mindset and our perception on life. Ultimately, gratitude is a key component of being happy. (1) A grateful person feels that they have enough and they are enough. A grateful person feels appreciation in the smallest things. They can find happiness in a moment simply because they choose to.

What gratitude pointed to, was an elevation in CONSCIOUSNESS. These benefits and changes that gratitude creates are influences on our happiness and sense of self. As highlighted earlier, there is an emotional struggle as individuals and as a collective: mental illness, stress, pain. Too many are living at a lower level of Consciousness than that which they are truly capable of.

In this book you are going to learn about how to elevate your Consciousness. I define Consciousness as mastering your psychology and finding alignment with yourself. To change your story, you cannot be ruled by anxiety, depression, anger, stress or hate. You must rise above the entrapments of lower Consciousness. When you do, you allow your best self to shine through: the hero of your story. When you align with a higher level of Consciousness, you Author Your Life.

My message of Identity was about finding purpose and direction in our existence. I spoke of connecting with and cultivating our identity and how doing so increased the richness of our pursuits. When we understand the uniqueness of our self, we understand the path we should take in life. The person who really knows themselves knows where they want to go; knows what they want to do; knows how they want to do it; and knows why they want to do it. This "knowing" is where our purpose and meaning come from in life.

When we know our identity, we know our CALLING. As described earlier, many people have found ourselves in an intellectual struggle: living without passion, stuck in jobs they can't stand, dreaming but never actualising. Too many have not been pursuing their Calling in life.

In this book you are going to learn about how to answer your Calling. I define Calling as identifying your personal mission and finding alignment with your work. Every hero has a quest. To change your story, you cannot be confused about what you are supposed to do, be stuck creating someone else's dream, or not doing what you were born to do. You must ignore the shiny objects and wrong doorways and keep on target. When you do, you express your best self out into the world: the hero of your story. When you align with a truer pursuit of your calling, you Author Your Life.

My message of Love was a message of giving. I spoke of the importance of finding love every day and giving love to those you meet. The magical experiences of life happen when we live in love. When we open our hearts to find fondness for friends, compassion for strangers, union with family and appreciation for teachers and mentors, we live with an incredible harmony within.

It might seem like love is the final destination. So many are on the quest for "the one" and love. Ultimately, when you strip away all the facade, at our core is the desire to be loved. However, even love is part of a wider construct: CONNECTION. In our world right now is a spiritual struggle of anger, intolerance and division. A world increasingly becoming "Us vs Them": Conservative vs Liberal, White vs Black, Christian vs Muslim, Male vs Female. Our world has lost a whole lot of connection. People have forgotten they are just a small part of a wider whole. This is the essence of connection, it is about this realisation that there is something bigger than us.

In this book you are going to learn how to deepen your Connection. I define Connection as embracing love and finding alignment with something larger than yourself. To change your story, you cannot live with intolerance and anger and you cannot be lonely and isolated. You must enrich the lives of the people around you and contribute to the world. When you do, you give your best self to world: the hero of your story. When you align with a deeper level of connection, you Author Your Life.

When these three principles of Consciousness, Calling and Connection come together in alignment, we enter a state of living called FUL-

FILMENT. It is a state where we have it all. The very breakdown of the word means to be "Filled-Full". There is nothing left to add, we are complete.

However, for too many of us, there is something missing. I have observed that there are three core pursuits for people: happiness, purpose and love. These are the outcomes we get when we live in alignment with one principle. Consciousness brings happiness. Calling brings purpose. Connection brings love. These things are good by themselves but it is not the complete picture. We are not Filled-Full. If we chase just one of these, we will still feel empty. That is why the amazing experience, the promotion and even the marriage do not make us complete. At best, they only fulfil one end goal, and often only fleetingly. The human condition demands more.

Many people manage to achieve two out of three — many people achieve greatness based on two out of three — but still something is painfully and obviously missing for them.

When an individual is aligned with Consciousness and Calling, I call them THE LONELY VISIONARY. For me the most famous example of this is Nelson Mandela.

Nelson Mandela is a role model and inspiration for me. I have a wall in my bedroom with pictures of inspirational leaders on it: Mandela is right at the top. If I can be half the man Mandela was and achieve half the impact he did, I will consider my life a life well lived.

Mandela was a highly conscious individual. He was perceptive, determined, wise, encouraging, strong and resilient. One of the reasons Mandela inspires me so much is because he also developed the power of forgiveness. After being oppressed and abused for most of his adult life, and then imprisoned for twenty-seven years, Mandela was finally granted his freedom. With that freedom, Mandela could've wielded the sword of revenge and justice, who would blame him for doing so?

Instead, Mandela made that famous walk out of prison, ready to forgive the men who put him there. Moreover, he didn't just forgive them. He wanted the Afrikaners to be a part of his vision for South Africa: he wanted to work with them to create the country he dreamed of. That is a level of consciousness, of spirituality, of enlightenment, that I can barely fathom and I'm sure you struggle to comprehend too. It astonishes me and I admire Mandela immensely for it. It was this quality that made Mandela a highly conscious individual.

Mandela was also a man greatly attuned to his calling. From an early age he recognised the injustice of his country and the mistreatment and oppression of his people. At a young age, a fire roared to life in his heart. He fought for the justice of black people in South Africa. He defended their rights as a lawyer; he sought political change through the African National Congress; he went to jail for twenty-seven years for what he believed in. He was a pioneer of the revolutionary movement in South Africa.

When he was released from prison, he was a pensioner; he could've been justified in saying that his part in the fight was over. However, he saw that there was still much to be done. He continued to pursue his vision of equal civil rights for Black and Coloured people in South Africa. In 1994, this vision was finally realised. Mandela had led his people to freedom and became their President.

Mandela was a highly conscious individual who achieved a monumental calling. He is my role model for these reasons but even Mandela only achieved two out of three factors of Fulfilment.

Reading Mandela's autobiography "A Long Walk to Freedom", Mandela speaks with great regret about the time spent with his family. (2) Even before he was imprisoned, Mandela saw very little of his family. By day, he worked as a lawyer defending the rights of Black citizens. In the evenings, he worked with the African National Congress to create political change. So often he returned in the late hours of the night and left again in the early hours of the morning. He saw very little of his wife and children during this time.

When he was imprisoned, he had little visitation rights and went for long stretches of time with seeing anyone from his family. In particular, he saw one of his daughters when she was three years old and didn't see her again until she was *sixteen*. That is a whole childhood missed.

Even when Mandela was released, he still had little time for his family. He was travelling to instigate the final stages of political change and then served as President for five years when he achieved that change.

What Mandela speaks about with a sense of regret, was this lack of connection. He valued and cared for his family but never got to enjoy that connection in the way he desired. Mandela was The Lonely Visionary: he had Consciousness and Calling, but lacked Connection.

Instead, what if someone finds Connection, they find Calling, but do not find Consciousness. This is the life I call THE TROUBLED GENIUS. The famous example of this for me was Robin Williams.

Williams enjoyed Connection. He had a loving family. He brought joy to everyone he met. He made people laugh. That was his gift — it was also his Calling. Williams achieved great things through comedy. He had his own stand-up tour, he appeared on television shows and he starred in many of the films I watched as I was growing such as *Aladdin* and *Mrs Doubtfire*. Williams won multiple awards for his comedy.

But Williams wanted more. What he really wanted was an award for not being funny. In 1997, Robin Williams won the Academy Award for not being funny: Best Supporting Actor for his role in *Good Will Hunting*. For those who have seen the film, who can doubt that he deserved that award for his performance.

Williams had Connection; he had a Calling; but he only achieved two out of three. Williams was able to make everyone happy...but himself. In 2014, we lost Williams when he took his own life. Williams's life was full of struggles with addiction and mental illness. He was never quite able to find the happiness within. He was never quite able to find Consciousness. Robin Williams was a wonderful man but a Troubled Genius and only found two out of three.

There is one last combination. It is when we have Consciousness and we have Connection, but we miss out on our Calling. This is the life I call THE WANDERING SOUL. There is not necessarily a famous example of this. So often fame comes from answering a Calling. Nevertheless, there is one prominent example for me. My dad.

Dad was a Conscious individual. He was insightful, tough, confident, witty and wise. He taught me so many lessons and gave me so many insights. Dad faced many challenges in his life and I benefitted from the lessons he was able to share from these experiences. In the last decade of his life, I observed a peace and contentment in Dad, where he seemed in harmony with himself.

Dad also enjoyed a deep Connection. This was not necessarily in the realm of romantic relationships, as his two ex-wives will tell you! Dad was sometimes a difficult man to get on with, but that mellowing in later life helped him foster positive relationships with extended members of the family, and of course with myself. He also had good relationships with my friends, and so often they would say "I need to come round soon David, I haven't seen Jim (Dad) in ages!".

The most fulfilling relationship I observed for Dad, however, was with nature. He was always walking in woods, by rivers and, in his younger years, up mountains. He liked to sit in silence and meditate in the beautiful surroundings of our home country, Scotland. Dad remarked of nature: "The silence is absolutely deafening". I know what Dad meant by this. There is an awe in nature, an intense realisation of the life all around you that is powerful and at times almost overwhelming.

My dad loved nature and nature loved him. It was here that he felt a connection with something larger than himself. He called it "energy". Others might call it Spirit, Universe or God. I believe this is the true essence of Connection; to be aware that you are a small part of a grander design. You don't need to be spiritual or religious to feel this connection. We all know that we are an individual out of seven and a half billion in our species. We all know that we share this planet with many other forms of life. We know that our planet is a minuscule part of a wider universe. When you recognise this grand design, you are embracing the deepest form of Connection.

This was the Connection my dad enjoyed; he was also a Conscious individual; but what my dad missed out on was Calling. Dad had huge potential within him but he never fulfilled it. In his 20s, Dad rose through the ranks to become the youngest Warrant Officer in the history of the British Army at the time. In his 30s he was a top performing salesman for an insurance company. In his 40s he discovered a gift for spiritual healing and hypnotherapy. In his 50s he invested his life's knowledge and wisdom into a new child…me. Dad displayed excellence in multiple domains but never quite found his Calling.

When I was young, Dad and I would listen to Wayne Dyer, a great thought leader. I think why I resonated with Wayne was because he was very similar to my dad. The strength they had taken from hardship was not that different. The insight and philosophy they had was not that different. The love they had in their heart was not that different. Dad was a mentor and leader to me but he could've been that to many more people. He could've served the world in the way that Wayne did.

A couple of months before he died, I interviewed Dad about his life and lessons. Towards the end of the interview, I asked Dad what he thought his greatest achievement in life was. He paused, thought for a moment, and said: "Sometimes David, I feel like I haven't achieved that much really."

That statement has really stuck with me. Dad never felt like he fulfilled his potential. That to me is sadder than the fact he is gone. When Dad lay on his deathbed and looked back on his life, I think he looked back with regret that he never quite found his Calling. I recognised this as I stood at the doorway of his hospice room and I vowed I was not going to let the same thing happen to me. I was not going to leave this world without answering my Calling. Because Dad had only achieved two out of three, and lived the life of the Wandering Soul.

What I'd like you to do before you continue reading, is to reflect on where you are in your life right now. What level of Consciousness, Calling and Connection do you rate yourself at? Which of these areas do you think is lacking or lagging for you?

What I want to help you accomplish in this book is to develop your Consciousness, discover your Calling, and deepen your Connection. To not just bring up your lowest component, but to raise them all, and bring you closer to that state of Fulfilment. To do so, there are three main obstacles you must overcome, three challenges that are preventing you from becoming the hero of your story.

To develop our Consciousness, we must overcome FEAR. We must stop letting the discomfort of change stop us from taking action. We must not be worried about failing. We must stop doubting our capacity to succeed. This book will help you push through that fear.

To discover our Calling, we must overcome CONFUSION. We must discover what truly motivates us. We must find the path to our particular form of success. We must cut through the noise and conflicting advice to identify what steps we need to take to get ahead. This book will help you clear that confusion.

To deepen our Connection, we must overcome ISOLATION. We

must realise that we are not alone and neither do we have to be alone. We must realise our ability to interact confidently with others. We must realise our capacity to serve others. This book will help you leave this isolation.

CONSCIOUSNESS. CALLING. CONNECTION. This is the triad that cuts through the pain. This is the triad that heals the hurts. This is the triad that allows you to rewrite your narrative. This is the triad that helps you become the Hero of your Story. This is the triad that leads to Fulfilment. This Triad allows you to Author Your Life.

Section 2: Develop Your Consciousness

"Our greatest fear is not that we are inadequate. Our greatest fear is that we are powerful beyond measure." **- Marianne Williamson**

To Author Your Life, you must first start with the hero of the story. You must first start with the mind behind the pen. You must take executive command over yourself so that you can take executive command over your life. Consciousness is all about mastering our psychology and finding alignment with yourself. What you'll be introduced to in this section is the three-part framework that will create this change for you.

The first step is to UNDERSTAND. Sadly, we are simply not educated on the way our mind works. In the U.K., psychology is not taught in the education system until the age of sixteen; even then, it is an optional subject. I believe that psychology should be a mandatory subject from the grassroots up. Knowing similes, Pythagorus's Theorem and the date of the Battle of Hastings is nice, but how well does that serve us in everyday life? We don't have imagery, right-angled triangles and French invasions bothering us day-to-day. But what we all have are habits we want to change, self-doubts we want to overcome, and emotions we want to process. If we do not know our own minds, then what hope do we have? To take our life to new levels we must first UNDERSTAND what resources we have been dealt with.

The second step is to UNLOCK. Many of us are only working at a fraction of our full capacity. We have incredible strength and power between our ears that is not being fully utilised. We cannot run anything effectively on 10% battery. Our society sadly operates on a superficial level: easy to access media; trite conversations; trivial tasks at work. We do not need our full brainpower to process these experiences, so why would we develop our minds any more? However, if you are reading this book, then this level of superficial living is not enough for you. You want more. In the pages to come you will learn how to UNLOCK greater capabilities of your mind.

Finally, when you have understood and have unlocked your potential, it is time to UNLEASH it. How do you take command of your brain to take command of your life? If you are familiar with personal development, you'll have been told countless times to "think positive", "develop good habits" and "accept your emotions". These cliches have merit but how do we fully embody them? What shifts do we need to make to live life on a more vibrant and joyful level? How do we take an almighty step into a new paradigm of living? We have to UNLEASH what we have within us.

The steps are simple, the process is difficult. Because as you read this book, you have been scripted by the story that has come before. The events, encounters and experiences you've had have shaped that two kilogram, tofu-like substance you carry around in your skull. You have the chance right here today to rewrite your story — but you do not get to "start again". There is no "clean slate" in the story of your life. Our past has already been written, it gives us great opportunity for reflection and learning, but it cannot be edited or erased.

What your past has scripted for you, in one way or another, is fear. As will be explained later, our brain is built on neural circuitry. Our brain is comprised of, on average, eighty-six billion neurons (1) and there are almost innumerable connections between them. These connections are built up through consistent disciplined practice — such as riding a bike — or by a single intense emotional experience — such as being knocked off one. Fear is one of the strongest emotions we experience and so it scripts our brain instantly. Furthermore, we have an entire part of our brain, the Amygdala, which is responsible for remembering our fear responses, so that fear script stays with us if we continue to reinforce and respond to it. (2)

It is fear that will block you from progressing along the UNDERSTAND, UNLOCK, UNLEASH framework. As you try to educate and train your brain to be more proactive, confident or joyful, you will encounter fear scripts that tell you to do and be the exact opposite. If you are not self-aware and resilient, these fear scripts will win. In particular, there are three fears that you must be vigilant against.

The first is the FEAR OF CHANGE. We as humans like to have certainty in our lives: it's comfortable; it's safe and secure; it's predictable. We like to know what deal we've got, even if it's a bad one. However, with change — even positive change — comes uncertainty. Uncertainty is not comfortable. It's risky. It's an unknown entity. We don't know how to prepare; how painful the process will be; and whether the end result will be worthwhile. So rather than risk putting ourselves through an ordeal for no reward, we stick to what we know. FEAR OF CHANGE wins.

Change is nothing to be feared. It is necessary...and it is *inevitable.* Nothing stays the same. This is a good thing. The human story is one of change and progression. Do you still want to be walking on the streets through your own filth? Do you still want to be beheaded for crimes you did not commit? Do you want to live in a world that doesn't have internet? Of course not. If you fear change, then you fear growth, and that is nothing to be feared. In this book, you will be shown how to manage the change. You will learn the mechanisms of change. You will be shown the scientific evidence of what end result your change will achieve (and its a good one!). You will be prepared as much as you possibly can be.

The second fear is FEAR OF FAILURE. Whilst we have grown and developed significantly as humans, some core parts of us have not. We are still primarily driven by survival: to ensure we protect ourselves and, at a stretch, those with genetic relatedness to us. Our ego fears anything that threatens it...and not just life-or-death-threats. It feels any wound, physical or abstract, real or imagined. So our ego protects itself with a cloak of fear.

It is this cloak of fear that makes us fear failure. I can guarantee that at some point in your past you had a painful failure. It wounded you physically, intellectually, emotionally or spiritually, and you don't want to feel that way again. So you don't try anything that might make you feel that way again. We fear failure because we think it demonstrates that we're not good enough. We fear failure because we don't want to get hurt. We fear that our hopes and dreams are not possible.

However, if we allow failure to rule us, we will never truly thrive. We will never take charge of our narrative. Failure is nothing to be scared of; all the people we admire and look up to have failed. In fact, most people succeed *because* of their failures, not in spite of them. These individuals did find that their dreams were possible, despite pain and challenge along the way.

What you will realise as you progress along your journey is to see failure as simply learning. In life we win, or we learn. Yes, sometimes the learning has a bit of pain associated with it but in this book you will develop your innate skill and ability to overcome such challenge. You will integrate failure into your learning and growth process. You will also elevate your level of thinking to the level of your dreams, so that fear doesn't hold you back from becoming the hero you were born to be.

On this note, our third fear is often FEAR OF SUCCESS! We have an unfortunate tendency in our society to demonise ambition, to mutter behind the backs of people who are trying to achieve big things for themselves. This has been called "Tall Poppy Syndrome": when one person is growing higher than the rest, people would rather cut that person down to their level than rise up to join them. We fear the success of others and so we also fear our own success, as highlighted in the Marianne Williamson quote at the beginning of this section. We ask who are we to dream for ourselves? We doubt whether we deserve success. We fear how people will judge us if we reveal our desires and goals. We fear not being able to maintain the success, that ultimately we will lose it and end up a failure.

If we fear success, then we fear the opportunity to have happiness, purpose and love in our lives. We fear being the person we want to be and living the life we want to live. In this book you will realise the wonderful quality you have within you and when you do you will want to share it with everyone. When we make significant changes and breakthroughs in our lives, we can't help but share it. Change is contagious and you will spread it. Some may mutter but most will accept and be inspired by you. This change is not a short term success, it's not something you lose in a market crash, divorce or cup final. This is inner work and you will develop the confidence, drive, intelligence, resilience and vision to create the success you want for yourself.

It's time to break through your fear, and learn how to Understand, Unlock and Unleash a higher level of Consciousness.

Chapter 4: Understand

"It is our choices, Harry, that show what we truly are, far more than our abilities." - **Albus Dumbledore**

The Author Your Life journey begins with Understanding. In this chapter, we will explore some important foundations for rising to a higher level of consciousness. You will learn about happiness, where it comes from, and that much of your happiness is about the choices you make. Next, you will learn about the mind, how it is formed and programmed, and how successful people think. Finally, you will explore how to live in alignment with some of your guiding values and will set the aspirations for who you want to become. With this foundational understanding, you will develop the springboard to elevate to higher levels of Consciousness.

Part 1: Deciding for Happy

The ultimate outcome of developing our Consciousness is happiness. "Happiness" can be a vague and layered term: it has different interpretations and definitions depending on whether you take a spiritual, philosophical, psychological, physiological or even economic view of happiness.

My version of happiness borrows from multiple schools of thought but what I will focus on most in this section will be what positive psychologists are telling us about happiness. Positive psychologists study human happiness and flourishing using scientific research and experiments. I believe that starting from this objective, tangible perspective will help provide a solid foundation for the next steps in your journey.

I define Happiness as being comprised of two components:

1. JOY: Experiences of positive emotion.
2. WELLBEING: An overall contentment with ourselves and our life.

This matches what multiple schools of thought tell us about happiness. Positive Psychologist Tal Ben-Shahar, who created the most popular course of all time at Harvard University, teaches the "Hamburger Model" of happiness. (1)

Ben-Shahar asks us to imagine we're hungry and we walk into a restaurant, where there is a choice of burgers we can have.

The first burger is a decadent masterpiece. It has multiple slabs of processed meat, high-calorie dressing and white processed buns. This burger will taste great *in the moment*, however, it will ultimately be detrimental for us *in the future*. This is a pursuit of happiness called HEDO-NISM. It is seeking joy in the moment at the expense of wellbeing in the future. This is living a life of partying, drug-taking and unprotected sex. When we choose junk food, cigarettes and alcohol we are choosing Hedonism.

The second burger we can choose is a veggie burger. It is dry, plain and tasteless. This burger will taste bad *in the moment*, but may ultimately be more beneficial for us *in the future*. This is a pursuit of happiness called THE RAT RACER. It is sacrificing joy in the moment in the hopes of wellbeing in the future. This is living a life of overworking, frugality and narrow focus. When we choose working for money instead of fulfilment; putting off our dreams until some vague tomorrow; or even starting a business; we are choosing "The Rat Racer".

The third burger we could have is an empty burger. It is two slabs of bread with a tiny bit of salad, no dressing, and no patty. This burger will taste bad *in the moment* and provide no benefit *in the future*. This is living in a state of NIHILISM. It is the belief that we will have nothing good in our present or future. It is a lack of connection and belief in life. This is the realm of grief, depression, addiction and hopelessness. When we give up on ourselves or our lives; lose faith in what is to come; or we are consumed by pain and emptiness; we are living in a state of Nihilism.

So what are our choices? Do we live fast and die young? Do we sacrifice our youth for the hopes of a tomorrow that never comes? Or do we just give up completely?

Fear not, for there is a fourth option. There is a burger with organic, grass-fed meat. It has a gorgeous natural dressing. Instead of two slices of processed bread, it is put between two large flat pieces of vegetable. It is gluten-free, dairy-free, soy-free, GMO-free, and everything-else-free. This burger tastes great *in the moment* and will also be good for us *in the future*. Ben-Shahar describes this fourth choice simply as HAPPINESS. My definition of Happiness as you can see is inspired by Ben-Shahar's Hamburger model. It is being happy in the moment and also moving towards happiness in the future.

To develop our Consciousness, we must have pleasure in the moment and optimism for the future in equal measure. However, as we know, this is not always the case. It's all very well being able to stuff our face with Hamburger Four when things are going good but often that choice is not available or apparent. We might be facing serious challenge or pain in the present, or see no hope or prospects in the future. Hamburger Four does not seem to be on the menu. Do we have to settle for a lower standard?

Ben-Shahar's hamburger model provides a signpost to what Happiness is and *what* it should look like, but it does not give us the *how*. If we are lacking happiness in the present and/or future, how do we change this?

How do we find happiness? Before we explore the answer, I'd like you study the list below. From the options listed, what do you think would make you happier? Make a mental or physical note of what option/s you would pick.

- A new relationship
- More flexibility at work
- New job
- Extra bedroom
- More attentive partner/spouse
- A baby
- Looking younger
- Losing weight
- Child excelling at school/work
- More supportive and loving parents
- Cure from chronic illness/disability
- More money
- More time

Funnily enough, there is actually one definitive answer as to what would make you happier. And that is…

…none of them! That's right. None of these things will make us sustainably happier over the long-term. We may experience some short term boosts, like when we eat Burger One, but ultimately our level of happiness will return to what it was.

Sonja Lyubomirsky is a positive psychologist at the University of Southern California and one of the most respected happiness researchers in the field. Lyubomirsky has conducted extensive research into different factors that make us happy and from this wanted to know, what is the equation for happiness? From looking at each of these factors, can we identify where happiness actually comes from? When Lyubomirsky ran the numbers, she found out you could, and this is what she shared in her book "*The How of Happiness.*" (2)

50% of our happiness is determined by our genes. So to a certain extent, we are born happy or we're not. I'm sure you know people who seem to be happy despite huge challenge, pain and adversity, and in turn people who seem to be unhappy regardless of how much abundance, achievement or love they receive. 50% of this can be explained by our genetics. We might see this as being beyond our control, but the field of epigenetics would suggest different.

Epigenetics is a field of research that is finding that our genetic expression can be turned "on" or "off" by environmental factors. (3) Two individuals might have the same genetic code (for example twins), but have very different perceptions of their lives because of the difference in how those genes express themselves.

To oversimplify things, let's say that there is a "depression gene". Two individuals have this gene.

One individual is brought up in a loving family. Their teachers at school nurture them. They find their passion early on in life. They enjoy great success doing what they love. They meet and marry a wonderful partner and raise a happy family of their own. They have the fairytale story. Even though they were born with the "depression gene", they were brought up in such a loving and empowering environment that the gene was rarely, if ever, "switched on".

Conversely, another individual with the gene is brought up in a broken home. They see violence and aggression from their parents. They experience sexual abuse. Their school is underfunded and their teachers never have time to support them. They are bullied by their peers. They experience depression throughout their upbringing and it doesn't change as an adult. They leave school and struggle to hold down a job due to their mental health. They self-medicate with alcohol, junk food and eventually drugs. They struggle to find and maintain relationships and become more and more isolated. Eventually, the suffering becomes too great for them and they take their own life. This person's depression gene was rarely, if ever, "switched off".

Our environment feeds into our genetic expression and so changes we make to our lifestyle and environment can feed right down to the cellular level. As Richard Davidson neatly summarises: "Genes load the gun, but only the environment can pull the trigger." (4)

This means we may have significant control over our genes and we don't have to accept the results of a bad "genetic lottery". A whole book could be written about epigenetics and there is still lots of fascinating research to come I'm sure. However, for the sake of argument, let's say that our genes are fixed, there is nothing we can do about them. 50% of our Happiness is beyond our control.

Well what can we control? What changes can we make to be happier people? Think back to the list a little earlier. How many of the changes do you believe would make you happier? Which of those changes have you already tried to make you happier?

If we are unhappy, so many of us try to change our external circumstances. We are not wrong to do so. It's not that external circumstances don't impact our happiness. I'm sure all of us would be happier living near a sunny beach than in arctic conditions. I'm sure all of us would rather live in a country at peace than a country that is war-torn. The little things such as having our hair just right, wearing clothes that suit us and having a bit of muscle tone to show off are nice. But we vastly overestimate the impact they will have on us.

That is why there are celebrities checking into rehab. They have money, cars, houses, fame, achievement, fans and everything else we might think we need to be happy, yet some celebrities struggle with their mental illness and addiction. Why is this? Because our external circumstances only have a small influence on our happiness. In fact, Lyubomirsky's research has found it accounts for just 10% of the equation.

Where the difference really can be made is in the remaining 40% of the equation: our internal state of mind. This is what we think and what we do on a consistent basis. This section is entirely under our control and it's where big shifts in our Consciousness occur. Lyubomirsky calls it *"The 40% Solution"*, it's where we find the "How" of Happiness.

Lyubomirsky's findings are backed up by neuroscience research conducted primarily by Richard Davidson at the University of Wisconsin-Madison. Davidson has spent decades studying emotions and finding the neurological sources of emotion since the earliest days of brain imaging technology.

He has found that a key difference between people reporting positive emotions and those reporting negative emotions is activation in their pre-frontal cortex (PFC). If you take your knuckles and (gently) rap them against your forehead the part of your brain immediately behind that part of your skull is your PFC. Davidson has observed that in people who report feeling more positive emotion, they show more activation in the left side of their PFC. (5) The left side of the PFC sends signals to the amygdala (the area of the brain associated with our fear response and producing stress chemicals) instructing it to quiet down. This allows individuals with high left PFC activation to reduce the effect of negative experiences and bounce back to positive moods more quickly.

Stanford Psychologist Laura Carstensen observed this in effect. She used fMRI (Functional Magnetic Resonance Imaging: this measures what parts of the brain are activated by a stimulus) scanners to study the brain behaviour of subjects presented with both positive and negative imagery.

She found that in young people, their amygdala showed activity for both sets of imagery. However, in the elderly, she only observed activity for the positive stimuli. Carstensen hypothesised that the elderly subjects had trained their PFC to inhibit the amygdala in the presence of negative stimuli. The elderly subjects were not happier because their life was any better. They were happier because of what they chose to focus on. (6) Moreover, what the age difference suggested was that this ability could be trained. We'll talk more about how you can do this in forthcoming chapters.

It sounds trite, but we really do *think ourselves happy*. This might sound like some warm and fuzzy self-help hype but this is what science is now telling us.

We cannot explain the variation any other way. We know genetics play a big part, but isn't the full picture. We know our external circumstances play a small part, but they don't explain the rest of the difference. Why do we have celebrities checking into rehab, and starving children in Africa smiling and dancing? It is all to do with the way they view and think about life. We too can change the way we view and think about our lives. A huge portion of our happiness is under our control. That is what you will learn as we dive deeper into the principles of Consciousness.

Before we do, however, there is some more foundational work to build. If you want to change what is going on between the ears, it is necessary to have a deeper understanding of what you have between your ears. It is a piece of equipment that far surpasses anything we can build, yet so many of us have little to no understanding of what it is and how it works. This will be rectified in the next part of the chapter.

Part 2: The Mozart Mind

I'd like to begin this segment by giving you a list of statements. Next to them is the option to say whether you agree or disagree with the statement. If you have a pen handy, circle or highlight your answer, or take note of your answer on a separate sheet of paper. Alternatively, keep a mental note of your answers.

1. "Failure is the limit of my abilities." YES/NO
2. "Failure is an opportunity to grow." YES/NO
3. "I'm either good at something or I'm not." YES/NO
4. "I can learn to do anything I want." YES/NO
5. "I don't like being challenged." YES/NO
6. "Challenges help me grow." YES/NO
7. "My abilities are unchanging." YES/NO
8. "My effort and attitude determine my abilities." YES/NO
9. "Feedback and criticism are personal." YES/NO
10. "Feedback is constructive." YES/NO
11. "I stick to what I know." YES/NO
12. "I like to try new things." YES/NO
13. "Other people's successes make me jealous." YES/NO
14. "I am inspired by the successes of others." YES/NO
15. "I can either do it, or I can't." YES/NO

I'll come back to these answers in a couple of pages. What we're going to be focusing on in this segment is mindset. "Mindset" is a term that gets thrown around a lot in the personal development field, without many students (and sometimes even the coaches and trainers who talk about it) understanding exactly what the term describes.

My definition is that "mindset" is how we use our mind on a consistent basis, it's like our default setting for the mind. Our default setting is how we will operate through most of our life, in particular, during times of stress and challenge. It is the setting that we will fall back on, even if we are striving to build a new, improved mindset.

Carol Dweck is a Stanford Psychologist who is one of the world's leading voices on mindset. In her extensive research she has identified that there are two primary types of mindset: The FIXED MINDSET and the GROWTH MINDSET. (7)

The fixed mindset is what has been fostered in most of us from an early age and it is based on the belief that we have a fixed set of skills and abilities that will never change. We either have something, or we don't; we're creative, or we're not; we're a people person, or we're not.

Because individuals with the fixed mindset believe their abilities are fixed they are constantly seeking situations where they know they can succeed. Since they don't believe they can improve, they only want to showcase themselves in a scenario where they know they can look good. They won't push their boundaries and challenge themselves. They will give up if things become too hard. They believe that talent, not effort, is the key to success.

This belief leads them to avoid situations where they may fail or look bad. If they have to put in effort, or if they can't overcome a challenge, they feel that this exposes their lack of ability. Individuals with a fixed mindset will blame and make excuses to try and hide their failures. They will also feel threatened by the success of others, as they see it as undermining their ability.

Now this is where well-meaning but poor parenting and teaching come in. When a child does well, we tell them they're smart. We tell them they're athletic. We tell them they're artistic. We prescribe fixed nouns related to their performance. We nurture and feed the fixed mindset in our young children. Then one day they will encounter a challenge that shatters their belief that they can get by on talent alone.

Even worse, we call our children "naughty", "bad", "disgraceful". I sometimes sit in an airport and cringe at how parents talk to their kids. I remember one particular flight where I nearly kicked the chair of the parent in front of me.

My partner and I were flying to Amsterdam for our first anniversary, and the trip got off to a slow start as our plane sat on the tarmac for forty-five minutes before take-off. These scenarios can be frustrating and boring, especially if you're a young child.

There was a young girl in front of us. She couldn't have been much older than six or seven. Summer was her name. I will never forget it, because of the amount of times her mother shouted it at her.

Summer was fidgeting and kicking in her chair. She was whining and complaining. Yes she wasn't being the model of good behaviour but she wasn't disturbing me even though I was just a row away. She was acting like any other six or seven year old would act in her situation. I know for a fact Summer wasn't a bad kid, she was just bored.

Her mother, however, did nothing to try and entertain her. She didn't play a game with Summer. She didn't tell Summer some interesting facts about the amazing city we were going to. She didn't even sympathise with Summer's frustration. She just shouted: "Summer be quiet.", "Summer you're going to upset your granny", "SUMMER YOU ARE THE WORST BEHAVED PERSON ON THIS PLANE."

That last line has stuck with me ever since. If it stuck with me, you can bet it stuck with Summer, either consciously or unconsciously. I couldn't believe a parent would say something like that to their child. What a terrible thing to tell them. When you tell your child such a disempowering statement, it sticks. What else has Summer been told by her mother? What fixed attributes will she prescribe to herself when she grows up?

I wish parents would realise the damage of prescribing fixed attributes to their children. Yes, a child may be behaving poorly, but they usually do this because they are bored or needing attention and love. How is a child who has been called "bad" since an early age ever supposed to believe they have anything worthwhile to give to the world?

We are scripted by the stories of the past. What stories have you been scripted by? Who told you that you weren't good enough? What beliefs do you hold about your lack of ability? When do you usually give up on something? If you have a fixed mindset, you'll struggle to change. However, don't worry if you do, because you can change it.

What we want to cultivate in ourselves, and I hope in the future we will cultivate more in our children, is the growth mindset. This is the belief that we can improve any of our current abilities and skills. If we're shy, don't understand technology or want to be more compassionate, that is something we can work on.

Because individuals with the growth mindset believe that their abilities can be improved, they seek out opportunities for learning. They aren't concerned about their starting level of talent, they just focus on getting better. On this quest for learning, they will explore the unfamiliar and challenge themselves. They will persist even when things are difficult because they believe that you succeed through effort, not talent.

When someone with a growth mindset fails, they understand that is just part of the learning process. On the next attempt they will try a new strategy or they will work harder. They are also not intimidated by the successes of others but inspired by them. If someone else has succeeded, then it means that there is a way for them to succeed too.

To summarise:

Fixed Mindset

- What I've been born with, I'm stuck with
- If something is too difficult, I give up
- Failure means I'm not good enough
- I win because I'm talented

Growth Mindset

- What I've been born with, I can improve
- If something is difficult, then I know I'm learning
- Failure just means I have to keep trying
- I win because I've worked hard

Remember those questions you answered earlier? Go back and total up the questions you answered "YES" to. If you answered YES to most of the odd numbered questions, that is evidence that you have a FIXED MINDSET, if you answered YES to most of the even numbered questions, you have a GROWTH MINDSET. If you haven't got one already, developing a growth mindset is key to the Author Your Life process.

When we talk about mindset, we can sometimes get lost in self-help hype. Statements such as Napoleon Hill's *"Whatever the mind can conceive and believe, it can achieve."* or Henry Ford's *"Whether you think you can or think you can't, you're right."* are sometimes voiced when the topic of "mindset" arises. Not that these statements don't have merit but I always like to have a tangible, scientific foundation behind the statement whenever possible. Carol Dweck is a Stanford Psychologist, and she has spent decades studying the science behind these two mindsets.

The first scientific concept to understand in relation to Growth Mindset is that our brain is not a fixed structure, it is like a muscle that can be trained and developed. There is this wonderful phenomenon called *Brain Plasticity* or *Neuroplasticity*. Brain plasticity describes our brain's potential to grow and develop new connections between the billions of neurons in the brain.

In blind individuals, their visual cortex becomes involved in tactile sensation, meaning blind people are able to perceive things through touch with far greater accuracy than non-blind people. (8) In deaf individuals, their auditory cortex retrains to detect visual signals, meaning deaf people have greater peripheral vision than non-deaf individuals. (9)

The implications for therapeutic interventions are fascinating. Edward Taub conducted an experiment to test a method of rehabilitating victims of a stroke. One of the common outcomes of a stroke is that the patient loses use of one arm, so Edward devised a way of gaining use back in that arm.

He put their good arm in a sling and put an oven mitt on their good hand for two weeks, forcing the individual to try and use their paralysed arm with a set of various rehabilitation activities. The results were astonishing. The patients began to be able to pick up cups, hold utensils and put pegs into holes using their damaged arm. Progress was slow and shaky at first, but they soon got to the stage where they could dress themselves, feed themselves, and perform most of their daily routines around the home. (10)

There is a second key process related to brain plasticity that was active in this study with the stroke patients. That is *myelination*. Myelin is a fatty substance that wraps around a nerve and increases the speed and intensity at which that nerve fires.

Now here's the thing about myelination. It's not something we're born with, it's something we develop. Every time a cell and nerve circuit fires, the myelin sheath around the neurons in that circuit thickens. The more that pathway fires, the thicker that sheath gets, and the faster and stronger that connection.

I like to use the analogy of the internet to explain myelination. When I was growing up, we used dial-up internet. You literally had to "call" you internet provider and wait until a connection was made. It was slow and cumbersome compared to today's standards. That is like a connection in your brain that you don't use very often. When you start playing the guitar, you are using a dial-up pathway.

However, the internet evolved. After dial-up came broadband, and after broadband, fibre optic. As engineers and technicians worked on the internet, they were able to make it faster and faster.

The same happens as you continue to work on your guitar skills. Eventually your neural pathways evolve from dial-up and become more like broadband, then fibre optic. The signals between your guitar-playing neurons travels faster and faster. Individuals such as Slash, Brian May and Jimi Hendrix all started with dial-up guitar neurons.

Therefore, when we say someone is talented or skilled, we are really just saying they are well myelinated. Let's take the example of Mozart. Mozart is considered a genius; a huge natural talent; he was able to play the piano at just three years old.

Mozart *was not a genius*, he was well myelinated. He didn't have the talent to play the piano at three years old. He had the talent *because* he played the piano at three years old. Mozart's dad drilled him for hours every day and Mozart's myelin grew like it was on steroids.

Geniuses are made and not born. That is why this part of the chapter is entitled the Mozart Mind. What I want you to understand is the phenomenal ability your brain has to grow, adapt and change. Coming back to the growth mindset, it is important to remember that every skill and quality can be developed. Not just practical skills like playing the piano: you can train yourself to be more confident, more expressive, or more loving. We will explore how you can do so in the chapters to come.

Before that, let's look at three broad components that separate the fixed mindset from the growth mindset, and what you can do to become more growth-minded.

Challenge

We live in a society where too many people like to quit. When the workouts get tough, people cancel their gym membership. When degrees get tough, students drop out. When marriages get tough, spouses divorce. People's health, education and relationships suffer because they have an aversion to challenge.

If you avoid challenge, you are running away from life. Choosing the easy option each time doesn't help you grow, it creates delusion and arrogance. You think life is better than it is and you think you are better than you are.

If you want to create a new story for your life, you're going to have to start doing some things you haven't done before. You're going to have to face challenge.

When I talk about challenge, it's important to recognise there are two types of challenge. First are the challenges life throws at you; these are random, unexpected, and sometimes not at all pleasant. Having to experience violence, poverty and grief is hugely challenging. It's true some people find incredible growth from incredible pain but I don't recommend seeking out danger, scarcity and heartbreak just to "build your character".

Second are the challenges we give ourselves. Life is going to give us challenges but we must also give ourselves challenges. The most successful people in life are those who challenge themselves most. Brendon Burchard's study of the top 15% of high performers in the world has found that these individuals have a bias towards action, even when the action's outcome is scary, risky, or uncertain. (11)

One of the ways you can develop a growth mindset is to start to see yourself as a person who takes on challenges. One way that I have developed this for myself is to get excited about discomfort. When I do hot yoga and the sweat is pouring down me and my head is swimming, I smile and stretch further into the posture, knowing that I'm pushing my capabilities. When I find a problem-solving task difficult, I rub my hands together and double my focus, knowing that I'm getting tested. One morning when I was meditating, my mind kept telling me that I had to start organising my first multi-day event. This sparked a heap of nerves and doubt for me, but as soon as I become aware of my discomfort, my excitement kicked in. Here was another challenge for me to face.

When you face discomfort in this way, you start to surprise yourself. We have this assumption in our society that "hard" equals "bad". Actually it is doing something hard that gives us our sense of achievement. Take a moment just now to think of the five things in your life that you're most proud of. I bet most, if not all, of those five involved overcoming some kind of tough challenge such as running a marathon, gaining a degree, or standing up to someone.

You learn quickly that when you push through a challenge, there is reward waiting for you on the other side. You feel more confident, more motivated and more meaningful. What you discover is that you are stronger and more able than you gave yourself credit for and that is very encouraging.

So how can we create challenge for ourselves? How do we hold autonomy over our challenges, rather than allowing them to happen to us?

The first component of a good challenge is it stretches you, but doesn't break you. Imagine my earlier example of yoga. If I sit cross-legged on the floor I'm not going to develop at all. On the other side of the spectrum, if I try to yank my leg behind my head I'm going to give myself an injury. I have to stretch the muscles and ligaments past their current level of flexibility, but not so much that I snap them. Use this principle with your challenges: what stretches you beyond your current boundaries but doesn't cause you to snap.

The second component is to be able to measure your progress. This helps you determine what is a feasible way to stretch yourself. In yoga, when you are trying to touch your toes, maybe you can only reach your knees to begin with. From there, you aim to be able to extend further down your shins each time you try until you can touch your ankles. Then you are able to reach your toes, then grip them, then eventually you can actually reach beyond your toes. Each section of your body provides a measuring stick that lets you know your normal range of motion and where to aim for to extend that range of motion.

With these two components, you can consistently challenge yourself and extend your abilities. However, it sounds simple when you put it down on paper, but there is another important aspect of the growth mindset that is involved in this process.

Effort

The huge advances in technology in the past few decades have brought a huge number of benefits. I am bringing this book to you using an Apple Macbook Pro, Amazon Bookstore and Social Media marketing. Each of these things is younger than I am. I'm deeply grateful that this book has been made possible by these things.

However, an unfortunate side effect of technology is that it has made a number of things ridiculously easy. We can order groceries straight to our door, be driven to our chosen location, and watch events halfway round the world in real-time. Because we are experiencing ease in a number of areas of our life, we start to assume that we should be experiencing this ease in other areas of our life.

With this in mind, is it surprising that we are developing an adverse attitude to effort? Why would we walk a couple of miles to the supermarket and carry back four bulging bags of shopping when we can get someone else to do it for us? Why would we bother putting in the effort?

That statement is dangerous, because we start asking ourselves that question in other domains of our life. "Running makes me sweaty and out of breath." *Why bother putting in the effort?* "I'm not getting any clients for my business." *Why bother putting in the effort?* "No one I'm going on dates with is compatible." *Why bother putting in the effort?*

Here's the key distinction that I think will hold true even as technology advances more and more. We can reduce the amount of effort it takes to get *things* but we need to increase the amount of effort it takes to get *results*. You can get that pair of Nike trainers easier than ever before but you need to put in more effort than you've done up until this point to get fit in those trainers.

Individuals with the growth mindset understand this equation, they understand that effort equals results. Angela Duckworth has demonstrated this with her research into achievement. (12) She notes that we all start out with a base level of *Talent*, our natural ability to do something. Here the fixed mindset does hold true, some people are born with more natural talent than others.

Duckworth notes that this is the beginning of the journey. Talent is not enough. To progress further, you must apply effort to that talent. When you do, it turns into a *Skill*. A skilled individual will beat a talented individual every time. The first round draft pick in the NBA is talented, but the first time they step onto court they will face a tough time against the higher skill of their opponents, as they have not yet turned their raw talent into refined skill.

However, skill is also not enough by itself. Every Olympic athlete is highly skilled but only one brings home the gold medal. Duckworth notes that you have to take your skill, apply effort, and that will turn into *achievement*. This process can be summarised in the following equations.

Talent + Effort = Skill
Skill + Effort = Achievement

In the process of achievement, innate talent is a factor. So too is skill. However, effort appears twice in the equation: this is because effort is twice as important as ability. Effort is the fuel of achievement. Imagine a car. You might have the best engine, chassis and tyres (talent and skill), but if you don't have any petrol, you aren't going to win any races.

Individuals with the fixed mindset never master this equation, so will struggle to match the achievements of those with the growth mindset. They view effort as the enemy, as a sign that you are getting further away from achievement, not closer to it.

This aversion to effort has been explored in a number of studies. One study, for example, asked a group of seventh graders how they would respond if they got a poor test grade. Those with a growth mindset said they would study harder. However, those with a fixed mindset said they would study less. After all, if they weren't born with that ability, why bother even trying? Some even said they would seriously consider cheating! (13) Those with the fixed mindset were looking to avoid effort at all costs because they believed it exposed their lack of ability.

The same trend can be observed in older students. On university campuses in the Northern Hemisphere, the period from February to March can be a challenging time. Project deadlines and mid-term tests are looming, and the lighter days and warmer weather of spring have not properly arrived. Rates of depression are higher during this time on university campus. (14) If an individual with a fixed mindset becomes depressed they display more negative self-talk, they take less action to solve their problems and they put in less work to their projects and revision.

However, if an individual with a growth mindset gets depressed, they have the opposite reaction. They take *more* action to confront their problems, put in *more* work to keep up with their studies, and apply *more* effort to maintain self-care. Individuals with the growth mindset know that to have any chance of rising out of their slump, they need to put in the effort. (15) Even in individuals with depression, for whom willpower and perseverance are generally difficult, there is a difference between those looking at their depression through the lens of the fixed mindset, and those looking through the lens of the growth mindset.

It's not particularly sexy to talk about hard work. Everyone wants a "hack" or a strategy to get them ahead faster. I'm going to offer some "hacks" and strategies to help you be more effective in this book. However, I warn you that none of them will work if you don't put in the effort. Great strategy is not a substitute for poor work ethic. If you are going to Author

Your Life, you'll need to work flipping hard for it. That is what individuals with the growth mindset do.

<u>Failure</u>

Overlook this part of the chapter at your peril. It might just be the most important thing I write in regards to Consciousness, and perhaps in this entire book. With this book I aim to help you grow, progress, and change in order to find success, however you define it. Nevertheless, I want you to know that failure is the most vital component of success.

Life as we know it is built on polarity. We have day and night; life and death; happiness and sadness...success and failure are no different. You cannot have one without the other.

On this journey you are going to fail and fail hard. You are going to have some soul-destroying, gut-wrenching, existential-crisis failures. Not very motivational I know but I'm not saying this to motivate you. I'm saying this to prepare you.

You need to know the truth and embrace it. Because it is true that you are going to have some horrible failures. It's quite likely that it was a horrible failure that made you pick up this book. Throughout this book I have and will share success stories, either my own or others, to show you what is possible when you apply the principles of Author Your Life. What I want to share now though, are the failure stories. I want you to know that I am nothing special. I have been humiliated, neglected and defeated in my life.

- At age nine, I went to a chess tournament. It was not my first and I had a respectable record at tournaments leading up to it. At this tournament, I lost my first couple of games and I let it get to me. I started to make stupid mistakes against inferior opponents and ended up losing all six of my games. I was utterly demoralised by this and gave up chess.

- On my first day of high school, I became infatuated with a girl in my year. She was one of the "cool" kids, which I certainly wasn't, and I could only ever admire her from afar. In our final year of high school though, we become really good friends and I wanted to tell her how I really felt about her. I never did. We moved away to separate universities. She entered a relationship soon after that which, as far as I know, she has been in ever since.

- At the University of Glasgow, where I graduated from, I was aiming for a first-class degree. To do so, I needed to secure mostly A grades across my third and fourth year. In third year, I was getting As for my coursework and Christmas exams. In my summer exams, I got four Bs and two Cs, my first Cs I had ever received at university. This essentially scuppered my chance of getting a first class degree as it sent my GPA plummeting.

- When my dad died, he left me with approximately £7500. At the time, one of my close friends wanted to start a business but needed some capital to buy tech. I loaned him £2000 of Dad's inheritance to help him do so. My friend took this loan for granted and made little effort to pay me back; eventually I realised that I had misplaced my trust and that this person's values were distinctly different from my own. I lost that friend and lost that money.

• I decided to launch my first incarnation of my business with an online course. I offered it for an introductory price of £1. Only five people bought it (one of whom was my mum!). I redesigned it and brought it out months later for £19.97. Only one more person bought it at this price.

These all stung. They hit right to the core of important aspects of the human condition: love, purpose, faith. I am a big failure…and I'm proud of it.

Those failures taught me how to be a success. I never got together with that girl in high school. It turns out there was another girl at that school, who at the time of publication I am now engaged to. I didn't get that first class degree. Instead I started a business, where it doesn't matter what a piece of paper says about you. I had totally the wrong strategy for the online course, so instead I wrote a book. Six months after the second launch of the online course, *The Last 60 Minutes* hit #1 on Amazon.

We learn and grow so much more from failure than we do from success. Furthermore, it is actually necessary to fail in order to succeed. One of the best analogies I've heard comes from Derek Rydall, author of *"Emergence"*. He reminds us that "walking is just controlled falling". (17) When we were children, the "failure" was to fall from one leg without getting the other in front of us to keep us upright. Yet as children, we take that failure and learn that if we do get that leg in front of us, then we can springboard to the next step.

The process of growth is a process of failure. When you attempt something important, perhaps even something unprecedented, you are going to mess up. Professor Randy Paush, in his famous "Last Lecture" at Carnegie Mellon University, talked about brick walls. He said that brick walls are a test to see who really wants it. (17) If anyone could become an Olympian, a F500 CEO or a Nobel Prize winner, we would not hold their achievements in such high esteem. It is because such individuals push through odds and challenges that others haven't that we admire them.

You are going to fail in this process. This you must know. But don't see it as the loaded word "failure". It is only a "failure" if you give up or do not learn from the experience. Failure is just an action ("I failed"), but too often it is seen as identity ("I am a failure"). This is a key distinction between a fixed mindset and a growth mindset. Individuals with a fixed mindset split life into "winning" and "losing". Individuals with a growth mindset split life into "winning" or "learning".

Failure is feedback, but individuals with a fixed mindset often ignore it. A study at Columbia University (18) gave participants a challenging test then measured their brain waves when they were given feedback on how they performed. Individuals with a fixed mindset only paid attention when finding out whether they got an answer right or wrong. When given feedback on how they could've gotten the answer right, they stopped paying attention. Because they believed their ability was fixed, they didn't believe they could do better on the test. In the growth minded individuals, the brain imaging showed that they were paying attention when receiving feedback on how to do better.

Of course, it can be lovely with the benefit of hindsight to look back on a failure and know that when that door closed, another opened. What is far more difficult is to be in the midst of struggle, challenge, and failure, and still be able to say to yourself: "Woo Hoo, a failure, this is going to lead to great future victories!".

I say that facetiously; I don't expect you to be so blasé and Pollyanna about the failure. Failures do hurt and it's important to process that hurt. With this in mind, I recommend three steps to follow when failure hits.

1. Take the hit: feel the pain

When failure arises, notice the emotions that arise: disappointment, anger, hopelessness. Give yourself permission to feel these emotions. Often we have the failure, and then kick ourselves when we're down by criticising ourselves for the way we're feeling about the failure. Accepting the emotion does not mean you are endorsing the failure, or promoting feeling that way. Schedule time that day for self-care and personal space. This takes the "sting" out of the emotion.

2. Focus on the solution, not the problem

When you've taken that "sting" out, you are in a better place to do something about the failure. I recommend the old cliche of "sleeping on it" and waiting until a fresh day to look at the failure (assuming nothing catastrophic is going to happen if you wait that period). If you continue focusing on the problem, you are only going to exacerbate it, as we will learn more of in the next chapter. Instead, what can you, and will you, do about it? What steps can you take, no matter how small, to start recovering from the situation?

3. Identify the learning

When you have achieved significant distance from the failure — this might be a couple of days, weeks or even months depending on the scale of the failure — return to the failure when the emotion has dissipated and you have a rational mind. Start to analyse and process the failure. Get your pen and paper and start journaling about the failure. What happened? How did it happen? Why did it happen? If you were in that situation again, what would you do differently? What action can you take to prevent or mitigate against that failure occurring again? What do you have now that you didn't have before the failure? What opportunity became available after that failure? In short, what "gain" came as a direct result of that pain?

Part 3: Know Your Value

Each of us has a set of values that make us uniquely us. We operate at our best when we operate from our values as often as possible. Being aligned with your values is going to help you thrive as a person, in your career, and in your interactions with others. Finding and living in alignment with your values will give you clarity on who you really are. Research has shown there is a positive correlation between self-clarity and self-esteem. Conversely, low self-clarity is strongly correlated with neuroticism and negative emotions. (19)

Finding and identifying our values is something we are not particularly encouraged to do or educated on at all. Consequently, I think it is important to begin with a few distinctions.

Values are not personality traits. Our personality is an expression of our values. For example, extroversion is a personality trait but it can originate from different value bases. Imagine the braggart who walks into a room and practically performs their own fanfare. They have the charm, charisma and confidence. They find themselves in the centre of the room holding people's attention. Their extroversion comes from a value set of pride and control.

Conversely, consider the extrovert who circles the room, constantly introducing themselves to new people and asking them questions. Their extroversion comes from a value set of curiosity and learning.

Furthermore, consider another extrovert who is the storyteller and joker, always capturing people's attention and making them laugh. Their extroversion comes from a value set of joy and creativity. So you can see that our personality is not our values. Yes you might want to express your extroversion but from what place do you want that extroversion to come from?

Values are also not interests. This is a big misattribution people make in the dating game. They go on a couple of dates with someone and say: "Oh my God I've found my soulmate. We're both vegan. We both love manga. We both study philosophy. We both volunteer for animal charities. I think they might be the one."

When that relationship ends a couple of months later, it can cause a lot of head-scratching. There may have felt like there was alignment. However, it was only the superficial level of interests; interests that came from different value sets.

One person might be vegan for ethical reasons. The other might be vegan just to jump on a trend.

One might love Manga because it activates their curiosity. The other might love it because it allows them to live out fantasies they don't have the confidence to pursue.

One might study philosophy because they want to find out more about themselves and the world. The other might study it because they want to appear intellectually superior to others.

One might volunteer for an animal charity from a place of love. The other might volunteer for an animal charity from a place of self-interest.

Interests do not equal values. Our values are the deepest part of us. It is where our personality and interests stem from. Two people might share the same value but express it in different ways. The key is to first identify what your values are, which is what the next few exercises are designed to help you do.

Begin with the End in Mind

"Begin with the end in mind" is the second habit of Stephen Covey's *"The 7 Habits of Highly Effective People."* (T7HOHEP) I agree with Covey that this habit is vital to growing and advancing in our lives and the first exercise is one that he shares in his book.

Covey asks you to picture driving along an old country road. Along the road you come across a funeral, and you leave the car to see what is going on. When you enter, you walk up to the casket, and see that the person in it is you. It is your funeral.

You sit down in the audience, read the order of service, and see that there are four people delivering eulogies.

1. A close friend
2. A lover
3. A work colleague
4. An acquaintance from the wider community (20)

Thinking of your funeral, many years from now, what would you want these people to say of you? What qualities would you want them to speak of? These are what David Brooks calls "Eulogy Virtues". (21) In life Brooks notes we are often aspiring for "resume virtues" such as intelligence, charisma and achievement i.e. things that look good to an employer and that compare favourably with our peers. However, when someone stands up at your funeral, you don't want them to say: "She had an IQ of 163" or "He broke the sales record for the company in 2019." You want people to talk about who you were as a person. These are you "eulogy virtues", for example kindness, courage or humility.

I read T7HOHEP, and this exercise, a couple of months after my dad died. This was hugely relevant and impactful for me. I was right back at the crematorium where I said goodbye to Dad. However, instead of me delivering the eulogy, it was me in the casket. Dad's death had already prompted me to consider the way I wanted the rest of my life to pan out but this started to help me solidify it.

I would encourage you to also go through this process and begin with the end in mind. As I have said before in this book, one day we will all be lying on our deathbed. Who do we want to have been during our life? What impact do we want to have made on the world? What influence do we want to have had on the people around us? This book is designed to help you tap into these answers throughout, but take some time here to think about them actively. What do you want those four people to say at your funeral? As you write down what you want them to say, look out for common words and themes. These commonalities point towards your values: what you should aspire to live to day-to-day.

5:5:5

The second exercise I call the 5:5:5 task. This is an excellent task that I recommend to people starting or near the beginning of their self-awareness journeys. The first part of this exercise is to simply write down five words that most define who you are. As we covered before, try not to highlight a personality trait or interest, take it a level deeper. Don't write down "extrovert" or "sporty". Where does that extroversion come from (joy, curiosity, love)? Where does that sportiness come from (challenge, teamwork, determination)? This is the first "5" in the task.

When you've found five words, consult with the five people who are closest to you and know you best, and ask them to describe you in five words, using the same parameters. This is the second "5" in the task.

When you've completed this, you will have thirty words describing who you are. You will likely find some of the words you wrote down were also used by those closest to you. Good, this means you're onto something, and that these words represent core components of who you are.

You might also be surprised to notice that others are repeatedly saying something you didn't notice yourself. This represents two things. Either you are not expressing yourself authentically and are showing a distorted sign of your true nature. Alternatively, the people around you see a quality that you don't truly appreciate yourself. Either way, this is why we get the opinion of those who know you best. You can make a judgment call about whether what they are seeing is a false self you don't want to project or a virtuous part you have not given yourself credit for.

Once you have this list of thirty, it is your job to cut it back down to five. There will be some you can double up or amalgamate, but then there will still be some left you have to make a decision on. Of these, which five words most represent who you are? These five words are five core values that you want to live from in all areas of your life. This is the third "5" of the exercise.

The 5:5:5 task identifies your five core values. Now these five values might describe who you are right now. However, you might also look at the words and notice there are some values that you feel do describe you, and certainly describe who you want to be, yet right now you aren't living in alignment with that value as you would like. This is good, this is you identifying your aspirations, which we will explore further in the next segment.

Set High Standards

This concept is key, not just to being more aligned with your values, but to everything that we cover in this book. If you want to Author Your Life, you need to set high standards for the type of story you want to create. I want you to be aspirational and think big for yourself.

This is something that can be uncomfortable for many of us. We were brought up to fit in and play along. We were chided by teachers, parents and peers for having "ideas above our station" or being "big-headed".

What has happened for a lot of us is that we have confused ambition with arrogance. Absolutely you shouldn't swagger around thinking that you are in any way superior to others, that is classic fixed mindset thinking. However, having aspirations for the type of person you want to be and the type of life you want to live is not arrogant at all. In fact, it is necessary for the advancement of humanity.

Aspiration makes people eat healthier and more sustainably. Aspiration drives doctors to invent new medicines and treatments. Aspiration motivates engineers and inventors to create new technology. Aspiration encourages people to educate themselves to higher levels. Aspiration elevates people out of poverty. Aspiration catalyses political progress.

There is a second barrier that holds people back from being aspirational. They worry about belittling and undermining others. We worry about making someone feel small. This is a very noble sentiment but ultimately misplaced. True greatness does not diminish, it enriches.

Young football players do not watch Cristiano Ronaldo and think: "man, I'm rubbish at football, I should give up." Young entrepreneurs do not listen to Richard Branson and say: "I can't sell a flipping thing, why bother." Young actors do not watch Meryl Streep and decide: "I'm a terrible actor, I'm never auditioning again." When you demonstrate your quality, it inspires others to emulate those qualities. Will you have some who feel jealous, resentful and upset when they observe your efforts? Sure, but that is their problem, not yours.

Research demonstrates that high-performing individuals report spending a lot more time thinking about their future, aspirational self than low-performers, as much as sixty minutes more every single week. (22) They can describe their future self faster, more confidently, and more articulately. (23)

Therefore, as well as identifying your core values, also identify the core values of your future aspirational self. How do you feel when you are living to your values more authentically? What do you do on a regular basis? How do you show up in your interactions with others? As well as your five values, also come up with three words that would summarise a greater expression of these values.

When you have the five words that summarise your current values, and three words that summarise your aspirational values (there can be overlap here), the next key step is to be intentional about living to them. You can activate them through priming.

Priming

Many people are out of alignment with themselves because they are not living to their values. People with a value of self-care who have let their exercise habits slip. People with a value of service working for a greedy employer. People with a value of freedom stay in a relationship with a restrictive partner. You need to be connected to your values on a consistent basis to make sure you don't fall into these situations.

A consistent difference observed by Brendon Burchard in his study of high-performing individuals is that high performers prime their values far more regularly than low-performers. Low performers self-monitor their values only a third to half as many times a week as high performers. (24) Identifying your values and aspirational future self is not sufficient by itself, you need to prime this identity for yourself.

The first technique I recommend is to set alarms on your phone. (25) You have your phone on you all the time don't you? And most of the time it is pinging nonsense and other people's agendas at you. So why not use this technology to your advantage? Set a regular alarm to go off every three to four hours. On this alarm you can have a reminder of your values. This might just be the word (e.g. "kindness") but I would recommend a statement ("I seek opportunities to be kind every day") or a question ("what can I do to be kind right now?"). This way you are checking in multiple times throughout the day to see if you are living in accordance with your values. This is actually a great method to practice and ingrain a number of the concepts and techniques we will talk about in this book.

The second technique is to create a value statement for yourself. (26) On a single sheet of paper, you write out your five values and your three aspirational values, and then what you do to express those values. For example, one of my values is "Joy" and the ways I activate joy for myself are optimism, gratitude and humour. The Value Statement is your "cheat sheet" for how to live in alignment with your values. Stick this somewhere you will see it everyday, such as your fridge, your desk or your bathroom mirror. Mine is in my bedroom so I see it every morning when I wake up. This acts as a primer every day for your values and how to express them.

The third technique is self-coaching. (27) This is verbalising to yourself what your values are. Self-coaching can be used when you are out of alignment and integrity with yourself. Sometimes I like to give myself a good talking to "Come on David, you are one of the most driven people I know, you'll find a way through this." or "David, you're being ungrateful right now. What can you do to bring this back to gratitude?". It's not a case of being hard on yourself, it is reminding yourself of who you are, and bringing you back into alignment with your best self.

<u>Understand</u>

Change begins from understanding. In this chapter, you have started to Understand your capabilities. In the next chapter, we will build on these and help you Unlock them.

In this chapter you have learned:

- Four different "hamburgers" of happiness
- How at least **40%** of your happiness is under your control
- Happiness is a choice
- The difference between the fixed mindset and the growth mindset
- How your mind is a muscle that can be trained and developed
- What values define you as a person
- How to live in alignment with your values

My biggest takeaway from this chapter is

_____.

Chapter 5: Unlock

"Compared with what we ought to be, we are only half awake." - **William James**

Many of our brains are running at a fraction of their potential. For many people, this is because our brains are not being looked after. Stress and negative thought patterns are clogging up our brain and preventing it from operating to its full capability. In this chapter, you are going to learn the chemistry behind your emotional states and how you can rebalance your chemicals to enter more positive states. You will learn how to readjust thought patterns that aren't serving you. You will learn about one of our most important practices that most people are not being intentional enough about. If you want to Author Your Life, then you must clear away the debris, reboot your operating system, and Unlock your full potential.

Part 1: Breaking the Bad (1)

It's time to put on the yellow biohazard suits and look into our brain laboratory. What is the chemistry of our brain? How does that impact our physiological and psychological state? In our brains and bodies we have something called neurotransmitters, which are chemical messengers that send important signals to the body. In this segment we're going to be focusing on some of the key chemicals that bring about happy states and responses.

We have some chemicals that don't make us feel so good. You will likely be quite familiar with these and the feelings associated with them. I've called these "stress" chemicals, as you will associate them with the overarching feeling of "stress".

Stress Chemical 1: Cortisol

Cortisol is receiving press at the moment as the "stress chemical" and getting painted as the bad guy. Remove cortisol from the picture and we'll be happier.

This is an accurate representation, but it's important to know the full nuances of cortisol, rather than just labelling it as the bad guy. The release of cortisol does make us feel stressed but not because cortisol is some sadistic tormentor who likes to spoil our day.

Cortisol makes us feel stressed so that we will take *action.* Cortisol is released because something in our body, mind or environment is not conducive to our wellbeing. The stress and negative feeling produced by cortisol makes us pay attention to the problem and attempt to remove it. If you are hurting yourself with a behaviour; if you have an approaching deadline; or if someone is giving you a hard time; then cortisol is released, motivating you to take action to resolve the problem. Cortisol is not bad — what is bad is excessive cortisol.

The brain stores memories of what previously brought you pain and this creates a neural circuit in your limbic system, its emotional centre. If at any time you encounter a similar situation, your cortisol will be activated. This can be helpful (a near miss causes you to drive more cautiously) or unhelpful (one breakup hampers your ability to find another date). We are scripted by the pain of the previous chapters of our life. This is where cortisol can be the bad guy. We want to move on from an event or make a change but trying to do so triggers our stress response: even though we have set the intention to change, that old circuit is still wired in our brain. This is what you can override when you start to Author Your Life.

Stress Chemical 2: (Nor)epinephrine

Epinephrine and norepinephrine are the two chemicals you will know as "adrenaline". You might say to yourself "but adrenaline makes me feel good" or "adrenaline makes me perform better". You might even actively seek adrenaline though something like extreme sports. Nonetheless, nor/epinephrine are released as part of our stress response. A state called "fight-or-flight".

Fight-or-flight is an ancient part of our make-up that was (and still is) vital for our survival. When we feel threatened, our body flushes with stress chemicals to prime us to defend ourselves, or run away. Cortisol is released to increase blood pressure and blood sugar and also suppresses the immune system. Epinephrine and norepinephrine are released which accelerates our heart rate and breathing as well as impairing all non-emergency functions such as digestion and peripheral vision. If we encounter a lion, this gives us the strength to sock it on the nose or pedal our legs away as fast as possible. However, this is an emergency response and takes a lot out of the body. It is not meant to be sustained for long periods.

We still have this response today, it is still useful, but more often than not it isn't. Our fight-or-flight response is triggered by the stresses of modern life: traffic, meetings, even what we see on social media, all of which aren't necessarily life-threatening. The fight-or-flight response is expensive for our body. It raises our stress and anxiety levels, which is important for life and death situations, but most of our lives are not a life-or-death situation.

This is how nor/epinephrine can be a negative force in our life. It leaves us constantly "wired", which is not a conducive state for overall health. Our secondary, but nonetheless important, functions do not run at optimal levels when we are in this heightened state. Adrenaline can keep us going at times, but *it's going to cause us to crash and burn in the long run*.

Stress Chemical 3: Endorphin

Similarly to nor/epinephrine, if you've heard of endorphin, you might believe it to be a "happy" chemical. "Endorphins" seems to be a generic term in pop psychology nowadays for "feeling good". People will say "that's good for you, because it releases endorphins in the brain" when the actual chemical is dopamine, serotonin or oxytocin (you'll find out about them shortly). There is a big difference between activating dopamine, what people usually label "endorphins", and activating actual endorphin.

Endorphin is the chemical that is activated when you take heroin. Still want to have the feeling of endorphins? Endorphin is short for "endogenous morphine" and gives us that euphoric feeling that heroin and its positive cousin morphine does. It is the chemical behind the anecdotal "runner's high".

So if it makes us feel good, why am I labelling it a stress chemical? That's because endorphin is released when we experience physical pain. We experience runner's high because we have pushed our body past its normal pain threshold and it has responded by releasing endorphin. We only trigger endorphin when we are in physical pain; so to keep on experiencing the endorphin hit, we have to keep putting ourselves in pain; not a good cycle to repeat. Alternatively, we have to take highly addictive drugs to create the feeling. Not good either! Some athletes and fitness enthusiasts will keep pushing themselves to recreate that high. Eventually they can reach a point where they break their body.

Endorphin of course does have its purpose. If we find ourselves seriously injured or ill, endorphin can give us a short burst of energy to try and find safety and help. There are also more innocuous activities that can give us trickles of endorphin. Side-splitting laughter and crying creates a trickle of endorphin. (2) It's interesting that when we feel sad, two common responses are to cry or to try to find some humour in the situation. Both of these behaviours release endorphin and so act as physical (and emotional) pain relief.

While these three stress chemicals have their function and role to play in our survival, we definitely don't want them to be regular contributors to our states of being. Too many people in society are living with high levels of stress chemicals. We want to get out our test tubes and bunsen burners and start addressing these chemical imbalances.

Just as there are three prominent stress chemicals, so too do we have three prominent "happy" chemicals. These are chemicals that make us feel good and promote positive behaviours and outcomes. Let's examine them in a little more detail and explore strategies for how we can increase the levels of these chemicals.

<u>Happy Chemical 1: Dopamine</u>

The first chemical of interest is dopamine. Dopamine is our "reward" chemical. It is dopamine that motivates and rewards our actions. If we didn't have dopamine, we wouldn't have any drive to fulfil our needs and would ultimately die. When we fulfil a need, dopamine is released and gives us a *"yay, I did it"* feeling. That feels good and so we are motivated to pursue that need again to gain that reward.

Dopamine helps us invest our energy and effort. If your body detects a reward within reach, it will drip-feed you dopamine to encourage you to pursue it.

Your dopamine circuits build over time. So if you find a consistent path to a desired reward, your dopamine will encourage you to keep on taking that path, as it knows there is a fulfilled need at the end of it. This is what builds healthy habits (e.g. meditation leads to feeling of calm) and unhealthy habits (e.g. smoking a cigarette leads to feeling of calm).

Dopamine is responsible for a lot of our addictive behaviour because we continuously seek that "hit" of a reward. Exercise, eating sugar, sex, shopping, drug-taking, playing video games and posting on social media are all examples of behaviours that can become addictive because they trip our dopamine receptors. There is a famous study of rats who had electrodes placed in the dopamine receptors in the brain. (3) The rats could press a lever that would activate their dopamine receptors and they would continue to press this lever, neglecting their physical and even sexual needs. (4) Just like the rat, chasing the feeling of reward can cause us to neglect our vital needs.

However, this is not to say that dopamine is a "bad" or "dangerous" chemical. Dopamine helped Thomas Edison invent the lightbulb, helped NASA put a man on the moon and helped Usain Bolt become the fastest ever human. Dopamine is the fuel that keeps us working towards our goals. When we achieve "micro goals" we get a spurt of dopamine and these spurts keep our drive alive in pursuit of the big goals. Let's look at three strategies for how we can boost our Dopamine.

Take Small Steps

Dopamine is triggered through the process of attaining a reward. Every step we take towards a goal is fuelled by dopamine. Our brain detects an upcoming reward and injects spurts of dopamine to move us towards the goal.

Imagine a monkey who sees a banana on a tree. When it sees the banana it gets a little spurt of dopamine which makes it anticipate the reward of the banana. As it approaches the tree trunk it gets another spurt. As it climbs the trunk, another. As it reaches the branch the dopamine burst gets stronger. As it moves along the branch the dopamine is coursing through the monkey. When it grabs the banana it gets the strongest injection yet. *"Yay, I did it."*

We can reproduce this process intentionally to trigger our dopamine and boost our motivation. We can do this by measuring our progress.

I first learned how to do this through lifting weights in the gym. As part of my New Year's Resolution in 2013, I started to record my workouts. Each workout I would record the exercises I did, the weights I used and how many sets and reps I did. I recorded these in a journal so I knew how I had performed in that workout.

When I next did this workout, I would know what numbers I was aiming to beat. I would try to lift a heavier weight or lift the same weight more times. As I neared failure, my dopamine would push me through to help me beat the previous week's numbers. If I had completed eight reps in the final set of an exercise the previous week, as soon as I reached eight, I knew I could achieve progress by pushing through and completing that ninth rep.

Finding a method to record your progress in this way will open up a drip-feed of dopamine and increase your motivation and progress.

Celebrate Small Victories

Later in this chapter we will discuss how our brain is wired for negativity and how we place more focus on the negative than the positive. Because of this, we have a tendency to linger on our losses; when things go wrong and when we mess things up. This lingering and negative focus can make us stressed and depressed. We can reverse this and activate our dopamine by learning to linger on our wins in the same way as we linger on our losses.

Just as we break down our goals into small steps to activate dopamine, so too must we focus on and recognise each small step we take. Have gratitude and appreciation each time you make progress, no matter how small and insignificant you may think it is. Too often we only wait until the completion or achievement of something before we celebrate. However, when we achieve something, the feeling is fleeting.

Even big achievements only provide short term feeling. This book is an eighteen-month project. When it is published, the feeling of accomplishment will be great. However, it's not going to last. As the weeks go by, as the tour dates are over, as the sales and reviews die down, the feeling will go. That's not me being defeatist or pessimistic, that is just how our neurochemistry works.

Therefore, I have been taking time to notice and appreciate the small moments along the way: times when I felt in creative flow; times when I found the clarity required to pull ideas together; times when I finished a chapter; when I wrote the concluding sentence of the book; each piece of feedback I received from my proofreaders. You have to take time to celebrate the journey, not just the destination.

Also remember that you can't count on other people recognising your achievements. That's not a criticism of other people, that's just because they have only seen a snapshot of your journey at best. Even big achievements do not receive the attention proportionate to the scale of the effort you put in, so you certainly can't count on people to recognise the little stuff. You are the only one who can fully appreciate the little victories you make along the way, so make sure you recognise them.

In life it's very easy to get down on ourselves, so take some time to big yourself up too. Your dopamine will respond to it.

Seek Novelty

Our brain loves novelty. It's one of the reasons we're constantly checking into social media. When we see a new wave of thumbs and hearts, our brain is going "bingbingbing" like it's a game show machine. It's one of the reasons we're at danger of becoming addicted to social media, because it activates our dopamine so consistently that it can create the habit and pattern of constantly checking our profiles.

I do not recommend plugging into social media to activate your dopamine but we can utilise the principle of novelty to activate dopamine in less addictive ways. We can do this in simple ways throughout the day: we can walk a different way to work, buy coffee from a different shop, or listen to a different genre of music.

To embrace novelty on a deeper level, increase the scale of change. Go to different restaurants for dinner; find different events and shows to attend; network in different social circles. Some of the best resources for this are the event-hosting sites Meetup and Eventbrite. They have a plethora of different categories to suit every taste and tell you what events and groups are in the city that match these interests.

Furthermore, it is not just doing these things that trigger dopamine. Research has found that the anticipation of reward is just as powerful in releasing dopamine as the actual experience. (5) This is that "Christmas Feeling" that many people get through December, knowing that Christmas is on the way. Anytime you have a big party or holiday in the calendar, you are creating some "Christmas Feeling" and releasing dopamine.

Happy Chemical 2: Serotonin

The next chemical of interest is serotonin. Serotonin is our "abundance" chemical. Serotonin is released when we are in a state or environment where we feel resources are plentiful, whether that be physical, social, or psychological. Serotonin lets us know when we are in a context that is positive for our wellbeing, and gives us that *"yay, this is good"* feeling.

Serotonin plays a key role in regulating our mood. Our body and mind function best when we are in a high, positive mood rather than a low, negative one. Antidepressant drugs operate primarily through promoting higher levels of serotonin in the body. Serotonin is active when we have just completed an action conducive to our survival, such as eating, exercise or earning someone's respect.

Serotonin also plays a key role in seeking social influence. One of the keys to fulfilling our needs is to enjoy a good social position. Being a key component of a group yields many rewards and our serotonin will reward our social efforts accordingly. Every time we feel in the "one-up" position, we get a squirt of serotonin. Being in the "one-up" position commands greater access to resources. Social dominance provides the calm, secure expectation that you will get what you need. Our mind is constantly evaluating our social position, and if it sees our position as healthy and prosperous, it will respond with a squirt of serotonin.

When we perceive ourselves to be in a position of scarcity, our serotonin will drop. This scarcity can be *real or imagined.* The person who is unpopular or the person who *thinks* they are unpopular will both experience a dip in serotonin. Whether we choose to compare ourselves positively or negatively also influences our serotonin levels. You might choose to focus on the fact that your friends have more money than you or the fact that you are the one they come to when they have a problem. How you choose to compare yourself will affect which way your serotonin level goes. Low serotonin can leads to issues with our mood, appetite, sleep and sex drive. (6)

Serotonin is important as it keeps us on the hunt to improve our prospects. It encourages us to grow physically (serotonin is released when we exercise), professionally (serotonin is released when we feel we have abundance in our career, whether that be money, freedom or time) and socially (serotonin is released when we feel we have an established position within a social group).

Let's look at three strategies to boost our serotonin.

Exercise

Exercise has such a dramatic effect on our serotonin levels, that it is cited as one of the most effective natural antidepressants. Indeed a study in 1999 compared using exercise and an antidepressant called Zoloft to treat patients with depression. After a four month period, what they found was that exercise was equally as effective in reducing the symptoms of depression as Zoloft, and equally effective compared to exercise and Zoloft combined. (7) Large scale randomised intervention studies show that exercise may be the most effective instant happiness booster of all activities. (8)

So upping your exercise is going to boost your serotonin levels. If you can do that in sunlight, even better, as exposure to the sun also seems to boost our serotonin. (9) In countries with short winter days, individuals can develop Seasonal Affective Disorder (SAD). This is a condition with symptoms of depression that scientists believe is related to the low exposure to sunlight and thus reduced serotonin production.

You've also got a double whammy with exercise, because guess what else it produces? Just six weeks of exercise has been shown to enhance dopamine production and receptivity in the brain. (10)

So what type of exercise is best? People will argue between the different types of training: cardio, strength or flexibility. It will seem that there is always a new style or class that is in vogue: zumba, crossfit, bikram etc. How can you know which type of exercise is best for you?

The answer is simple, whichever one you do. How do you know which one to do? It's the one you enjoy most. Whatever you enjoy most will be the one that you are most likely to stick to, and the one that makes you happiest.

Enjoy your social position

The way our society is set up, we're always striving to be on top. Being on the bottom can be frustrating but so can being on top. Each part of the hierarchy comes with its own set of challenges. If you speak to the oldest, middle and youngest child, each of them will tell you they've got the worse deal.

So instead of focusing on the drawbacks of your current social position, focus on the benefits of your position moment to moment. If you're in a subordinate position, see that as an opportunity for learning and growth. If you're in a dominant position, feel empowered by the respect and responsibility.

Notice your social influence

Sometimes we don't give ourselves enough credit for the social ripple effect we have. Every person that we encounter and interact with in life is impacted by us in some way. So take pride in yourself when you are able to be socially valuable.

Notice when others are influenced or helped by something you say. One of my favourite ways to do this is when I am able to connect people during networking. If I'm talking to someone, they may mention that they are looking for a particular type of person who I can link them up with or I realise I know a person that I think they could have a great conversation with. In this scenario, I'll help them exchange contact information or introduce them in a group message. Doing this always gives me a buzz, as it makes me feel socially valuable.

Also notice when others mirror your good example. Sometimes we get resentful or defensive when someone copies us but instead learn to be flattered by it. It shows that we're successful at whatever it is we're doing or who we are. See it as a form of service to others, that you're providing them with a template that helps them be a better person.

One of our highest human needs is to feel we've made an impact on the world, so notice when you've made yours and you'll spike your serotonin.

Happy Chemical 3: Oxytocin

Our third happy chemical is Oxytocin. Oxytocin is our "connection" chemical and is stimulated through bonding behaviour. Oxytocin is released when we feel part of a group or valued in a relationship and it gives us that *"yay, I'm loved"* feeling.

Oxytocin helps us to build trust. At a primal level, being able to survive necessitates knowing who you can trust and who you can't. When someone displays behaviour to us that suggests we can trust them, there is a squirt of oxytocin. This gives us the feeling of "yay I'm loved", and we associate that good feeling with that person, and that deepens our relationship with them. We know who we can rely on to support us. Equally, when someone breaks our trust, it results in stress chemicals being released, and we know who to avoid in future. Research has also suggested that oxytocin plays a role in our generosity, (11) where we show that we are trustworthy to others.

Oxytocin also helps us to reproduce. When we engage in mating behaviour our oxytocin is stimulated (*I'm not just talking about sex!* This also includes flirting, cuddling, kissing and holding hands). This helps us feel close to that person. Talking from a primal, evolutionary standpoint; if we feel close to someone, we are more likely to produce offspring with them and more likely to ensure the survival of our genes (that is goal #1 of evolution and natural selection).

Leading on from this, oxytocin helps us form attachments to others. It helps us feel closer to our romantic partner and to the children we have with them. We only have limited time and resources to share with others; oxytocin helps us recognise who is most important to us in our lives. Oxytocin is also involved in forming "in-groups" and "out-groups". In-groups are people who we feel share the same values (e.g. community-minded, passionate, inquisitive, creative) or characteristics (e.g. culture, class, political or religious affiliation) as us.

In popular media, dopamine and serotonin seem to command more of the headlines but I actually think oxytocin is the most interesting of the three. The release of oxytocin has some really interesting side effects in the body.

When oxytocin is spirtzed into the noses of study volunteers (this allows it to go directly to the brain) it reduced activity in the amygdala, which is one of the key players in our fear responses. (12) The release of oxytocin also decreases blood pressure and reduces the level of cortisol. (13)

MDMA (ecstasy) is a popular street drug because it raises oxytocin levels. Interestingly, MDMA has passed phase three clinical trials for being used as an astonishing successful treatment for Post-Traumatic Stress Disorder (PTSD). Studies report a 50-60% decrease in severity of symptoms, with as many as two-thirds of patients no longer meeting the criteria for PTSD a year after treatment. (14)

It is research such as this that makes me think oxytocin is arguably our most important happy chemical. Regardless of what new findings emerge, know that oxytocin is important as it allows us to form deep relationships with others. It enables us to identify social allies and people to form groups with. It also helps us find and commit to a romantic partner, then support them and our children.

Let's look at three strategies to boost our oxytocin.

Massage/Physical Therapy

Physical touch stimulates oxytocin. If you think about it, as a relationship develops, we touch each other more: we therefore associate touch with connection and trust and our oxytocin responds. So start bringing more physical contact into your life.

One method is to book more pampering. Treat yourself to spa and massage days. Your oxytocin will like that physical touch. Also hug and hold hands more. I try to use hugs rather than handshakes whenever I feel I can get away with it. It creates a stronger and faster connection than handshakes. (15) You can even self-massage through practices such as Qi Gong. Attached to this book are free online resources which you can access at

http://davidmccrae.thinkific.com/courses/author-your-life-book-resources

There is a video in these resources where I will demonstrate a Qi Gong practice you can use.

Embrace Proxy Trust

"Proxy Trust" means developing trust at a lower level than that which we experience in close, deep relationships. That type of trust is something that develops over a long period of time and is not something we can develop with everyone. However, we can develop proxy trust much easier and begin the process of increasing oxytocin.

One method is through getting a pet or using someone else's. Getting a mammal as a pet that you can stroke and cuddle (fish and reptiles just don't cut it) is a great quick win for oxytocin. If you have a friend who has a pet, visit them more often so that you can play with their pet (and see them, of course...but mainly the pet). Alternatively, there are cat and dog cafes you can go to in a number of cities where you can play with and feed resident animals.

A second method is to spend time in crowds such as networking, concerts and seminars. Being in a group doesn't stimulate oxytocin as much as a person-to-person connection but it also isn't as difficult to create. If you can find a group of like-minded people; who are in the same profession; who like the same music; or have the same goals; that will automatically give you a head start on connection. You can also do this to a lesser extent with digital friends. Join and contribute to Facebook groups or Reddit forums to also feel a small sense of connection and community.

Build Stepping Stones of Trust

From the foundations of proxy trust, you can start to build deeper levels of trust, and do so gradually in a way with minimal risk. Often what holds us back from developing trust is the fear that trust might be broken. So we take small steps to confront that fear.

The way to be in control of such fear is to be trustworthy yourself. This is something that is entirely your responsibility. You can do this by making and honouring commitments. If people feel they can trust you, they will automatically open themselves up to deeper connection with you.

You can also reverse this process by testing people on small commitments, which will have minimal consequences if they don't follow through (e.g. emailing you something, attending another meeting). This is really useful to gauge the exact level of trust you stand at with someone. There are some people you can trust to buy you a coffee but not to look after your kids.

When we start to understand the way that our chemicals affect our body, we can start to take steps to readdress the balance. However, where do these chemicals come from? They are not just released at random. They are released for a reason...because of the way we think. Every thought we have, positive or negative, releases chemicals in our brain. It is sustained patterns of thinking that release enough stress or happy chemicals to change the way we feel. Therefore, if we want to exert greater command over the way we feel, we have to go to the source. We have to engineer the way we think. That is what we will cover in the next segment.

Part 2: Neuter the Negative

To Unlock our inner abilities, we often have to get out of our own way. However, as I will stress multiple times in this book, this process is not easy. Whilst we want to be happy and positively minded, our brain is not actually built for this. You see, our brain is not a happiness machine: it is a survival machine. To develop our Consciousness, we have to override the natural default of our brain.

This is because our brain possesses an inbuilt negativity bias. It is easier for us to notice negative stimuli rather than positive ones (16) and we place more attention and energy onto the negative. (17)

Let's imagine you visit a restaurant ten times. The first nine times, you had great service, the food was delicious and the ambience was relaxing. However, the tenth time you go, everything goes wrong: the waiter spills some wine on you; the wrong food gets delivered to your table; there's a screaming child on the next table.

What story are you likely to tell your friends? About how you went nine times and really enjoyed the experience or the one time you went and throughly detested it? It's the one negative time right? You might slander the restaurant at every opportunity and, based on that one experience, might decide to never go again.

This is the negativity bias in play, it is an ancient survival mechanism that has served us well. If we ate a plant and it was poisonous, it was important to pay attention to what we ate in the future. If there was a rustling in the bushes, it was important to be aware that it might be a predator rather than assume it was the wind. Our attention to the negative was key to avoiding and reacting to the threats and dangers around us.

However, nowadays we have much less real threats in our environment but more innocuous things still trigger our negativity bias. Now it's not poisonous food or hidden predators, it's mistakes at work, lying politicians and trolls on Youtube. Our negativity bias is still well nourished.

If we want to be happy, we need to have strategies in place to protect against this bias. Mainstream psychology has spent a number of decades examining how to address negativity and cure illness (only recently has positive psychology started examining the opposite: how we enhance positivity and promote wellness). This focus means that there are plenty of scientifically validated techniques to address our negativity bias. We will explore some of these techniques now.

Distraction

Our negativity bias is reinforced by a process called rumination. Rumination describes the process by which animals such as cows and sheep chew their food. To break down the grass they eat and begin the digestive process they chew in large circular motions. This motion is similar to how we have a negative thought go round and round our head: that nasty thing someone said to us plays on repeat; we rewind that mistake we made again and again; our worrying about the bills stays stuck at the forefront of our mind.

Rumination is an incredibly damaging mental process. It doesn't help us solve the problem but it ramps up our stress and anxiety levels. Rumination increases our likelihood of becoming depressed and prolongs the duration of depressive episodes when we have them. (18)

When we ruminate we are stuck in our heads in a disempowered intellectual state. In order to break the pattern, we need to shift our state. We can shift into a physical state or an emotional one.

We can shift into a physical state by exercising. You might be someone who, when upset, angry or sad, goes for a run or hits the gym. You likely do this because at one point you tried it, and it worked in changing your mood. As we have covered, exercise increases levels of serotonin, dopamine and maybe even a bit of endorphin too if you push yourself hard.

However, what it also does, is it shifts our focus. We move out of our heads and into our bodies. You might notice you struggle when you first try to exercise and you're in a state of rumination. You aren't really "feeling it" and it takes more effort than normal to get your body to perform. Nonetheless, as you persevere, your attention begins to shift and you make a proper connection with your body: you get into the zone. This represents the shift from intellectual into physical; you break the pattern of thinking and remove the power the rumination had over you.

An alternative is to shift into an emotional state. You might be someone who, when upset, angry or sad, seeks the company of others. Just like with the folk who exercise when they're down, you do this because it works in changing your mood. Again social interaction changes our physiology in a number of positive ways. As we have just covered, it raises levels of serotonin and oxytocin and again maybe a little endorphin if you laugh or cry.

Outside of these effects, just like exercise, it also shifts our focus. We move out of our heads and into our hearts. When you're first talking to someone you might not really feel in the mood or be very responsive. However, as you share stories, insights, news and humour, your attention shifts. You shift from the intellectual into the emotional, again breaking the pattern of thinking and removing the power that cycle of negative thinking had for you.

Both techniques are effective, so what I like to do to compound the effect is to combine them by bringing movement and social connection together. This could be through playing team sports, attending a fitness class or being part of a running club.

One of my favourite ways to combine the two is through dancing. If I feel I'm in a low mood or fixating on a problem, I will put on my Spotify, crack the volume up full and dance like a maniac around my living room. I jump and turn and shake out my whole body to one of my favourite songs.

I was speaking at an event with another speaker named Jermaine Harris. Harris told us "no one has ever been depressed whilst shaking their ass", and we all proceeded to get up and shake our asses. I have found this to be very true in my personal life.

If you would like to give the neighbours something to think about, have a selection of songs on a playlist that trigger strong positive emotion in you: that song that always gets you up on the dancefloor; a song that reminds you of a great holiday you had; a song from an artist that you saw live. When you dance to this song not only does it generate the physical shift in your body, it also has that emotional component for you as well, which will have a powerful effect on breaking that thought pattern.

Anchor

Some of the most powerful practices I have found in my life and the lives of others are when we blend science and spirituality. When we take a spiritual practice and apply scientific rigour to it, we develop a practice that is applicable to both the physical, rational-minded person, and the esoteric, intuitively-minded person. The prime example of this is meditation, a traditional spiritual tool for thousands of years, that has been brought to the masses thanks to scientific evaluation.

The Peace Begins With Me (PBWM) meditation is another example. (19) This is a form of Kundalini meditation comprising of a moodra (emotion) and mantra (phrase). Kundalini practitioners use it to activate and release spiritual energy. The meditation involves pressing your thumb and fingers together whilst repeating a mantra.

NLP (Neurolinguistic Programming) practitioners use a technique called an anchor. (20) This involves connecting a linguistic command (affirmation) with a physical action (anchor). One such anchor involves pressing your thumb and finger together whilst repeating an affirmation.

Sound familiar? The spirituality of Kundalini and the science of NLP point to the same truth, we can connect language and an action to change our state. By blending these two disciplines, we create the PBWM Anchor.

First, we must create the anchor before we can use it. You can watch an instructional video in the online resources or read the instructions here.

http://davidmccrae.thinkific.com/courses/author-your-life-book-resources

Begin by holding your dominant hand palm upwards and press your thumb and index finger together, like you are pretending to be a buddhist monk meditating. Next press your thumb and middle finger together; then your thumb and ring finger together; then your thumb and pinkie. Finally, return your thumb to your index finger. This is the pattern you will repeat throughout this anchor: this is the physical component.

The linguistic component is that each digit has a word assigned to it. Your index finger is "Peace". Your middle finger is "Begins". Your ring finger is "With". Your pinkie is "Me". When you create this anchor, you say the words out loud and this is good practice whenever you do the anchor. If you are in a public setting and feel self-conscious, you can say this in your head but speak out loud whenever possible. As your thumb presses against each finger, you say the word associated with it: creating the mantra/affirmation "Peace. Begins. With. Me."

We now have the physical and verbal component of the technique, the final aspect is an emotional one. When you first start creating the mantra, complete a few cycles of moving your thumb and repeating the mantra, start off slowly. When you have your rhythm, close your eyes and bring up a vision of something that brings a high level of positive emotion for you. This might be a place you went on holiday, a time you accomplished something or a person who always brings you up. Focus on this positive stimulus as you continue to move your thumb and repeat "Peace Begins With Me."

Connect with the feeling this vision brings up for you. Imagine this feeling gathering in your heart as a ball of light. This ball of light can be whatever colour and size feels right for you. Hold this light at your heart for a few moments, feeling its energy. Then imagine this light spreading across your chest on the side you are performing the anchor on. Imagine it going through your shoulder, down your arm and gathering in the palm of your hand. Hold this energy in your hand, directly connected to your heart and the essence of this feeling. Infuse the anchor and the mantra with this energy. Keep the anchor and mantra going.

After a few minutes of engaging in this, you will notice a change coming over your body. You will feel calmer, clearer, focused, energised, whatever feeling is best associated with the vision and memory you created. Now close your hand into a fist and imagine that ball of light being absorbed into your hand. This feeling is always available to you now. Whenever you feel in a state of stress, begin the process again. If done correctly, the emotion will be attached to the physical action of bringing the digit together, and the verbalisation "Peace Begins With Me." Performing this anchor will now conjure up the emotion for you.

What I love about this technique is how discreet it is. You can do the anchor in your pocket. You can do it under the desk at work. You can do it behind your back standing on stage. It is a great technique to have in your tool box to shift your state on command.

ANT Spray

Dr. Daniel Amen is an American neuroscientist and psychiatrist. He is one of the few psychiatrists who actually looks at the organ he is diagnosing. Can you imagine going to the cardiologist and they didn't measure your heart or going to the chiropractor and they didn't examine your spine? Yet this is what most psychiatrists do: they make diagnoses based on what you tell them and what boxes are checked on a sheet without taking a look at the brain. Amen (and myself) believe this is nonsensical and at Amen Clinics, he uses brain scans to inform diagnoses and treatment plans.

Amen often works with patients with chronic mental health issues: suicidal ideations, huge mood swings and intense obsessions. After a particularly hard day at work, he returned to his home to find that his kitchen had an infestation of ants. Now this would've been the straw that broke the camel's back for many people but, for Amen, it was a revelation. In that moment he saw that just as his kitchen had an infestation of ants, so too his patients at the clinic had an infestation of ANTs...Automatic Negative Thoughts.

As we discussed earlier, our default setting for the brain is negative and often our negative thoughts arise unexamined and unchallenged. So Amen has devised ANT Therapy (21) to combat these negative thoughts.

The premise of ANT Therapy is to challenge our negative thoughts and look to replace them with a more positive pattern of thinking. Amen uses four questions devised by Byron Katie to challenge an ANT. (22) I teach a modified form of these questions which you can work through below.

This is a process I recommend writing down when you first start, then as you become more familiar with it you can verbalise it or work through it in your head. Let's say the thought is "Work stresses me out."

1. Identify consistent negative thought

What at work stresses you out? As you observe your thinking patterns and reflect on your days, you realise the prevailing thoughts are about your boss: "They're always on my case. They treat me unfairly. They're rude and bossy." Summarising your consistent negative thought might end up being something like: "My boss is a nasty person."

2. Who would you be without the negative thought?

How would your day be different if you didn't have the negative thoughts about your boss? How would your time at work be? Perhaps there would no longer be a sense of dread as the alarm went off in the morning. Perhaps you'd enjoy the conversations with your colleagues more. Perhaps you would no longer tense up every time your boss strides into the room.

3. Write down positive alternative

Think what the positive alternative to your negative thought might be. Now this doesn't mean an unrealistic, polar-opposite approach. Our boss doesn't go from devil to angel here. We simply identity a new thought that has moved along the spectrum into a positive zone. For example, our new line of thinking might be: "Maybe my boss has a lot going on in their personal life just now. Maybe they're getting pressured from their boss. Perhaps my boss has never been taught the best way to motivate and lead others." See how this isn't dressing the situation up in sunshine and rainbows? Yet it is a far more empowering way to think about the situation.

4. What would it be like if you believed the positive alternative?

How would your day and work be if you believed the positive alternative about your boss? Perhaps it would help you communicate better with them. Perhaps it would inspire you to help ease the pressure on your boss. Perhaps the understanding and compassion you show would end up resulting in you becoming friends with your boss.

Using this technique, we can begin the vital process of reprogramming the default setting of our mind. This default setting, frankly, is not really the way we want it. We have a mind geared for the negative, not the positive. If you want to Author Your Life, then you need a mind that is going to work with you, not against you.

It's like when you get a new computer and the first thing you do is change the default browser to Firefox or Chrome, adjust the mouse speed and download your favourite apps and games. Why do you do this? So that the computer is how you want it. You run some performance diagnostics to see if it's running at the specification you desire and you install an antivirus to make sure that nothing bad is damaging the system.

Imagine today that you have just got a new computer. It is the finest processing machine known to mankind: your brain. You want to customise the brain in the way that works best for you. You want to ensure that you don't have parts that are broken or malfunctioning. You want to ensure that there are no viruses clogging the system. That is what the strategies in this chapter enable you to do, to optimise your brain functioning so that you can approach your journey with courage and confidence.

Let's continue the computer analogy as we look at the third section of how to Unlock you full level of Consciousness.

Part 3: Power Down to Power Up

I argue that sleep is the single most important behaviour we have. You will spend more time sleeping than doing any other single activity, even watching Netflix! If you don't get this right, all the rest of the things in your life are going to suffer. Your body is not stupid, there is a reason that it spends a third of your life in sleep mode. If it wasn't important, evolution would have selected against it a long time ago.

To be frank most people are poor sleepers. We abuse our sleep. There is even this badge of honour about how much we abuse our sleep. Someone says to you in the office: "oh man I had a rough night last night, only got five hours of sleep." To which you reply: "That's nothing, I only got three hours of sleep last night". We boast about pulling all-nighters and functioning day after day on low sleep. "Plenty of time to sleep when you're dead" the popular mantra goes. Well with that kind of thinking, you'll be enjoying that long lie sooner than most.

After twenty-four hours without sleep, you have the same reaction time as a drunk driver (23). After forty-eight hours without sleep your levels of white blood cells plummet. (24) After seventy-two hours without sleep, you start to hallucinate. (25)

If you have health goals, poor sleep will affect your ability to exercise and make good nutritional choices. You will not have the energy to stick to and perform exercise. Your willpower will be sapped and you will make poorer nutritional choices. There goes the new body you'd like.

If you have career goals then know that sleep deprivation means you will make riskier decisions in the workplace. You will lack the ability to focus and motivate yourself. This is going to hold you back from creating the calling you want.

What about relationship goals? If you are tired you will be more likely to snap and shout at colleagues, friends and partners. If you're tired, you may not have the motivation to attend dinners and get-togethers in the evening. Even if you do, a shattered companion is not an exciting one. In your intimate relationships, being tired is not conducive to a great sex life. How can you enjoy the richness of relationships if you can't keep your eyes open?

Consistent poor sleep impairs our brain functioning (26) and causes brain cells to die. (27) There is a reason that poor sleep is linked to many of the common mental health illnesses. (28) Not sleeping properly damages your mental capacities on a temporary and permanent basis.

I hope I've shocked you a bit with this research, because the sad fact is that the majority of people do not prioritise their sleep. So they suffer all these psychological and physiological impairments that hold them back. You might even say: "Well actually David, I've done just fine on five hours of sleep a night". You may well have done. My response would be: "Imagine how much more successful you could be if you got seven?"

However, it's not all doom and gloom, because the reverse is true. If we have good sleep, then we will have *more energy, more focus, more motivation, more patience* and *more calm.* From here on we will investigate a variety of practices and strategies that will supercharge your sleep.

First, it's useful to know that we have several different cycles of sleep. Each cycle takes about ninety minutes to complete, so you can already realise, that less sleep, means less cycles. Each stage, we go deeper into sleep and our physiological processes change. Stages one and two are lighter stages of sleep, Stages three and four are our most restorative stages of sleep, also know as Slow-Wave-Sleep (SWS). From Stage four, we then rise back up the stages, and from stage one we then move into our lightest stage of sleep called Rapid-Eye-Movement (REM). This is the state in which we dream. Because of this, it has been suggested that the REM stage plays a component in our ability to be creative.

There is an important hormone involved in this whole process, it's called melatonin. The simple way to see melatonin is as our body's sleeping pill. The levels of melatonin are low during the day, and begin to rise as we get near sleep time. It then kicks in to move us through these stages of sleep.

One of the primers for melatonin is light. Back before we had lamps and alarm clocks, that was how the body regulated sleep. When the sun rose, we woke up. When the sun set, we went to sleep. That is still how melatonin functions.

Through understanding our sleep stages and our melatonin production, we can understand why we may not be sleeping well, and how we can improve it. There are three important factors that influence the quality of our sleep.

Blue Light

Light can be measured on different coloured spectrums, the brightest of which is a spectrum of light called blue light. This is the light that comes from the screens on our computers, phones and TVs.

When our melatonin detects blue light, it thinks it's daytime, so its levels drop. The problem is that if you are exposed to blue light just before going to sleep, your melatonin levels plummet and you will no longer have the natural sleeping pill to take you through all the stages of sleep. You will miss out on your two most important stages: SWS and REM sleep. You might be asleep for the same amount of time but you will not have the same quality of sleep. I'm sure you've already found this: where you sleep for eight, nine or ten hours but you still feel tired when you wake up. That's because your melatonin levels weren't optimised.

Too often nowadays we're on our phones or laptops until the moment we go to sleep. We're harming our poor melatonin and giving ourselves a fractured sleep cycle. However, there is an easy way to remedy this.

It's called the digital sunset or technology blackout. At least an hour before you try to go to sleep, preferably two, shut down all your tech. Shut the lid on the laptop. Put your phone on airplane mode. Do not have the temptation of hearing a notification or vibration. This is your time, to take care of yourself, by getting a good night's rest. Whatever work or communication you think you need to be doing at 1030pm, can wait until 9am the next morning. You will get more done during a well-rested tomorrow, than what you will achieve cramming into the last hour or two before bed.

Liquids

There's two commonly ingested substances that are harming your sleep: caffeine and alcohol.

I'm not against caffeine, it's useful for our mental performance in small doses. However, when consumed in excess, especially approaching bedtime, it disrupts our sleep. Caffeine has a half-life of approximately six hours, which means it takes six hours to process half of the caffeine you consume in one sitting. So if you have a cup of coffee at 4pm, half of the caffeine is still in your system come 10pm. And that's just one cup. Are you drinking more than one cup a day, or worse guzzling energy drinks which have chronically high levels of caffeine? That caffeine has not left your system when your head hits the pillow.

Caffeine is a stimulant, which means you will go to sleep physiologically stimulated, even though you feel tired. It will disrupt your ability to enter the more restorative stages of sleep. (29) Stimulated sleep equals less restful sleep. Less restful sleep equals feeling more tired the next day. Which equals...more caffeine to stay awake and so the vicious cycle is perpetuated.

So what can we do to prevent this? We have to watch our consumption of caffeinated products. This includes coffee, green tea, black tea, dark chocolate and other chocolate bars such as Mars bars, fizzy drinks such as Coke and Diet Coke, energy drinks such as Red Bull and caffeine pills such as Pro Plus.

Obviously you know that chocolate bars, sodas and energy drinks aren't healthy for you, but I would encourage you to consider the sleep implications of these products if the other health implications haven't swayed you from them. I'm not saying you have to cut out all the other stuff, however. I love green tea and dark chocolate but try to keep them to the first half of the day and certainly aim to have a caffeine curfew at 4pm. This gives you a good six-hour window before going to bed to allow the caffeine to leave your system.

Substance number two is alcohol. There is a sad myth that alcohol helps us get to sleep, which is why many people enjoy a little nightcap of wine or whiskey. It doesn't help us sleep, it helps us *pass out*, there's a difference. Even just a couple of units can disrupt our body's ability to fall into the most important stages of sleep, particularly REM sleep. (30) Have you had the experience of waking up after a drinking session and not feeling quite right? You didn't get drunk but there is a hangover-like feeling. That's because the alcohol, even at those low levels, disrupted your sleep.

So what can we do to prevent this? I'm not telling you not to drink, but try to keep alcohol consumption contained between 6-7pm and just have one really nice glass or pint. That then gives your body a solid three hours to process that alcohol before bed. Secondly, watch your frequency of drinking. If you keep on having one or two glasses or pints each night, your sleep will suffer each night. So by all means treat yourself but try to make sure you have several alcohol free nights during the week to allow yourself to get a REM rebound: nights where you are spending more time in REM sleep.

Sleep Hygiene

We covered two preventative practices that will improve your sleep. So you might be asking "David, what am I going to do before bed instead of have my glass of wine and watch Netflix?"

The key is to develop a sleep hygiene routine, your body likes to be eased into sleep. Here are some practices that you can do to prepare yourself for a good night's sleep.

Hot Bath

When you have a bath your core temperature rises and when you get out again it drops. This synchronises with our body's natural cycle of lowering our temperature before sleep. Your temperature will drop more rapidly after having a bath, which has a relaxing effect on you. Try having a bath for at least 20-30 minutes 2-3hrs before bed. (31)

Herbal Tea

If you look at the many brands of "sleep tea" you will see a number of common ingredients such as camomile, valerian, lavender, cinnamon and passion flower. With many of these ingredients, the research linking them to calming, sleep-promoting properties is inconclusive.

Nonetheless, I would still recommend trying herbal teas before bed. There may be some direct sleep promoting effects in sleep teas but I also believe there are *indirect effects*. By drinking a herbal tea before bed, you are creating a nighttime ritual. The brewing and drinking of the tea is a behavioural trigger to your body that you are preparing to sleep. This is also a way to effectively transition from having caffeine or alcohol directly before bed.

Meditation

As will be further discussed in the next chapter, meditation has a host of health benefits, one of which is improved sleep. Meditation has been found to have a greater effect on sleep quality than sleeping pills (32) making it an effective intervention for individuals reporting sleep problems. Meditation has also been found to boost levels of melatonin by an average of 98%. (33)

Read

If you need to engage and unwind without using a screen, books are your best bet. Of course, I'm talking about the physical copies, not putting your eyes in front of the light on the Kindle screen. Furthermore, I'm not talking about newspapers and magazines full of stories of scandal and war; this will rile you up and send you to bed with messages of negativity.

Grab yourself a good story, or books that interest and inspire you such as autobiographies and self-help books. We often say we cannot find time for books during the day but as part of a good sleep hygiene routine we can always earmark 15-30 minutes at the end of the day. This is not just a good practice for sleep but also for your general development too.

Journaling

If you find your head hits the pillow and your mind is racing, take some time to write these thoughts out. I'm not talking about trying to do creative work before bed but just get whatever's on your mind out onto paper. If you're upset about something, write out your feelings. If you're worried about what you're going to do tomorrow, write down a couple of steps to do the next morning. The act of journaling helps to externalise what is happening in our heads in a methodical and structured way. There is nothing we can do about a situation when we are trying to get to sleep, so park that thought on the paper and address it the next day.

Another type of journaling that I swear by is a gratitude journal, we will talk about this more in the next chapter. This journal involves taking five minutes before bed to write about three things you're grateful for. This helps to reorientate our focus at the end of the day. If we've had a day full of negativity, taking these five minutes changes our mindset. Instead of thinking of everything that didn't go our way that day, we instead go to bed thinking about what we can be grateful for. I believe this may explain why studies have found that individuals who write a gratitude journal before bed report improved sleep quality. (34)

With some simple strategies you can significantly improve the quality of your sleep. If you can get your sleep right, you will find your other goals in life, whether that be your health, your career or your relationships, that much easier. We cannot expect our minds to operate effectively if we do not give it the rest it needs. To use the computer analogy, your laptop can only run for so long before its battery runs out and it's no longer effective. Your mind is no different.

Unlock

Your brain is capable of operating at a much higher level than it is now. With the concepts covered in this chapter, you will learn how to Unlock that potential. When you have found that potential, the next stage is then to Unleash it, and that is what you will learn how to do in the next chapter.

In this chapter you have learned:

- The different types of "stress chemicals" and "happy chemicals".
- How to readdress your chemical balance for more positive emotion.
- To recognise your in-built negativity bias.
- How to use distraction, anchors and ANT spray to shift your thought pattern.
- Why sleep is one of your most important behaviours.
- How to improve your sleep by removing blue light, caffeine and alcohol and creating a sleep hygiene routine.

My biggest takeaway from this chapter is

_____.

Chapter 6: Unleash

"Everything can be taken from a man but one thing: the last of the human freedoms — to choose one's attitude in any given set of circumstances, to choose one's own way." - Viktor Frankl

There is the potential within us to live life on a completely different level of Consciousness. There is a fuller expression of ourselves to give to the world. As the title of this book implies, there is a hero within you waiting to be unleashed. In this chapter, we will explore three of the most powerful practices for increasing your happiness. You will learn how changing your perspective on life significantly boosts your health and happiness. You will learn about the "magic pill" that everyone should be taking. You will learn about one of the most important emotions you can experience and how to create more of it in your life. This chapter is going to show you how to Unleash a new level of Consciousness in your life.

Part 1: 100% Glass

With a different perspective on life, you can increase your life span by 19%. This is achieved through means known and unknown. Some of the factors we can link to this change are decreased risk of illness, (1) increased chance of recovery from operations and major diseases such as cancer (2), and reduced risk of developing mental illness, in particular depression. (3)

What is this incredible change? Quite simply, it is optimism. Research has shown that optimists, on average, live 19% longer than pessimists. (4) Research has found optimism to be associated with all those lovely health benefits highlighted above. Furthermore, optimists are more successful professionally, academically, athletically and socially than non-optimists (5). The tendency to view our life in a positive light increases our prospects physically and psychologically. People talk about seeing the glass half-full or half-empty. Optimists recognise that the glass is 50% water and 50% air…the glass is always full.

An important distinction to make here is the difference between positive thinking and optimism. I think the teaching and message of "positive thinking" has given the concept of optimism an unfortunate barrier to overcome. Positive thinking is a well-intentioned, and largely accurate, message to spread. It is based on the principle that we can more positive than we are. That we think negatively too often and we can be happier if we change this situation. This was a concept we talked about in the previous chapter in the "Neuter the Negative" segment. We need to stop being so negative.

Nevertheless, I think the "positive thinking" ethos has taken this too far in the opposite direction, preaching an unrealistic, sunshine and rainbows, view of the world. Positive thinking doesn't solve anything, it just ignores and bandages over the wound. "Positive thinking" doesn't put money in the bank when you're broke; it doesn't strip the fat from your belly; it doesn't bring someone back to life. Positive thinking is a perfectionist pressure that we place on ourselves to be in a happy stupor all the time.

Optimism is different. Unlike positive thinking, it is a perspective that neither ignores or attempts to cover up our life circumstances. Rather it is a perspective that we can rise above our problems, and find the positive stimuli despite our current circumstances. Optimism is simultaneously a problem-solving and joy-finding perspective. Optimists believe that they can overcome their challenges and find greater fulfilment either in the process, or on the other side, of their struggles.

A common misconception of optimists is that they don't feel unhappiness or suffering. They do. What differs is their perception of unhappiness or suffering. When they are in such a state, the optimist thinks "what can I do to improve this situation?". An optimist has problems and doesn't ignore them. Instead the difference is they believe in their ability to solve them.

When outlining the difference between positive thinking and optimism, I like to use the analogy of seeing a bear in the forest. When a positive thinker sees the bear, they think "I'm going to make friends with that bear". When an optimist sees the bear, they think "I believe I can escape from this bear." Optimists always look for the positive in a situation, even when they recognise that a situation is a negative one.

An example that I believe typifies the power of optimism is the story of Viktor Frankl. Frankl was a Jewish psychiatrist who was imprisoned in Nazi concentration camps. In these camps, Frankl lost his entire family. He saw so many of his fellow prisoners suffer the same fate. However, Frankl also saw something else.

In the camps, he observed that there was a difference between the prisoners who were able to survive and those who did not. Even in the most atrocious suffering, Frankl observed that there were certain parts of the human condition that the Nazi guards could never take away from them. Frankl observed that the prisoners could not choose what was happening to them but they could choose their attitude towards what was happening to them.

This was not a positive thinking "sunshine and rainbows" impression of the camp, which it clearly wasn't, but the prisoners could choose what to focus on. They focused on seeing sunlight or on feeling the wind on their face. They focused on the hope of seeing their loved ones again, or that this entire experience was going to have some significance or meaning to it. It was this latter perspective that really inspired Frankl. When he was free he wrote *"Man's Search for Meaning"* (6) and developed an entire therapeutic practice based on the power of meaning called *Logotherapy*.

Frankl's key observation was a statement I shared with you at the beginning of this chapter: *"Everything can be taken from a man but one thing: the last of the human freedoms — to choose one's attitude in any given set of circumstances, to choose one's own way."*. We cannot always choose what happens to us but we can choose our attitude to what happens to us. Frankl's story is something I find deeply impactful and quite often a wake-up call for me.

The way I see it, if those prisoners, subjugated to some of the worse treatment, pain and suffering that humanity has known, can choose their attitude to what was happening to them, what excuse do we have? What do we have happening to us that compares to the Holocaust?

What I hope to demonstrate, through Frankl's example, is that we have the power to choose our response to situations. Too many people are constantly looking for, and thus seeing, the worst in everything. If we want our lives to be happier, then we know that a lot of that outcome comes down to the way we perceive life.

So how do we take on a more optimistic viewpoint in life? Martin Seligman, pioneering positive psychologist and author of *Learned Optimism*, (7) reports that optimism comes from our perspective on three key criteria: whether something is Permanent (how long will this affect me?); whether it is Pervasive (how much of my life does this affect?) and whether it is Personal (how much will this affect me?).

Let's look at this criteria through a relatable scenario. You approach someone you find attractive and ask them for their number. They give you a bit of a rough turndown. The pessimist may respond in this way.

• They may believe this situation is *permanent* and think: "I will never find love."

• They may believe this situation is *pervasive,* and think: "Getting turned down romantically is going to affect my health, my job, and my happiness."

• They may believe this situation is *personal*, and think: "I am an unattractive and horrible person."

Do you recognise this self-talk? This would suggest you have a pessimist viewpoint on life and you are allowing your biological negativity bias to take control of proceedings. Instead, could you reconfigure this response into a more empowered one?

- This situation *isn't permanent*: "I can still find love".

- This situation *isn't pervasive*: "This is not going to affect my health, job, or happiness. It's not even going to affect my success in the dating game. It's just one person."

- The situation *isn't personal*: "I just wasn't what that person was looking for, it's not representative of my value as a person."

Do you see the distinction? Who do you think has a better chance of finding love? The pessimist or the optimist? The optimist right? Not because they are any more attractive physically or emotionally, it's because their mindset allows them to recover from failure and try again.

Let's flip the switch and see how the pessimist and optimist respond to a positive event. Let's stick with the dating analogy and imagine that someone we're attracted to starts chatting with us. Here's what could be going through a pessimist's mind.

- Permanence: "They'll stop talking to me soon, this is just a one-off."

- Pervasive: "I'm never going to manage to speak to someone this attractive again."

- Personal: "They're probably only talking to me to make someone else jealous."

Do you also recognise this self-talk? Not being able to accept when something is going for you. Have you ever been complimented on something you were wearing and replied by saying "oh I just got it in a sale". You immediately seek to devalue the positive.

Embrace the positive. Accept it. That's what optimists do. Imagine an optimist is speaking to this gorgeous individual, and here's what they're thinking.

- Permanence: "Wow, this is a person I could form a long-lasting relationship with."

- Pervasive: "Spending more time with this person would make the rest of life so much more enjoyable."

- Personal: "This individual clearly values me as a person."

Is the optimist more likely to "get lucky" with this gorgeous individual? Yes or no? Well it's funny that term "get lucky", because the harder we try the luckier we get. If our optimist hooks up here, there won't be a whole lot of luck involved, it will be because they embraced a mindset that increased their chance of success.

Those are the three Ps. Analysing our thoughts using these three categories can help us self-monitor whether we are in a pessimistic or optimistic mode of thinking. However, what can we do to train ourselves to be optimists? Three techniques are listed below.

Best Possible Self

The Best Possible Self (BPS) diary is a practice that involves taking 20-30 minutes each day to write about your Best Possible Self of the future. What would you be doing? How would you feel? Who would you be in your interactions with others?

Research by Laura King has demonstrated that just four twenty minute sessions of this activity lead to immediate increases in positive mood, improved ratings of happiness several weeks later and even a reduction in physical ailments several months later (8).

Sonja Lyubomirsky notes that the BPS diary allows you to organise and structure your future aspirations. For example you recognise you don't want money for the sake of it, you want it to be able to travel regularly. It also makes you recognise your own personal power to create your future. Your dreams aren't reliant on a lottery win, stock market bubble or political election. They are created and crafted by you. (9)

To develop a more optimistic self, begin by engaging in the BPS diary. It's been shown to be one of the most scientifically effective ways to increase optimism.

Positive Brainwashing

This next suggestion may seem like an oxymoron. "Brainwashing" is traditionally associated with cults and dystopian novels. However, I think we can take the mechanisms of brainwashing and utilise it to positive ends.

As we learned in the previous chapter, our brains have an in-built negativity bias. This negativity bias is fed by many of the inputs in our environment: politics, celebrity scandal, environmental disaster, crime, gossip, work stress. The internet, the media and the people around us can constantly drip-feed us negativity if we don't take steps to monitor and regulate this input.

"If it bleeds, it leads" the popular broadcasting mantra goes and this shows the thinking behind our media. They know they can attract your attention with negative stories because your brain is primed for negativity. Because of this I don't read newspapers, watch television or subscribe to news websites because they are a constant source of negative information.

Research has shown that the average person in the UK spends four hours a day watching television (10) (that's not counting computers and phones) and that the average mood when watching television is mild depression (11). This is because our news tells us about death and destruction; our entertainment is based on conflict and criticism and our advertising aims to make us feel inadequate and incomplete. For this reason I stay away from traditional broadcasting. Sometimes this results in me being a bit behind major events but if it is important enough, I'll soon catch up on it. This doesn't mean I don't care about events in society and the world, I just prefer to research such matters on my own terms.

Am I telling you to boycott traditional media the way I do? No. Am I putting on my tinfoil hat and claiming the media is deliberating trying to feed us negativity and brainwash us? No. I'm just highlighting that the media has a negativity bias that reflects the same bias you have in your brain and that if you want to change that bias, you should be feeding yourself different information.

This is where positive brainwashing comes in. It is choosing to feed your mind with positive information and to reconfigure the bias you have in your brain. So instead of newspapers, I read books that teach you how to improve yourself and autobiographies of people who I admire. Instead of the news, I listen to podcasts that interview inspirational people. Instead of tabloid alerts on my phone, I set myself reminders that ping at regular times during the day with a positive message or motivational call to action.

In years gone by, the self-help field recommended affirmations; saying positive messages such as "I am rich and famous" and "I am full of joy, hope and love" to yourself. I have never really warmed to affirmations because I have viewed them as being forced and inauthentic. Research has actually supported my suspicions, demonstrating that affirmations such as these reduce self-esteem, the very opposite of what they are supposed to achieve. (12)

I think the intention behind affirmations was well-placed, just the implementation was off-target. The proponents of affirmations recognise that to change the way you think, you need to give your brain some different programming. The chosen method of repeating positive programming to yourself just missed the mark. Sitting with bills on the table and telling yourself you're rich, swallowing an antidepressant and telling yourself you're happy and standing in the house alone telling yourself you're charismatic is kidding yourself on.

What I like about positive brainwashing is that it is not kidding yourself on. If you are reading a book and finding the strategies in it helpful, then that is a real experience you are having. If you are listening to a podcast and you are finding a guest inspiring, that is an actual perception you have. If you have a reminder ping on your phone and it motivates you to take action on something, that is real cause-and-effect. These influences are creating real behaviour, thoughts and feelings for you.

Start designing your life to have more positive input, and your brain will start to respond to the influences it is receiving on a consistent basis.

Smile

If you want to be more positive then act more positive. That sounds like the most trite advice in the world, and possibly hypocritical given what I've just said about affirmations, but hidden in that witticism is some fundamental truth. We often think that feeling creates action: that when we feel happy, we will act happy. However, neuroscience is repeatedly demonstrating that the opposite is also true, that action creates feeling. This is why I recommend smiling more frequently. This is because smiling is not just the result of happiness but the cause of it too.

A simple experiment with a pen illustrated the powerful effects of a smile. Participants were asked to watch cartoons whilst holding a marker pen in their mouth. One group gripped it sideways between their teeth, which forces your face into a smile. The other group held it longways so it was hanging out their mouth, which forces your face into a frown. The group which had their mouth forced into a smile rated the cartoons as much funnier than the group with faces forced into a frown. (13)

When studying the effects of smiling, it is important to note the distinction between a genuine and forced smile. A forced smile comes just from the mouth, a genuine smile (also known as a Duchenne smile) crinkles the corners of the eyes. A fake smile produces no brain activity, whereas a genuine smile activates the left pre-frontal cortex, (14) which as you might remember from an earlier chapter is associated with positive emotion.

Over the passage of time, you will actually start to develop wrinkles around your "smile lines" or "frown lines" depending on what your primary emotion usually is. A startling study was conducted to see what happens if you take away the wrinkles caused by frown lines.

This study gathered ten patients who were experiencing treatment-resistant depression, where neither medication nor therapy was working. The period of depression ranged from two to seventeen years. These patients were given injections of Botox to the areas associated with "frown lines" (the bridge of the nose, between the eyebrows and slightly above them). Two months after treatment, nine of these ten patients were no longer depressed and the tenth had improved mood. (15) Years of depression were removed simply by ironing out some frown lines.

Based on this research, I have made smiling my default behaviour. I smile when I'm walking. I smile when I greet someone (I also smile when I'm nervous or offended, which maybe isn't quite so helpful!). It is one of my primers that I use to trigger happiness for myself on a consistent basis.

If you are able to shift into a more optimistic outlook, then the research demonstrates you will be a healthier and happier person. Healthier and happier people are able to develop themselves and their lives faster. Optimism means you will be able to take charge and Author Your Life.

Part 2: The Magic Pill

"Suppose you read about a pill that you could take once a day to re-duce anxiety and increase your contentment. Would you take it? Suppose further that the pill has a great variety of side effects, all of them good: in-creased self-esteem, empathy, and trust; it even improves memory. Sup-pose, finally, that the pill is all natural and costs nothing. Now would you take it? The pill exists. It is meditation." - Jonathan Haidt (16)

It is tempting to be facetious and just finish this part of the chapter with that quote. I think that is the shortest and most powerful summary of why it is necessary to have a meditation practice. There is no single prac-tice that you will read about in this book that will have a greater effect on your health, career and relationships than meditation. This isn't my opinion or self-help hype, this is what science is overwhelmingly telling us.

The huge advancements in brain imaging technology has allowed us to see directly how meditation changes the brain and changes our experi-ence of life. Meditation has been shown to increase cortical thickness in the prefrontal cortex, improving decision-making and focus. (17) It in-creases grey matter in the hippocampus, improving our capacity for memo-ry. (18). Furthermore, it decreases activity in our amygdala, which plays a key role in our fear response. (19)

It's no longer monks smiling at us with quiet contentment; it's no longer New Age mystics crooning at us; it's the people at the big-name universities with an alphabet after their name that are telling you to medi-tate.

A study measured the effects of an eight-week program of Mindful-ness-Based Stress Reduction (MBSR). This is a form of meditation focused on non-judgement and acceptance of your thoughts and experiences. After this eight-week intervention, anxiety symptoms had fallen by 12%. Activation in the left pre-frontal cortex had tripled (remember this is associated with positive emotion). There was also reduced activity in the right pre-frontal cortex (as you might have guessed, this is associated with experiencing negative emotion). On top of that, subjects were injected with a flu vaccine and those who had completed the MBSR course produced 5% more antibodies to the vaccine than controls. (20) One study saw the positive effects (such as decreased anxiety) of a few months of a MBSR program last more than three years. (21)

Richard Davidson measured Buddhist monks who had accumulated over 10,000 hours of meditation. One of these monks was Matthieu Richard, a Western scientist and Eastern monk who has been dubbed "The Happiest Man in the World" (22) because his brain scans reveal extraordinarily high levels of activation in the regions of his brain associated with positive emotion.

Our brain has different wave lengths, which represent different levels of activity.

- The lowest form is Delta, which has a frequency of 0.5-4 hertz and is usually associated with deep sleep.

- The next lowest is Theta, which has a frequency of 4-8 hertz and is observed during dreaming, hypnosis and often meditation.

- After theta is Alpha, which has a frequency from 8-12 hertz and is observed during periods of relaxed concentration, such as daydreaming.

- What we spend most of our time in is Beta, which ranges from 13-30 hertz and comprises most everyday, conscious activity.

What Davidson and Ricard found was that during meditation of expert meditators, Gamma activity was greater than had ever been reported in the scientific literature. (23) Gamma is what happens after 30 hertz and we rarely access it in everyday life.

Davidson was excited to observe what he described as: "massive, far-flung assemblies of neurons firing with a high degree of temporal precision." (24) What that means in layman's terms is that multiple parts of the brain are talking to each other at the same time. This allows for new and exciting connections to be made. It's like living in a village for all of your childhood and never getting to speak to people who lived beyond the bounds of your village. Then one day you move to the big city and a whole new set of interactions and experiences open up for you.

What was also observed was that whilst this Gamma activity peaked during meditation, when the monk's baseline state was measured outside of meditation their Gamma activity was still significantly higher than controls. This was evidence that meditation not only spikes Gamma activity, it boosts long-term Gamma activity too. This has very exciting implications for our ability to be creative, productive and decisive. This may explain why college students who undertook a programme to learn about and practice meditation showed bigger improvements on an intelligence test as well as in their course test grades than a control group. (25)

So how can you experience these glorious effects for yourself? You can start with a five-minute meditation practice every day. Don't think you have five minutes? Yes you do. If you have a Facebook profile, then you have five minutes. If you have a Netflix account, then you have five minutes.

One of the things I hear people say is "I'm too busy to meditate." To which I reply: "You're too busy not to meditate." If you have a life that is go-go-go, then meditation is going to help you avoid anxiety, release tension, improve focus and raise energy. Meditation is like taking an anti-anxiety pill and a cognitive-enhancement pill at the same time, with longer lasting benefits and no side effects.

When people say "I'm too busy to meditate", what they really mean is "I'm choosing not to prioritise meditation." If you are not meditating for five minutes, it's because you're choosing to do something else for five minutes. If you are honestly working from wake to sleep, then you still have five minutes, because you can set that alarm clock to ring five minutes earlier. What you might find surprising is if you take that five minutes to recharge your mind, you will start to find yourself completing tasks faster and moving through things with greater energy; that five minutes is buying you so much more time later in the day.

A second excuse I hear people say is: "I try to meditate, but I can't concentrate or sit still." If this is the case, then you need meditation most of all. It's like saying "I try to run, but I get out of breath and my heart hurts." If that is what you feel whilst running, that shows you are unfit and need to run.

Similarly, if you feel this way whilst meditating, it shows that your brain is overstimulated and you need to meditate. If you can't sit still and concentrate for five minutes in a meditation practice, how do you expect to be able to focus on achieving your health goals, advancing in your career, or developing your relationships? So just as you've got to struggle through some runs before you get fitter, you've got to struggle through some meditations before you get calmer.

As meditation is time with yourself, I think it is a personal practice and you should do it in the manner that you feel suits you best. What I share below are three different styles that you can easily employ in a five-minute window. Each style begins with sitting in a comfortable position, on a chair or the floor, legs crossed or feet on the floor, hands resting in your lap or on your thighs. Whatever combination feels most comfortable for you.

Progressive Relaxation

In this style, start by focusing on your toes. Imagine the muscles in your toes relaxing and the tension disappearing. When your toes feel relaxed, move up to your feet. Imagine the muscles in your feet relaxing and the tension disappearing. Repeat this process for your calfs, thighs, tummy, chest, shoulders, neck, arms and hands.

If it helps, imagine a coloured light, or cool sensation running along your body as it progressively relaxes. Keep your attention on a body part until you feel it relaxing. Give that body part the time it needs to release whatever tension is stored there. If at any time your mind wanders and you lose your place, simply return to the last body part you were focused on and continue the process. When your body feels completely relaxed, just take time to sit with that feeling, until you feel ready to return to your day.

Counting Breath

In this style, you generate a point of focus with your breath. Inhale to a count of three through the nose; imagine cool, white light entering your body. Breathe into your belly, not your chest, this allows the full expansion of your diaphragm. Hold for a count of two, then exhale through the mouth for a count of three. Imagine hot, black air billowing out as you do so.

Repeat this breathing pattern, counting your breaths as you do so. Count each inhale as an odd number and each exhale as an even number. Inhale one. Exhale two. Inhale three. Exhale four. Continue this process until you reach ten, then start the cycle again from one. If at any point your attention wanders and you lose count, simply resume again from one. As you get more experienced, you can inhale/exhale to the count of five, or seven, and extend your breath hold to three or four.

Mantra

In Sanskrit, mantra means "a tool of thought." This style involves concentrating on a single word to focus the mind. This is why if you watch a Buddhist group meditation, you will hear them chanting "Om" in unison. Your mantra does not have to chanted out loud but said in your head. "Om" is one such example. You could use "Peace", "Calm" or any other word that feels appropriate to your motivations for meditating. As you breathe, simply repeat this word in your head, focusing on the energy and feeling of this word. If at any time your attention wanders, simply return to the mantra.

These are three simple techniques that you can use to begin your meditation practice. Start with just five minutes a day. That dissertation of health and wellbeing benefits are waiting for you when you do so. To help you get started, I have recorded three downloadable recordings of each of these styles that you can access in the book resources:

http://davidmccrae.thinkific.com/courses/author-your-life-book-resources

Part 3: Truth #1

At age twenty-two, I learned three fundamental truths that allowed me to unleash my potential, helping me develop my consciousness to a new level. The first of these truths was gratitude.

Gratitude developed my mindset and cultivated my happiness in a phenomenal way. The more I have explored and studied it, the more fascinated I have become with the power it has. I will go as far to say that you cannot be happy if you cannot be grateful. A big claim I know, but I feel comfortable making this claim given the amount of scientific research there is pointing to the transformational effects of gratitude.

I explored gratitude deeply in my book *"The Last 60 Minutes"*. I do not want to repeat verbatim what I outlined there. Firstly, it is boring for those of you who have already read my previous book. Secondly, it spoils the surprise for those of you who haven't. However, I do believe it is important to revisit key principles and ingrain key foundations. That is what I will do here by reaffirming some of the key points I made in my previous book, whilst offering fresh perspective on what I've learned since.

Let's begin by looking at how gratitude affects us. We can observe that gratitude brings about positive experience. When we enter a state of gratitude, we are able to see and appreciate what we have achieved and what other people have done for us, boosting our meaning and self-worth. (26) It also allows us to savour positive experiences through fond memorising of the past or grateful awareness of the present. (27) When we enter a state of gratitude, one of our happy chemicals oxytocin is released. (28)

Gratitude also acts as a buffer against the negative. Gratitude has been shown to diminish feelings of anger, bitterness and greed. (29) It also can be an effective coping mechanism in times of stress and trauma. Research has demonstrated that traumatic memories arise less often and are less intense in people who regularly express gratitude. (30)

Thirdly, gratitude has social benefits. Through appreciating the presence of others in your life, you nurture and strengthen the connection with them. It also prevents negative social comparison, as you are more likely to focus on and appreciate what you have rather than envy what others have. (31) Grateful people are also more positive people and positive people are more liked by others and are more likely to make friends with people. (32)

The research demonstrates that gratitude is one of the most pervasive and positive influences in our lives. With some simple yet powerful practices, we can bring the power of gratitude into our lives.

<u>Gratitude Journal</u>

One of the key practices that everyone should have in their life is the gratitude journal. If there is any such thing as a "hack" for happiness, this is it. Martin Seligman and his colleagues conducted a study into college students to investigate the effect of a gratitude journal on happiness. Participants in this study had their happiness scores rated on questionnaires and were then split into two groups. The first group were asked to do nothing for the next seven days; they were the control group. The second group for those next seven days were asked to spend five minutes at the end of each day to write down three things they were grateful for.

At the end of the week the happiness scores for the two groups were measured again. Unsurprisingly, the group who had been asked to do nothing showed no change in their happiness scores. Conversely, the journal group showed a 2% increase in their scores. A small change but a significant one, and significant considering that they were only spending five minutes a day doing the journal.

Here's where the study got interesting, because it was only supposed to last for seven days. However, the college students had felt so much benefit from doing the journal that they kept on recording it, even though they were no longer obliged to. Therefore, Martin Seligman and his team realised they had a great opportunity, so they continued to monitor those students. When they measured the happiness scores after a month of doing the gratitude journal, those scores were now up 5%. The students continued to record the journal and after a six month follow-up, those scores were up 9%. (33)

That's nearly a 10% increase. That increase comes from doing something for just five minutes per day. As I often say to my audiences, if I offered you a way to lose 10% fat in just five minutes a day, you'd bite my hand off. If I offered you a way to increase your income by 10%, you'd ask where you could sign up. What I'm telling you now if that you can increase your happiness by almost 10% with this one five-minute intervention. If you are looking for one "hack", one simple change with dramatic results, this is it.

Gratitude Intervention

Another way to bring the power of gratitude into your life is with the gratitude intervention. It is easy to feel grateful when everything is going right for us: we've got good health; work is going well; we have fun times with our friends and family. What is more challenging is to find gratitude when times are tough but this is when it is most necessary. The importance of gratitude is not in finding good in the good times but finding good in the bad times. When we are able to find gratitude in the midst of difficulty it creates a reframe for us. It shuts down our negativity bias and puts us into a more positive state of mind.

I'll share an example with you. One Monday morning, as my partner was getting ready for work, the shower broke. The dial to turn the shower on and off broke away in her hand, so she was unable to turn the shower off. As she had to go to work, I was left to deal with this.

Immediately my negativity bias kicked in: "what a way to start the week", "great, I'm the one who has to deal with this", "As if I haven't got important things to do too". However, I recognised the ANTs and shut them down. Thinking negatively wasn't going to help me resolve the situation, so instead I switched into problem solving mode. I called our estate agent, who called the plumber, and they told me they could be there in a couple of hours.

There was nothing I could do for the next two hours, so I switched to gratitude. I realised that I had a continuous source of clean, warm water cascading out of the shower-head. This is a "problem" that billions of people without clean running water would kill to have. To solve this problem I didn't need to take a crash course in plumbing, get the wrench out myself, and bang the pipes. I could ask someone else to fix the problem. Did I have to leave my home and walk miles to fetch this person? No, I simply had to pick up the phone.

How blessed was I? I embraced the power of gratitude to realise that my "problem" wasn't a problem. I had water; I had skilled help; I had technology...plenty to be grateful for.

This is the type of shift that I try to perform whenever I'm experiencing challenge or I'm descending into negativity. Life is not what happens to us, it's what we make of what happens to us. This is a lesson that I learn over and over again. When times are tough for you, try to find the gratitude and your perspective will shift.

A simple way you can practice this is to notice an ungrateful thought you have each day (e.g. "I didn't get the promotion" or "My hips are too big") and find a grateful thought to substitute it with ("yeah but I've progressed so far in my career" or "yeah but my hair looks great").

Heart Reset

There are two organs in the body that emit electrical signals: the brain and the heart. Thanks to today's technology, we can measure these signals using an (EEG) for the brain and electrocardiogram (ECG) for the heart. What you will usually find is that these signals are out of sync, particularly when we're angry, scared or unhappy. When the signals are like this, it indicates that our body is in a high-arousal, stressed state.

On the other hand, when these signals are in sync, this creates an optimum state for the body and research is just starting to explore the fascinating implications for what this can do for our body. (34) Scientists can measure the signals from the brain and heart and watch them synchronise with each other.

A technique that you can use to bring these signals into alignment is what I call the heart reset. This is a technique that I learned from Tony Robbins. (35) The heart reset is a gratitude technique to take you out of stress and into bliss. When we're in a stressed state we are generally feeling one of two emotions: anger or fear. Gratitude is the antidote to both. You cannot simultaneously feel angry and grateful at the same time. You cannot simultaneously feel fearful and grateful at the same time.

This exercise is best described through audio. You can find an instructional video that will take you through the entire process in the online book bonuses.

http://davidmccrae.thinkific.com/courses/author-your-life-book-resources

You can also listen to this exercise in the audiobook version. I will write down the process here and you can record yourself doing the exercise, or listen to myself in audio.

Sit in a comfortable position, close your eyes and place your hands on your heart. Take a deep breath through the nose and imagine the energy of that breath going into your heart. We call this "breathing into the heart". Let out a long exhale out of the mouth. Repeat this two more times.

Bring your attention now to your heart. Feel the power of your heart. Your heart beats 100,000 times a day. It pushes one and a half litres of blood through 60,000 miles of blood vessels every minute. If you put your blood vessels end to end, they would stretch around the entire world at the equator...twice.

Your heart does this for you every single day without you having to ask it to. Your heart is always working for you. Despite the stress and mistreatment we sometimes give our heart, it is always doing its best for us.

You didn't have to ask for this heart; you didn't have to acquire this heart; you didn't have to achieve this heart. This heart was a gift to you. It was given to you the moment you came into this world. In fact, you were defined as coming into this world when your heart started to beat and you will be defined as leaving it when it stops. Your heart will be there for you, from the very first moment, to the very last.

Feel immense gratitude for your heart now. Immense gratitude for this wonderful gift you have. Breathe again into your heart and feel its power.

I'd like you now to take your attention to something you can feel so grateful for. An experience that brought you joy. An accomplishment you were proud of. A person you love. Notice now how you can feel incredible gratitude for this. Other people may have had that experience; other people may have had enjoyed that accomplishment; other people may have loved and been loved by that person, but your perspective on it is unique to you. This feeling is yours and yours alone. It is another gift. Treasure it and feel grateful for it. Breathe into your heart again and feel this feeling flow through your body.

As you breathe into your heart, I'd like you to think of a time when your heart led you somewhere. So often in our lives we operate from the head, using logic and reason. Our head is great but sometimes it is limited. Our heart often knows what is right far more than the head. I'd like you to think of a time when you listened to your heart and it led you somewhere. Perhaps your head was telling you one thing and your heart was telling you something else. You chose to follow your heart and from that came good fortune, a coincidence, an opportunity, that wouldn't have come about if not for your heart. Feel the gratitude for your heart's wisdom.

Your heart is always there for you. It knows what is best for you. If you take the time to listen to it, it will keep you right.

This exercise only takes about five minutes or so but by the end you will have noticed a significant shift in your physiology. This is your body entering a synchronised, optimal state. This exercise can be used to shift you out of negative states, but also to prime yourself for something important. If you need to enter a state of creativity, productivity or negotiation, you can run through this exercise to enhance your capacity to do so.

Unleash

There is a whole new level of consciousness waiting for you. You can live a life that is more vibrant and joyful. In this chapter you have learned how to Unleash that level of Consciousness. Through doing this, you have taken the first stride towards becoming the hero of your story. You have started to Author Your Life.

In this chapter you have learned:

- The benefits of Optimism and why it is not the same as "Positive Thinking"
- The three "Ps" that separate optimists from pessimists
- How to develop a more optimistic outlook with the BPS diary, positive brainwashing and smiling
- The power of meditation and why it is the "Magic Pill"
- Three different ways to start your meditation practice
- That gratitude is one of the most powerful emotions we can experience
- How to enter a state of gratitude through keeping a journal, performing gratitude interventions and using the heart reset

My biggest takeaway from this chapter is

_____.

Section 3: Discover Your Calling

"When you have a dream in your heart, the whole universe conspires to bring it into reality." - Paulo Coelho

Author Your Life is all about becoming the hero of your story. To become the hero, we must do something heroic. This is not the stereotypical idea of fighting dragons or running into burning buildings. To be the hero of your story is simply to do something meaningful and to fulfil your own personal destiny. We all have our unique impact to make in the world. In this section, you are going to learn how to make yours.

The first step is to align with your PURPOSE. We sadly live in a world nowadays where many people are off purpose. Individuals are living without direction and meaning. An astonishing Gallup poll has found that 85% of workers are "emotionally disconnected from their workplaces" and

23% are "actively disengaged" which is scientist-speak for "hate their jobs". (1)

In my work, the top two issues my students report are: "I don't know what I want to do in life" and "I don't know how to motivate myself". Both of these issues indicate a lack of alignment with our individual "Why". Our "Why" is what drives and motivates us. Our "Why" is what defines us. Sadly, many people have not been given the empowerment and opportunity to find and express their "Why". In our society we are pushed down a set path.

1. Get good grades at school.
2. Earn a respectable qualification.
3. Get a well-paying job.

Given that 85% of people of people are not satisfied with the outcome of this process, this clearly isn't effective. In this section, you are going to tap into the fuel behind the Author Your Life movement: PURPOSE.

The second step is to develop PROFICIENCY. There are a number of people who do have dreams and aspirations for their life but they don't understand the process required to bring these into reality. Meaningful success is a long and difficult path. Fulfilling your purpose requires commitment, discipline and, to be honest, a bit of luck as well. To build a tall building you must first lay deep foundations. If you have high aspirations you must develop deeply ingrained fundamental principles and practices. Without developing these key concepts, you will be like a ship without a sail, hoping the tides of fate push you to your desired destination. Author Your Life is about taking command of your story and we do so by building the necessary PROFICIENCY.

The third step is to improve PERFORMANCE. Ultimately, we want to produce the outcomes we desire. Why do nine in ten people want to write a book (2) but only about one in ten thousand of those people actually write one? (3) It's because they are not productive. The graveyard is the richest place in the world because it's here that you'll find all the half-started projects, inventions and movements. Too many people are not able to bring their purpose into reality and this is not the fate I want for you. Therefore, you are going to learn how to create the outcomes of Author Your Life through developing greater PERFORMANCE.

I'm sure this is not the first self-help book you've read. You've watched the self-help gurus on Youtube. You've attended the motivational seminars. You've received coaching. You've had plenty of frameworks and programs pitched to you. The PURPOSE, PROFICIENCY, PERFOR-MANCE framework is yet another. If others before have not created the outcomes you want, why should this one? Already, perhaps, you have your doubts.

That doubt is the heart of the problem. Because it is CONFUSION that misdirects us on the path to our Calling. We get lost in the options, the decisions and the mystery. We lose, or do not even find, the clarity and conviction to proceed. Confusion can be like a spider's web: the more we wriggle, the tighter it constricts us. Specifically, there are three forms of confusion that will bind you in place.

The first is CONFUSION OF THE WHY. This is the most insidious form of confusion, where we can feel utterly lost and meaningless because this is when we have lost connection with the deepest, most authentic parts of ourselves. It is when we don't know who we really are, or what we want to do. It is in this state that we feel demotivated and lethargic because we are not truly connected to what lights us up as individuals. Individuals in this state know their current lifestyle isn't want they want but don't quite know what they want instead.

Our "Why" is deep within us and to burst through this confusion we must reconnect. Your "Why" has never left you, it's just that somewhere in your story so far you forgot how to connect with it. We all have a "Why": it is our reason for existing. If you didn't have a "Why", a reason for being, then you would not be alive. You can be as atheist or nihilistic as you like but you cannot deny that everything in nature and the world around us has a reason for its existence. Plants feed the animals; rain waters the plants; chargers power up phones; roadsigns provide directions: everything we see around us has a reason for its existence. You are no different. In this book you will discover that reason and ignite your inner flame. In this book you will learn how to tap into your drive and motivation in a consistent manner. You will create and work towards a vision of who you want to be.

The second barrier, is CONFUSION OF THE HOW. We want to create a better life for ourselves but we don't know how. This is an intense frustration with our current circumstances. We know we're not happy but we don't particularly know how we go about changing it. We have a spark of motivation within but we don't know how to fully ignite that spark. It is in this state that we can feel trapped. There is the desire to change but no path to achieve it.

Our "How" is not some mystical, elusive quality. Everyone achieves success the same way. They start on Day One and build from there. You must build with consistency, patience and, most importantly, faith. When you analyse the lives of famous, successful people — individuals that we so often hold up on a pedestal — you regularly find their "ordinariness". They did not possess abilities different to ours. They did not have resources different to ours. They did not lack the fears and doubts we have. All they did was build upon what they had, to add "extra" to their ordinary...extraordinary. In this book, you will learn how to adopt the exact same principles and practices that served them so well. You will learn how to build the foundations for your change and rise above your current circumstances.

The third barrier is CONFUSION OF THE WHAT. Sometimes, we are simply not doing what we are supposed to be doing. We get distracted, sidetracked, or misinterpret the path. We invest time, attention and resources on activities and tasks that have little real importance in the grand scheme of things. There are a number of motivated, talented people out there who never make their mark on the world. Why is this? Because they either didn't know or didn't properly focus on what they needed to do to make their impact on the world.

Our "What" is generally simple and sometimes its simplicity tricks us. We are often lead to believe that the secret to success is some hidden "hack", "framework", "program", "drug", or "mastermind". Often the answer is directly in front of us. Often we actually know what we need to do but we deliberately procrastinate and distract ourselves from it. We know what we need to do but we don't do it effectively. What we need to do on occasion is kick ourselves up the backside and take action. Ultimately, nothing happens if you don't take responsibility and make it happen. In this book you will learn how to identify what needs to get done, focus on that action, and execute it effectively.

It's time to clear the confusion, and find the Purpose, Proficiency and Productivity to carry out your Calling.

Chapter 7: Purpose

"What we must decide is what to do with the time that is given to us." **- Gandalf the Grey**

The Author Your Life journey is fuelled by Purpose. A hero becomes a hero because they are driven by something greater than themselves. Sadly many people in the world right now are not clear about or connected to their purpose. In this chapter you are going to learn how to find your personal quest, to get clear on what your mission is. You'll learn that motivation, often mystically branded and put up on a pedestal by our society, is actually quite simple. Motivation is something you already have, you just need to generate it. You will also learn how to create a vision for yourself, to put the passion and enthusiasm of your purpose in a clearly defined direction.

Part 1: Finding the Quest

It's all very well urging you to pursue your Calling in life, "but what is my Calling?" you might well be asking. If you are, you're not alone. 50% of people report not getting a sense of meaning from the work they do (1) with just 13% reporting being "actively engaged" in their work. (2) One of the key components of suicide, to which we are losing about six thousand people every year in the UK alone, is to perceive a lack of meaning in life. (3) At an anecdotal level, the most frequently asked question I receive is some variation of "David, I don't know what I want to do with my life." You might be joining the Author Your Life journey clueless, cloudy or clear on what your Calling is. Wherever you might be, I believe you will find the following concepts and exercises valuable to become clearer on what your personal quest is.

Ikigai

The concept of "Ikigai", and its relation to purpose, comes from an unrelated piece of research. A number of studies have been conducted in areas of the world where people have the highest life expectancy. What particularly interests researchers is that there are small pockets of people who live significantly longer compared to other communities and groups near to them, known as "blue zones". (4)

One such place is the island of Okinawa, just off the coast of mainland Japan. Okinawa has five times as many centenarians per head of population than mainland Japan (which already has the highest national life expectancy in the world (5)), as of 2002 there were 34.7 centenarians for every 100,000 inhabitants, which is the highest ratio worldwide. (6).

Researchers have tried to isolate what factor is responsible for this increased longevity and they have looked at a number of factors including nutrition, climate, access to medication, disease and even social ties. (7)

Even when accounting for these factors, a variable that seems to explain some of Okinawa's longevity is a concept called "Ikigai". Ikigai translates roughly from Japanese as "reason for being". It means what an individual's purpose in life is. The residents of Okinawa live for longer because they connect with their Ikigai and seek to express it everyday. The people of Okinawa understand their place and importance on Earth and thus have more connection and drive towards living longer.

So how do we find our Ikigai? Our Ikigai is made up of four components: (8)

1. Doing something you love.
2. Doing something you're good at.
3. Doing something the world needs.
4. Doing something you can get paid for.

If you find yourself in a role that fulfils these four criteria, then you are likely living your Ikigai.

To find your Ikigai you can grab a piece of paper and write these components down as four headings, or draw a Venn diagram composed of four circles. In these sections, write down all the major things you do in your life: your job, hobbies, activities, interests and clubs. For each item, write it under all the headings that apply.

When you've written them all down, look at how many sections these pursuits fill. Do you have something that fulfils all four criteria? That's great. This thing, or something close to it, will be your Ikigai.

However, perhaps you've got something that fulfils three, or maybe just two components. This is also good, you just need more exploration to get to your Ikigai. How can you take that pursuit and add to it so that it fulfils all four criteria? This is a problem that many startup entrepreneurs face. They have something they love; something they're good at; something the world needs, but they don't know how to monetise it. If they can work out that last piece of the puzzle, then they'll be living their Ikigai. If you can work out the last piece of your particular puzzle, then you can be too.

An important point to note is that Ikigai is not a grandiose or self-important notion. When we use language like "reason for being", we can start thinking we need to save the world to justify our existence. Sometimes the individual recognises their Ikigai as more humble roles such as "fisherman", "pot maker" or "gardener".

Your Ikigai might be "only" a coffee barista. You might love the smell of coffee and the art of making it. You love knowing about the origins of the beans and what new flavours you can create.

You might be good at making coffee. You know how to use different filtration processes and combine different beans to make multiple varieties of coffee.

You are serving a need with your coffee. Your coffee is part of someone's morning routine. Your coffee gives people a boost to complete an important project. Your coffee is something friends share when they meet each other.

You can get paid for making coffee. This might "only" be working in Starbucks but for that you receive a wage to sustain yourself. Alternatively, you might open your own artisan coffee shop or run an online store selling coffee blends.

Your Ikigai is simply the best expression of who you are and what service you can provide. The world needs its baristas just as much as it needs the doctors, lawyers and politicians.

Interestingly, the people of Okinawa have no word in their language for "retirement". Your Ikigai is not something you retire from like a job, it is something you carry out until your last day. To retire from your Ikigai is to retire from your life and to extinguish your reason for being. If you are doing something you want to retire from, then you are not fulfilling your Ikigai.

Find the "One Word"

"Follow your passion" is the theme of many a motivational speech. It is a message to follow what is in your heart. To do what you truly want to in life. It is a message that many of us subscribe to but not enough of us are living.

When we were young, we had an idea of what we would like to be. You don't meet a child who wants to be a "project manager", a "customer service assistant" or an "associate". Children want to be astronauts, cowboys, inventors, presidents, stuntmen, singers, actors or Jedi (this was my back-up career path). These ideas of fancy are entertained for a while but eventually passion is replaced with practicality. Parents, teachers and even peers demolish our dreams with warnings about real-life and comments on the limitations of our ability.

You are pointed towards high-income (medicine, law, engineering, finance) and/or high-security (teaching, government, local council) careers and steered away from the low-income (support work, charity, hospitality) and low-security (art, music, entrepreneurship) careers. You are discouraged from following your heart and instead following your head: what is "sensible", "practical" and "realistic".

I'm not suggesting here to follow the American Dream ideal that anyone can become the President. That job only opens up every four years (usually) and only one candidate is accepted. If a class of thirty children all want to be President, then they will not all be President. Not everyone can become an astronaut. Not everyone can be a gold medallist. I absolutely agree that we cannot be delusional about following our passion. But I disagree that we have to extinguish the fire of passion all together.

Here's what I believe. I believe that when we are young, we have a yearning in our heart for what we want to do. Our heart knows what it wants to do. However, as a young person, we don't have the maturity to fully understand, articulate and express what that feeling is. That is why we state outlandish desires to be an astronaut, a cowboy or a princess. We see something that activates that feeling and we state that to be our desire, because of the way it makes us feel.

One young person has adventure in their heart. They get read a bedtime story about astronauts and that activates their desire for adventure, so they think they want to be an astronaut.

Another young person has the desire for justice in their heart. They watch *Toy Story* and see Sheriff Woody, who activates their desire for justice, so they think they want to be a cowboy.

These children know what they feel and they chase the feeling. We then interfere with this feeling by telling them they can't be an astronaut or a cowboy, rather than nurturing the feeling behind the wish. Most children know their passion but they don't know the expression.

When I was young, I wanted to be an author (*ta da*). I felt that I wanted to write stories and sell books as a living. Naturally I got steered away from this and ended up pursuing psychology. When I turned eighteen, however, I started to get an itch. The itch was that I was procrastinating on being an author. I was already putting off writing until I got my degree. Well what about when I had my degree? Would I put it off until I had a secure job? Until I had a family? Until the kids left home?

I realised that if I wanted to be an author, I could start right then. So I began writing. I started working on a novel idea that had been circling my mind for years. This became my first book, which I self-published at age twenty, and the second followed at age twenty-one.

However, I was not following my passion.

I thought the passion in my heart was "fiction author". I was wrong — close — but wrong. What I now realise is in my heart is "storyteller". At the age of five, that feeling in my heart latched onto the closest thing it knew: the books I was reading and having read to me. I chased that feeling in the only way I knew how.

Being an author is a means to express my passion, not the passion itself, a big distinction. Now I find myself a non-fiction author and an inspirational speaker. My passion was not the job title "author", it was to help people "author" their lives: right word, wrong context. That is how I am connected to the feeling in my heart, through the word "storyteller". I'm sure how I express this will continue to evolve and adapt as time goes on but the feeling in the heart doesn't change.

What my story illustrates is the journey of finding our passion. There is a process. It is not grades and promotion as the current system tries to enforce. It is more nuanced than that. Angela Duckworth says that "passion for your work is a little bit of discovery, followed by a lot of development, and then a lifetime of deepening." (9)

It begins with chasing a feeling. At the age of sixteen, I had a feeling I wanted to be a psychologist. I chased that and learned how to create change in myself and others. At the age of eighteen, I had the feeling that I wanted to start writing books. I chased that and learned how to write and publish books. At the age of twenty-two, I had the feeling I wanted to be an entrepreneur. I chased that and learned how to start a business. At the age of twenty-three, I had the feeling that I wanted to be a speaker. I chased that and learned how to share on stage.

When I recognised how all these skills combined, I doubled down on them. I continued to study psychology. I continued to write. I continued to speak. I have been developing these skills for years now.

What is up ahead is a lifetime of deepening. It is understanding the mind more. Writing more books. Speaking to more people. I understand my passion. Now I find the truest ways to express it.

To follow your passion, you begin by following the feeling. When something excites you, do more of it. When something intrigues you, do more of it. Let that feeling guide you without allowing the head to come in and question it ("but I could never be good at this." "how could I earn money doing this?" "How is this relevant to anything else I do?"). Embrace the discovery stage and try new things, see what continues to light you up.

As you continue to try and discover new things, monitor yourself day-to-day. Where does your mind wander when you're daydreaming? What do you find yourself looking forward to? What you'll find is that your head starts to catch up with your heart; it will start focusing on what you are feeling in your heart.

When we are following our passion, even if we haven't yet "found" it, we are getting excited about the things we are doing and the things we want to do. We are aligning with our purpose.

If you are still in the discovery phase of your passion, I have some further suggestions for you.

The dilemma that faces you in the discovery phase is that there are so many potential routes to follow. You have so many different passions, which do you choose to explore more?

If this sounds like you, then I encourage you to arrange your passions into three categories.

Interests

These are your low level passions. These are things you enjoy engaging in but you don't do it on a regular basis, and you aren't particularly motivated to do it on a regular basis. You also don't feel the urge to "give" this to the world.

One of my interests for example is history. I enjoy finding out things about history, but I don't feel compelled to join a history club, nor teach history to others.

Hobbies

These are mid-level passions. Hobbies are things you partake in regularly and get a high level of engagement and enjoyment from. You will encourage others to engage in the hobby and might invite them into a community. However, this hobby is still mainly for you, again it is not something you are going to "give" to the world.

One of my hobbies is yoga. I have a regular practice and I will encourage anyone I meet to give it a try. I will offer advice and insight from what I know about yoga. However I'm not going to become a yoga teacher because that is not my deepest passion.

Contributions

These are your deepest passions. This is something you enjoy, you engage in regularly and, most importantly, you have a burning desire to "give" to the world.

My contribution is Author Your Life. It is helping people create new stories for themselves through writing, speaking and teaching. This is something I have a burning desire to give to the world.

Many people try to make an interest or hobby into a contribution and find themselves losing that passion, or not being fulfilled with what they are doing.

Of the various passions you might have right now, most of them will be interests or hobbies for you. What is important, to take your life in a new direction, is to connect with your contribution. That is what people mean when they tell you to "follow your passion".

To help you work out the different levels of your passions, I point you towards a wonderful analogy from Will Shortz: "How to solve the *New York Times* Crossword Puzzle": (10)

1. Begin with the answers you're surest of and build from there

There are things you know you definitely hate doing and life is often just as much about finding out what you don't like as what you do like. Conversely, there will be things that you feel more attracted to and interested in: start there.

2. Don't be afraid to guess

There is a lot of trial and error involved in finding your passion. Unlike a crossword, there is no right answer, so it can take longer to find out if something is really a good fit for you.

3. Don't be afraid to erase an answer that isn't working out

You have to persevere when exploring your passion but there is a difference between sticking at something and banging your head against a brick wall. When something isn't working, try, try, and then try something else.

Part 2: Your Inner Wiki

When you find yourself with the brand "motivational speaker" (a term that I don't like or find particularly accurate) you inevitably field a number of questions on motivation. I often get asked questions such as "David, how do I get more motivated?" or "David, I've lost my motivation, how do I get it back?". Motivation is my second most frequently asked question (funnily enough behind variations of questions on purpose, covered in our previous part of the chapter).

These questions display a huge error in thinking in regards to motivation and something that I feel is perpetuated by a number of "motivational speakers". Motivation is not a "thing". It is not something that is given to you like a doctor's injection. Somebody doesn't hand you a piece of paper saying "congratulations, you are now a certified motivated individual". People often say they have "lost" their motivation like it's a set of car keys. Motivation is not something you get, it is something you *generate*.

This is why I don't like the term "motivational speaker". It suggests I have something that you don't and that I have the power to give it to you. Your motivation comes from you. It is the only sustainable form of motivation there is. Yes you can get small bursts of "motivation" from caffeine, or music, or somebody standing on stage getting you to jump around and scream affirmations. As I'm sure you know, such motivation quickly fades and it's on to the next "hit".

There are two different types of motivation. You have *extrinsic motivation*, which is the traditional view of motivation, and you have *intrinsic motivation*, which is the type of motivation that most people don't harness. Guess which one is more powerful?

The prevailing view of motivation over the last century has been the "Carrot and the Stick" model. (11) This model has been used to make athletes perform, workers focus and children behave.

The premise of the Carrot and the Stick model is that we do more of something if we are rewarded for it and less of something if we are punished for it. We offer the athlete a higher salary if they help win the title; we offer a worker a promotion if they put in the hours of overtime; we offer the child a sweet if they clean up their mess. Conversely, we can threaten the athlete with a lack of playing time or a trade/transfer if they aren't being a team player; we can threaten to suspend or fire a worker if they can't keep up with the workload; we can threaten a child with a grounding or spank if they misbehave.

The Carrot and the Stick model makes logical sense. Of course we would want to do something more if we get a reward and less if we get punished. Because this system makes logical sense, that is why it has been employed in such a ubiquitous fashion across the years. Yet the Carrot and Stick model is severely limited. If the Carrot and Stick model worked, the highest paid athletes would always win, the 2008 Banking Crisis would never have happened and there would be no one in prison. We know that there are plenty of people who do bad things despite the presence of punishment and plenty of people who do good things despite the absence of reward.

The Carrot and Stick model does not adequately explain motivation nor is it a good model to try and motivate ourselves. This is because the Carrot and the Stick model is something that is known as *extrinsic motivation* in psychology. Extrinsic means "external". Extrinsic motivation comes from outside of us.

Whenever you try to use stimulants, accolades, money or violence as motivation, you are using extrinsic motivators. Extrinsic motivation does create action but it is a finite and weak source. A cup of coffee gives you an extra spurt of energy but it quickly fades. A Christmas bonus feels good but in January you're lethargic again. A kid will stop talking when the teacher shouts at them but start whispering again as soon as their back is turned.

You see, even though extrinsic motivation is commonly employed, it is far less effective than the second type of motivation: *intrinsic motivation*. Intrinsic means "internal". Intrinsic motivation comes from within. Because it is generated from within, it lasts longer and is far more powerful than extrinsic motivation.

Intrinsic motivation kept Nelson Mandela going during twenty seven years of imprisonment. Intrinsic motivation drove the founding fathers to write the American Declaration of Independence. Intrinsic motivation helped J.K. Rowling write Harry Potter as a single mum on benefits. Intrinsically motivated individuals and groups will nearly always outperform extrinsically motivated individuals and groups in the long run. (12) There is a famous example of this effect in motion.

In 1995, Microsoft launched its Encarta project. This project was designed to capitalise on the rapidly growing internet and digital technology, creating the biggest encyclopaedia in the world. Microsoft poured all its resources into this project. It hired the best designers, engineers and researchers and offered them all the rewards and resources they wanted.

In 2009, Microsoft announced it was shutting down its Encarta project because it could not compete with its rival. Who was its rival?

It wasn't one of the other giants in IT. It wasn't Apple, Google, Yahoo or Facebook. It wasn't the "disruptive" startup that Silicon Valley loves such as Uber or Airbnb.

The rival was Wikipedia. When you type a name, object, event, company, film, biological process or theory into Google, one of the top three search results, if not the top, will be the Wikipedia entry for that search term.

How did Wikipedia defeat the mighty Microsoft? Does it have more money than Microsoft? No, Wikipedia is sustained entirely by donations. Does it have a better team than Microsoft? No, Wikipedia is run entirely by volunteers, many of whom volunteer 30-40 hours a week for Wikipedia. Logically, Wikipedia shouldn't have stood a chance. Psychologically, however, its victory was inevitable.

The difference was that Encarta was fuelled by extrinsic motivation: Wikipedia was fuelled by intrinsic motivation. People don't work for Wikipedia for money or accolades, they work for Wikipedia because they believe in what it stands for: democratisation of information, love of knowledge, access to learning. People donate to Wikipedia based on those same principles. (13)

Intrinsic motivation is triggered by these inner values. This is what drove Nelson Mandela, Martin Luther King and Mahatma Gandhi to achieve the social change they did. This is what drove Winston Churchill, Abraham Lincoln and William Wallace to achieve the military victories they did. This is what drove Usain Bolt, Roger Federer and Muhammed Ali to achieve the athletic heights they did. Such individuals did not require reward and punishment to motivate their actions, they possessed a deep sense of what was important to them and why they were pursuing the outcomes they were.

When you generate a connection with deep values, "motivation" is not a problem. What I'd like to impart to you now is a few techniques to help you connect to your inner values and your inner motivation.

Three "C"s of Motivation

Research has found that there are a number of predictors for intrinsic motivation, the three strongest being creativity, (14) challenge and contribution. (15)

Creativity taps into our innate drive as humans to bring forth new things into the world. When Roger Federer hit a shot between his legs, he was tapping into his creative expression. When Martin Luther King wrote "I have a Dream", he was tapping into his creative expression. You can tap into your drive for creative expression by answering this question:

"How do I want to add to the world?"

Challenge taps into our innate drive to grow and improve as beings. When Winston Churchill was devising how to protect Britain from the Nazi onslaught, he was tapping into his drive to overcome challenge. When Muhammed Ali was taking punch after punch from George Foreman in Manila, he was tapping into his drive to overcome challenge. You can tap into your drive for challenge by answering this question:

"What have I always wanted to master?"

Contribution taps into our innate drive to serve and improve the lives of others. When Lincoln split his country in two to abolish slavery, he was tapping into his drive to contribute. When Mandela sat down at the table with his oppressors, he was tapping into his drive to contribute. You can tap into your drive for contribution by answering this question:

"Who do I want to be a hero to?"

You might have started to sense by now, either implicitly or explicitly, that intrinsic motivation comes from a sense of purpose. Interestingly, if you are searching for motivation, you are actually searching for purpose. When you have a mission in life, the desire to act automatically follows. This is not to say that you feel "psyched", "buzzing" or "pumped" every second of every day, but this deeper sense of purpose keeps you going even when you're not feeling your best. With this in mind, there are two extra questions that you can answer to get a sense of where your intrinsic motivation might be:

"What gets me out of bed in the morning?"

I don't mean "because I have to go to work", or "I need to get the kids to school", or even the flippant "because my alarm clock goes off." What makes you want to engage with life? What makes you want to be awake in the morning, rather than pass away during the night?

At the age of nineteen, I experienced a period of depression. During the worst times of this, I was waking up in the morning and wished I hadn't woken up at all. I wished I could escape to the fantasies of dreamland rather than having to battle through another day in the real world.

Do you feel like this? If you don't, then what is actually getting you out of bed? If you do have to get up for work, is that your opportunity to be creative? If you have to get the kids to school, is that your opportunity to contribute? What is the deep reason or value that makes you throw off that cover, even when sometimes you don't want to?

"What keeps me up at night?"

With this I don't mean your list of chores, who disrespected you at work, or your neighbour playing loud music. I mean what does your mind want to explore when it finally has a bit of space to do so? Are you inventing and imagining new ideas? Are you visualising competition or adventure? Are you sending thoughts to a special person or persons? The space between our waking and sleeping state is often where we are tapped into a deeper level of thinking. When you are connected with this higher thinking, what are you choosing to think of?

You Have a Dream

Martin Luther King has come up a few times in this chapter. When we're talking about motivation, it's hard not to think of the person who delivered what might possibly be the most motivational speech of all time. If anyone can be labelled a "motivational speaker" it was Dr King.

"I have a Dream" is a six-minute segment of a seventeen-minute speech that provided fresh impetus and hope to the Civil Rights movement. In the speech King paints a vision that resonates beyond either African Americans or individuals living in 1963. Martin Luther King passed long before I was born and I have never been subject to the injustice he was fighting against, yet the "I have a Dream" speech resonates hugely with me. When I need a little injection of extrinsic motivation, watching that black and white video on Youtube is one of my go-to sources.

I know I am not the only person who is similarly inspired by the speech. There are a huge number of non-black, post-King individuals who are also moved by the speech.

Why is this?

In the speech, King speaks from his inner values. He speaks of hope, freedom, and unity. He speaks to values within all of us. He paints a vision that we would all like to see. We also know where that speech led. In 1963, Martin Luther King stood on the steps of the Lincoln Memorial and spoke of character overcoming colour. Forty-six years later, at the opposite end of the Washington Mall, America inaugurated its first black President.

I point to "I have a Dream" as a prime example of intrinsic motivation in action. I believe we all have a dream within us: we all have something we want to create in the world; we all have a challenge we want to overcome; we all have people we want to help. Therefore, I created the "You have a Dream" activity.

I want you to imagine that you too are standing on the steps of the Lincoln Memorial. There is a crowd gathered in front of you. TV cameras are pointing at you and every person not present in the crowd is watching you on television. Translators from every known language are on hand. You have the opportunity right now to address every living person on Earth. The catch is that you have the same amount of time to share your message as Dr. King…six minutes.

If you had six minutes to address the world. What would you say? What lessons, teaching or vision would you want the other humans of the world to know?

What I also challenge you to do is to write this speech in just six minutes, to not overthink or overcomplicate the message, just to express from the heart. By enforcing this time constraint, you pull yourself out of the intellectual and resorting to clichés such as "be a good person", "help others" or "do your best". You have little time to think and process, so you have to go straight to the heart. It is here we often have the answers.

When I do this with a live audience, I encourage some of them to read out their answers. To date, I have never heard a message that doesn't have power and a wonderful poetic quality. There is something about this exercise that taps into something deeply meaningful.

I would encourage you to take time for this exercise. When you finish this chapter, take a piece of paper and write down your six-minute dream.

Motion-vation

Intrinsic motivation is valuable but I won't pretend it's infallible. Even when you are deeply connected to an "Inner Why", it's sometimes still not easy to get things done. Your energy and focus are just not on point. In all honesty, this is the norm. When it comes to getting important things done, we often don't "feel like it".

I have been working out in the gym since the age of sixteen. I know it is undeniably good for me. I know I feel better afterwards. I know that working out improves my performance throughout the rest of the day. I generally work out three times a week but perhaps only once out of those three times do I "feel" like working out. Yet there are only two or three times during a year that I won't follow through on a workout because of my mood. Why is this?

This is because I know that we cannot count on "having" motivation, but generating it. When you play around with the word motivation, you begin to see why.

Motivation = motive: motivation simply describes our reason for doing something. e.g. I workout to improve energy and health.

Moti~~vat~~ion = motion: motion is required to have motivation. Motivation does not precede action, it follows action.

E-motion: You need to have motion in order to generate e-motion.

Therefore, to generate motivation, we must have a reason to act and then act. It doesn't matter whether we "feel" like it or not. "Feeling like it" will come when we are already taking the action.

This is why I complete the vast majority of my workouts that I don't "feel" like doing. It's how I've written this book despite not "feeling" like writing each time I sit at the laptop. I use a technique I call "The twenty-minute rule".

When you're not "feeling" like doing something, first take a moment to prime the motive for the action you want to take. In my workout example I remind myself "You'll have better energy after this", "You'll generate momentum for the rest of the day" or even "You can have an indulgent meal after this this" if I need something a little more superficial.

When you've reminded yourself of the importance of the action, then begin the action. Make a promise to yourself that if you're still not feeling like it after twenty minutes, then you can leave it to another time. For me in the gym, this is usually a case of making it through the first couple of exercises and seeing where I'm at.

Ninety-nine times out of a hundred, after twenty minutes, you will decide not to stop. By then you have started to get into the swing of things and you're starting to "feel like it". You've broken a sweat in the gym, got some words on the document, even some dishes on the draining board. When you've made that small level of progress, the natural instinct is to want to build on it. That motion has then generated the e-motion.

One time out of a hundred though, you still won't feel a difference. Your head and body just aren't in it. That's okay. A couple of times a year, I will walk out the gym near the start of the workout because I will recognise that something more than motivation is in play. If my body hasn't woken up after twenty minutes, then I know that is it telling me it is not in a fit state that day to work out. If the words aren't coming out on the page, then I know my mind is telling me it's not in the right state for creative endeavours.

Using this technique, however, you will create results on 99% of the occasions when your lack of "motivation" would have stopped you creating them. Sometimes such efforts do not create our best work or results but this is what makes the difference between those who discover their Calling and those who never really find it. A winner is not someone who does great when they feel good, it is someone who does okay when they feel bad.

The sports team generally does not win the title by dominating the opposition in every game. It is usually decided by the victories they were able to scrape when they weren't on form. The marriage is not sustained by extravagant dates and amazing sex but by taking time to give affection when tired and to have difficult conversations when stressed. A business is not built on viral videos and blockbuster partnerships. It is built through the consistent content and individual meetings. Use "The twenty-minute rule" to start creating results out of nothing.

Part 3: Jim Carrey Commitment

When we understand what we want to work towards, and how to create the motivation to progress, all that is left is to work out is what we want the outcome to be. Nelson Mandela wanted "one man, one vote" in South Africa. Abraham Lincoln wanted to abolish slavery. Usain Bolt wanted to become the fastest man in history. Each of these individuals had a vision for what they wanted to achieve and every action they took was in alignment with this vision.

Nelson Mandela turned down a number of "power-sharing" compromises offered to him because it did not come with the "one man, one vote" he was aiming for. (16) Lincoln was prepared to take his country to war rather than continue to tolerate slavery. Usain Bolt (as far as we know) ignored any temptation to take drugs because he knew that would call into doubt any record he broke. When you have a clear vision of what you want to achieve it makes decision-making much easier because you will only take action that is aligned with your vision.

There is a popular anecdote told in the personal development space about the power of vision. When the actor and comedian Jim Carrey was a young man, he was a LA stereotype. He had moved to the City of Angels to pursue his dreams and hit the big time but he was struggling to make ends meet. One night, Carrey drove up to Mulholland Drive — where the A-list celebrities live — envisioning himself becoming successful enough to own a house on this prestigious street. He got a blank cheque and wrote on it "ten million dollars, for acting services rendered." He dated it for Thanksgiving 1995. (17)

In 1994, Jim Carrey was cast in his three breakthrough roles in *Ace Ventura: Pet Detective*, *The Mask* and *Dumb and Dumber*, for which he was paid $7.9M ($7M for *Dumb and Dumber* alone). In 1995, he earned another $7M for *Batman Forever* and $15M for *Ace Ventura: When Nature Calls*. By Thanksgiving 1995, he had earned just shy of $30M…three times the amount he had written on that cheque. (18)

Now before we launch into talking about the power of this type of visualisation, I have some qualifiers to make. Jim Carrey himself will tell you that he didn't write that cheque and sit on his backside waiting for that movie role to show up. He was still putting in the work and showing up to every audition he could. This is something that I feel the popular "Law of Attraction" and "*The Secret*" movement have miscommunicated to people.

I feel that the "Law of Attraction" is too often communicated and interpreted as personal development's "Get Rich Quick" scheme. The Law of Attraction is the idea that if we desire something enough and visualise it coming into our lives, it will come.

Now I actually believe in the Law of Attraction. I believe then when you put a certain type of energy out into the world, you do start to manifest things in your life. When you create a vision in your mind you start to bring it into reality. However, the caveat is that you need to also take action on that vision.

There's a reason why it's called "attrACTION", the action needs to come next. This is what I believe is missing for too many followers of the Law of Attraction. They make their vision boards and say their affirmations but then just wait around and hope that the universe delivers for them. This is why it is personal development's "Get Rich Quick" scheme. People think that abundance will be delivered to them just because they asked for it.

I think it is a shame that the Law of Attraction was dressed up in this way, because when applied correctly, it can have some powerful outcomes. I have experienced some of these in my own life.

At age thirteen I weighed seventeen stone (107kg) and I decided that I was fed up looking the way that I did. I started to make changes to my diet and exercise. I remember one day watching a triathlon on television and saying "these guys are the ultimate athletes. I would love to be able to do a triathlon." At the age of seventeen, weighing thirteen stone (83kg), I completed a 51km Triathlon.

On New Year's Day, 2015, I wrote down a list of goals that I wanted to have achieved by New Year's Day, 2018. One of the most prominent was to find "The One". Throughout 2015, a series of events worked in strange collusion and I started dating Kerrie. In 2018, I proposed to her and she agreed to marry me.

In September 2016, I created a new vision board for myself and one of my primary goals was to make the book I was writing *The Last 60 Minutes* a number one bestseller. In January 2017, a week after publication, *The Last 60 Minutes* hit number one on Amazon in the Death and Grief category.

At seventeen stone, did I continue to eat and exercise the same and expect to be able to do a triathlon? No. At the start of 2015, did I stay the same person and do the same things and hope "The One" would find me? No. When I had finished *The Last 60 Minutes*, did I just stick it up on Amazon and expect it to sell itself? No.

Before going on to talk about vision, I want to just hammer home this point about taking action. This is something we'll cover plenty more in the next few chapters to help you take effective action but know that this is a necessary part of the Author Your Life process. You need to pick up that pen and actively write your narrative.

So how do we tap into the same force Jim Carrey used so effectively? It's important to know that everything is created twice in life: once in imagination, once in reality. The chair (or bed) you are sitting on right now was imagined by someone, then built. The clothes you are wearing right now were imagined by someone, then manufactured. The words in this book were created first in my imagination, then written. To bring anything into our life, we must first imagine it.

The imagination is an interesting place, because our mind cannot tell the difference between real experience and imagined experience. Have you ever been nervous about going to a party because you imagined making a faux pas or seeing someone you don't like? You feel the fear as if you are actually at the party. Conversely, have you ever thought about being with someone you are attracted to and found yourself getting aroused? You feel the arousal as if you are actually with that person.

This manipulation of the imagination has been used in some profound ways. A research study by Dr. Judd Biasiotto, professor at the University of Chicago looked at improving the free-throw shots of basketball players. Three groups of people were gathered and tested on how many free-throws they could make.

For the next thirty days, each group were asked to follow a different intervention. The first group were the control group and did nothing. The second group were asked to visualise the process of executing a perfect free-throw but not physically practice. The third group were asked to practice their free-throws on the court for an hour each day.

Unsurprisingly, when measured again at the end of the thirty days, the control group showed no improvement. Also of little surprise was that the group who had physically practiced improved their accuracy by 24%. But of greater surprise was that the group who had just visualised had also improved their accuracy by 23%, just 1% less than the group who had physically practiced. (19)

Another study asked a group of volunteers to learn a five-finger piano piece. They practiced over and over and the experimenters observed using brain scans that their motor cortex had expanded. A second group was asked just to imagine playing the notes, yet the same expansion had occurred in their brains. Their imagination was growing their brain. (20)

On an anecdotal note, I perform a similar visualisation process before I speak on stage. I visualise the process of moving across the stage, how I want to say a line, and the reactions I want to generate from the audience. What I often find on stage is that I have moments of déjà vu, where I am in the exact spot, delivering a line in the exact way, and getting the exact reaction that I envisioned. It is these moments when I am most in "flow" on stage (we will talk about "flow" in the next chapter). When we visualise, it helps to prepare the process required to succeed.

What I'd like to do now is take you through a creative visualisation exercise that will help you clarify your future direction. This process doesn't work well being read and undertaken at the same time, so I recommend recording yourself reading the exercise first, then listen to it. Alternatively, you can access the recording in the online resources attached to this book:

http://davidmccrae.thinkific.com/courses/author-your-life-book-resources

When I use the word "visualisation", you might worry that it won't work for you because you are not a "visual" person, and perhaps process and understand the world in an auditory or kinaesthetic way.

What I'm really describing with the word "visualisation", is a multi-sensory experience. The following visualisation exercise will tap into all senses and processing styles to suit the way your mind works.

Because of this, don't worry if you find times during this exercise where you struggle for clarity. Your mind will be using its imagination in ways that it is perhaps not used to and it will take time and practice to develop it. Just use your mind to the best of its current capability.

I'd like you now to close your eyes. We are going to take you into a more relaxed state with some simple breathing. When we bring our brain into a calmer, more relaxed state, into the alpha brainwave, we create the best conditions for creative visualisation.

Let out a big exhale. Imagine the stress and tension in your body flying out as you do so. Relax the muscles in your face and jaw.

Inhale deeply, hold for a count of two, and let out another big exhale. Imagine that stress and tension whooshing out with that exhale. Relax the muscles in your neck and shoulders.

Inhale deeply, hold for a count of two, and exhale fully again. Feel the last bits of stress and tension fly away. Relax your arms. Relax your torso. Relax your legs.

Now you should be feeling more relaxed and more receptive to the work we are about to begin. I would like you now to imagine a TV screen in front of you. Imagine the biggest screen you've ever seen. It's HD, 3D, 4D, Surround Sound, all the things you look for in a cinematic experience.

On this screen is a situation you want to change in your life right now. You can only watch one channel at a time, so pick something specific in your life. Pick something that is bringing you pain and frustration right now.

See this scenario or situation playing on the screen. Really feel the pain that this situation is bringing you. This is not just a visual experience: it is an emotional one. Pain can be an incredible motivator in our lives, tap into this force now.

Connect with how this situation makes you feel, whether that be angry, fearful or sad. Observe how you feel as you connect with this emotion now. This is not the way you want to feel. This is not how you deserve to feel. This feeling is going to change.

Now imagine you have a whiteboard eraser in your hand. You can use this eraser to rub out this current picture. Rub at the screen until the whole image of your current circumstance is completely gone.

With this eraser, I also want you to erase your conception of the past. It does not exist. You are not governed and controlled by the things that have happened. With this eraser, I also want you to erase your concept of the future. When you visualise your new desired circumstances, I don't want you to imagine it as some future outcome that is disconnected from who you are right now. I want you to see and feel your desired outcome as vividly as you will when you reach it. Understand that the past, present and future are false divisions we make as humans to a continuous process.

With this in mind, I'd like you now to change the channel on that big TV screen. On this screen I now want you to see your desired circumstances. See them in that high quality, ultra-defined manner. See the wide array of colour. See the minute details on people and objects. How can your life look so much different than it does now? Where do you live? Who do you spend time with? What are you doing from day-to-day? On this screen you see not just a single experience or change but you see how the entire paradigm of your life has shifted. How do you want your life to be? See that on the screen now.

Remember that this is more than a visual experience. This screen provides multi-sensory stimulation. Hear the sounds accompanying this desired outcome. Do you hear the laughter of others? Do you hear your favourite music? Do you hear the sounds of nature, of rivers and birds? Can you hear the way you speak and the things you say in this experience? Can you hear the way people talk to you?

What are the smells and tastes of this new paradigm? What are you eating and drinking on a regular basis? What nourishes you and makes you feel great? What is the smell of home? Are there smells associated with the activities you do? Perhaps freshly cut grass on your beautiful lawn; perhaps incense candles and massage oil of regular pampering; perhaps the rich scent in your favourite coffee house.

What do you feel in this experience, both physically and emotionally? Do you feel the hugs of those you love? Can you feel the instruments of your favourite craft or hobby in your hands? Do you feel the warmth of the sun in an exotic location?

Take these feelings deeper. Notice how this paradigm makes you feel intellectually, emotionally and spiritually fulfilled. How does this new paradigm make you feel? Do you feel joy, excitement, gratitude or love? Embrace the intensity of this feeling. This visualisation is not a logical process, it is an emotional one.

Understand that you are not detached from the vision on the screen. This vision is already in your mind: you can see it, hear it, taste it, smell it and feel it. You can immerse yourself in this desired experience right now. Understand that there is no difference between how this experience feels now and how it will feel. The potential for this experience is already there because your mind can create it and your heart can feel it.

Just as you felt the pain and frustration of your current circumstances, feel now the pleasure and satisfaction of your new circumstances. Feel the positive emotion with the same or greater intensity. Notice how we change the way we feel through the power of our attention. Observe the power our mind has to change how we feel.

The process of visualisation is designed to tap into the power of our minds and release its unused potential. As I aimed to assure you at the beginning of the exercise, do not worry if you felt resistance or blockages during this process. If we are not used to using our mind in this way, it can feel strange or not provide the vivid clarity we might like. This is why visualisation should be a regular practice. You may wish to do a deep immersion as we have done today, or a sixty-second snapshot.

The more frequently you engage in this process, the faster you will train your mind to create the circumstances you desire and will create a stronger emotional connection to drive and motivate you. I hope you have found this process useful, now go out there and make your vision a reality.

<u>Purpose</u>

Discovering your Calling begins by getting clear on your Purpose. When you are connected to your "why", that gives you the fuel for all your future progress. However, the journey ahead is still long, and there are fundamental principles you will need to embrace to succeed. That is what you will learn in the next chapter on Proficiency.

In this chapter you have learned:

- That you have a specific purpose and mission in life
- How your purpose becomes more clear with exploration and to listen to the feeling in your heart
- That intrinsic motivation is far more powerful than extrinsic motivation
- How to tap into your drivers of intrinsic motivation
- How to generate motivation when you don't "feel like it"
- There is no point having vision without action
- The power of your imagination

My biggest takeaway from this chapter is

_____.

Chapter 8: Proficiency

"We are what we repeatedly do. Excellence then is not an act, but a habit." **- Aristotle**

What becomes clear when you study people who undertook great Callings in their lives is that they had a guiding set of principles that helped them succeed. They employed these principles with discipline and commitment. We are going to look at these principles in this chapter. The first thing we will look at is the notion of Grit, how successful people possess two vital traits: passion and perseverance. Secondly, we will examine mastery, the process through which someone becomes highly adept at something. Thirdly, we will examine the state of flow, a unique physiological and psychological state in which we experience optimal performance.

Part 1: PxP

"Grit" is a term coined by the psychologist Angela Duckworth that describes a constellation of traits common to successful people. (1) The pioneering research into Grit came from Duckworth's study of West Point Cadets. West Point is an advanced military academy which only takes the cream of the crop. Not only must you score highly on intelligence, fitness and aptitude tests to be accepted, but you must also be nominated by a Member of Congress, a Senator or the Vice President of the United States.

West Point training is a gruelling program, pushing the limits of physical and psychological endurance. Even though it only selects the best of the best, one in five drop out before graduation. (2) Furthermore, the score on the tests the applicants complete do not predict who will actually complete the training. A "Whole Candidate Score" (WCS) is compiled based on all the different metrics of a cadet. This "Whole Candidate Score" is a modest predictor at best of who will ultimately graduate. Those who ace the tests can drop out and those who sneak in can complete the training.

West Point weren't happy with this unpredictability, and this is where Duckworth came in. She believed the tests were missing something, an attribute called "Grit". She believed that "Grit" would predict who did and didn't drop out with far greater accuracy than the current tests.

Grit is made up of two key traits, passion and perseverance. To succeed at something an individual must have passion for that pursuit, a burning desire to pursue their chosen path. However, it's not enough to just have the passion, they must have the perseverance to push through when things get tough.

In 2004, Duckworth got to test her hypothesis that the level of a candidate's Grit would predict their likelihood of graduating from West Point. The usual tests were administered, giving the cadets their traditional WCS. Additionally, Duckworth's Grit Scale was used to measure each individual's passion (rating the truth of statements such as "I have been obsessed with a certain idea or project for a short time but later lost interest" and "I often set a goal but later choose to pursue a different one") and perseverance (rating the truth of statements such as "I finish whatever I begin" and "I have overcome setbacks to conquer an important challenge.").

They found that the WCS bore no relationship to the Grit Score. How talented an individual was had nothing to do with their level of Grit. That year, the WCS was again not effective for predicting who would drop out but the cadet's Grit score was highly accurate in predicting whether they would. A cadet with low Grit was much likelier to drop out then a cadet with high Grit, regardless of their WCS. It was not survival of the fittest... it was survival of the grittiest. (3)

We have covered the first part of Grit quite extensively in the previous chapter. How closely you are connected to a deep sense of purpose and intrinsic motivation makes up the "passion" component of Grit. Having that energy and vision is great but what can you do with it? How do you turn a dream into reality? It is not enough to be passionate, you have to have the determination and resolve to bring it into reality. That is what we are going to explore now.

The difference between Passion and Perseverance

Warren Willingham was the director of the Personal Qualities Project, the most ambitious attempt ever to identify the determinants of success in young adulthood. Willingham's team followed several thousand high school seniors for a period of five years. College application materials, questionnaires, writing samples, interviews and school records were used to collect data on each student. From this, over one hundred personal characteristics were identified and measured. What Willingham's team wanted to do was to put each of these variables to the test. Which ones mattered and which ones didn't?

Willingham's team measured success in three ways: academic distinction, demonstrations of leadership and significant accomplishment. On these parameters, one characteristic was miles ahead of the rest for predicting success. Willingham called this characteristic "follow-through".

"Follow-through", after controlling for high school grades and SAT scores, predicted graduating from college with academic honours better than any other variable. "Follow-through" was the single best predictor of holding an appointed or elected leadership position in young adulthood. "Follow-through" predicted notable accomplishments in a myriad of domains, from science to the arts to sports to business. (4)

What is "follow-through"? Willingham defined it as: *"evidence of purposeful, continuous commitment to certain types of activities versus sporadic efforts in diverse areas."* (5) Where the research team was observing this was in extra-curricular activities such as sports teams, student newspapers and community projects. Students with the highest follow-through ratings participated in two different extra-curricular activities for several years each and in both of those activities had enjoyed significant achievement (named captain, winning an award, reaching a major fundraising goal etc). They had picked an activity and stuck at it consistently.

This notion of "follow-through" neatly illustrates the difference between passion and perseverance. Plenty of people get passionate about things. Lots of people become "passionate" about weight loss on January 1st. Lots of people become "passionate" about politics near an election.

Lots of people become "passionate" about someone after a successful first date. However, for many that passion fizzles out. When the hype is gone or the going gets tough, they lose their passion and move onto something else. Passion alone will not help you succeed.

Perseverance is about sticking with passion. The road to success is a tough one. You will be tested again and again. Your limits will be pushed. Multiple times you will want to give up and end the struggle. What defines the successful is that they push through the challenges. This is perseverance. It is a stubborn tenacity to keep going even when there seems to be no reason or reward to do so.

Are you able to take your breakthroughs and insights from the previous chapter and follow through on them? If you realised what drives you, what your unique contribution is, what the word in your heart is, are you going to commit to that? Are you going to keep on working, honing and developing? That is the difference between successful people and unsuccessful people. They are able to match their passion with perseverance. Can you do the same?

Necessity

In his book "*High Performance Habits*", Brendon Burchard outlines the results of research conducted across thousands of "high performers", people who represent the top 15% of their industry. From this research, he has identified six habits that correlate with high performance. The third habit is "Necessity". (6)

From the data, Burchard was able to observe that high performers feel an urge and a duty to pursue their chosen path. This is not an external pressure from others like parents and teachers, it is an intrinsic part of who that person is. When high performers were asked in interviews why they work so hard and how they stay so focused and committed, they reported answers like:

"It's just who I am"
"I can't imagine doing anything else"
"This is what I was made to do"

There is also a sense of obligation and urgency:

"People need me now; they're counting on me"
"I can't miss this opportunity"
"If I don't do this now, I'll regret it forever" (7)

People who report strong agreements with statements like this report greater confidence, happiness, and success over longer periods than their peers. (8) What I believe Burchard has captured in this research is the essence of Grit: the burning desire within and the inspired action that comes as a result.

If you want to get ahead in your life, you need to make progress an utter necessity for yourself. I hear a lot of mantras in this regard that I don't like: "You need to give 110%", "If your commitment isn't a 10/10, don't bother", or even just "hustle" (one of my least favourite words in the motivational lingo). The more I hear this from someone, the more I see them as trying to prove to others they are committed, rather than being deeply committed themselves. The person shouting affirmations the loudest at a seminar is probably the person least likely to take action. The person posting the most motivational quotes on social media is probably doing the least to actually live up to the message of these quotes.

When someone is in this state, I believe they are making it too much about themselves. If you want to develop real necessity, make it about someone else.

The reality is that we will often do more for others than we'll do for ourselves. We'd take a bullet, jump in front of a car or go to jail to protect someone we care about. That is real necessity. You want to talk about having a commitment of 10/10? When the parent runs in front of a car to push their child out of the way, their commitment is a ten. There is no hesitation and no second thinking.

The irony of Author Your Life is that the phrase suggests it's all about you. However, if you really want to get ahead, you need to make it about someone else. But that someone else doesn't need to be as separate from you as you think it is.

There are three people who drive my necessity. The first is my dad. Thinking of him reminds me that life is precious and that I have work to do during my time here on Earth. In everything I do, I aspire to live a life that Dad would be proud of. When I'm struggling, I remember that Dad held on for me so that I could get those last sixty minutes with him. Whatever complaint I have compared to that isn't a real complaint.

The second is my partner. Thinking of her reminds me that I'm creating a livelihood for more than myself; I'm creating it for her and our family. I want to be the best partner, friend and lover for her that I can be. She was there for me during one of the most difficult periods of my life and has been there for me ever since. I will be there for her too.

The third person who drives my necessity is me. Yet didn't I just say not to make it about yourself? The two are not as mutually exclusive as you think, because what drives me on is young David. I think of David as a young adult. He was someone with potential and good qualities but he needed to release his fear and get out of his own way. He was cheerful but allowed his negativity to override that. He had a passion but didn't commit himself to it. He was nice but obscured that with cockiness and false confidence.

I want to reach the young Davids of the world. I want to help them break through their limits. I want to help them connect with their purpose. Most of all, I want to help them become the good human beings that we all are at our core.

These are the people who fuel my necessity. I'm going to push through the struggle the way my dad pushed through for me. I'm going to stay committed to what's meaningful the way my partner has stayed committed to me. I'm going to keep striving for excellence, because there's a young David out there who needs my help.

If you want to develop this necessity for yourself, then who are you championing? Who are you working for? This can be a loved one(s) but as my example shows, you can also champion yourself. You do so not in a self-serving way but in a manner that serves others. Whatever challenges you have gone through, others have gone through too. There are people you can help and inspire through your example.

The benefit of this approach is that you can have real empathy for the person you are working for. You might say "I want to be a champion for starving children in Africa". This is very noble, but if you haven't been a starving child in Africa, or even spent any time with such a child, then you are too detached from their plight for it to activate a strong emotional drive in you. On the other hand, if you are fighting for a younger version of you who was a child of five with a single mum on social security who occasionally went hungry, you can empathise with that a lot more, and thus you will fight for that person a lot more.

The Missing P

I think there is one more "P" to consider when talking about Grit. That is "Patience". Passion is the energy and enthusiasm that starts something; Perseverance is to keep doing something; Patience is the ability to wait for the results. A stock trader might persevere in buying shares, but patience is what will allow them to make a profit.

Impatience is one of the biggest challenges I have had to face in myself. I am a millennial and as such I am used to things happening quickly and on demand. On top of this, I am a hugely driven person. I want to create a huge impact with my work and life and I want to push that through as fast as I can. I have an urge to grow and progress.

I was running my first full-day seminars by age twenty-three. I was a #1 bestselling author at age twenty-four. I have mentored people more than twice my age. Yet despite this positive impact at a young age, I was (am!) impatient for improvement: to host seminars more regularly; to have more people reading my book; to mentor more people. I have reminded myself many times to chill the flip out and be patient. To allow the business and impact time to grow.

One analogy that I found really useful to help me be patient is the degree analogy. I thought back to my time at university and recognised that it took me four years to earn my degree in psychology (technically five as I changed universities after a year). Four years is the exact amount of time it takes to earn that degree. You can't shortcut, "hack" or accelerate that learning process. You attend the classes each week; complete the coursework each month; and finish the exams each semester. If you do that successfully for four years, they give you a pretty piece of paper at the end. In each of those years, you are a different person, with a different perspective.

Clueless First Year

In first year, you are still learning about yourself and finding your way around. You've moved away from home. You're exploring a new place and making new friends. You're learning how to look after yourself, how to prioritise and how to manage your lifestyle. During this time you make some mistakes and have some struggles. It's the early initiation and you have limited experience and skill. You're approaching a new subject or a familiar subject at a deeper level. You don't really know what you're doing but you find a way to stumble through.

Curious Second Year

In second year you are exploring and having fun. You now have some foundations and are a bit more stable. You know your way around and you're no longer the new kid on the block. You start to find out a little more about yourself and your chosen area of study. You start thinking about what your next steps will be. You start to select a few interests and explore them further.

Competent Third Year

In third year you are starting to clarify what you are aiming to do. You know the drill by now, it's just a case of mastering it. You know what's expected of you and where you need to improve. You are able to look after yourself and focus on what needs to be done.

Confident Fourth Year

In fourth year you know what you're doing and are focused on creating the end result you desire. Everything has started to click now. You can work on a project and know that, as long as you put in the work required, you're probably going to get the result you're looking for. You have a deep understanding of your subject and have developed a number of specialties. You now are focused on bringing everything you know together to bring about the accomplishment at the end of the journey: your degree.

I started to look at my business in the same way as my degree. What if my business was also a four-year project? My business degree started at age twenty-two, the moment I walked out of Dad's hospice room. For the first year I did a lot of learning and trying to find my way.

In the second year I began to explore writing, speaking and online training and started to have a lot more fun than the first year of trying to get to grips with everything.

In the third year I started to gain clarity on my message, the concept of "Author Your Life" and how to make an impact with this message.

I'm now in my fourth year and I've learned how to make things work. I have developed my own unique style and expression and I've gained confidence in my abilities to write, speak and train.

In July 2019, four years after I walked out of Dad's hospice room, I am hosting the Author Your Life Summit, my first multi-day event. This event is a significant date for a number of reasons, but one reason is that I see it as a mark of my graduation. That I have completed the business degree and I'm now ready for the next stage.

If you want to make significant change in your life, you need to prepare yourself for the same journey. If you want to make radical changes to your health, career, or relationships, you need to earn the degree to help you do so. At first you are going to be a clueless first year; then you will be a curious second year; then a competent third year; then a confident fourth year.

Part 2: Mastery

Mastery is the process through which we become highly proficient at something. There have been a number of notable figures throughout history who have displayed outstanding levels of excellence in their lifetime such as Leonardo Da Vinci, Wolfgang Amadeus Mozart and Albert Einstein. Current examples could be Elon Musk, Usain Bolt and the late Stephen Hawking. Students have looked at such masters and wondered "how did they achieve such levels of excellence?" From the study of such masters, certain traits, practices and principles in common can be identified and these provide the clue to how we achieve our own level of mastery.

Fundamentals

What becomes apparent looking at masters is that they have a set of fundamental practices that they perform religiously. Whether these fundamentals relate to their energy and vibrancy; their knowledge and craft; or their influence and impact; they definitely have them.

- Sir Alex Ferguson, football's most successful manager, travelled to multiple games each week to watch the upcoming opposition and scout potential transfer signings. (9)

- Warren Buffet, the second richest man in the world, reads 5-6 hours every day. (10)

- The Dalai Lama meditates for four hours each day. (11)

In order to generate the mastery you desire, you must establish and practice the fundamentals that form the building blocks to your success. Many people want the end result without the journey. The master honours and welcomes the journey. Brian Johnson, host of the Optimise Podcast, calls the fundamentals "fun-dies" as you should approach them with a sense of fun. (12) You should relish the basics, because you know that these are what help you to develop mastery.

We can look at two forms of fundamentals: general and specific.

General

General fundamentals are what we all require to grow and thrive. You can remember this through the acronym P.I.E.S.

1. Physical
2. Intellectual
3. Emotional
4. Spiritual (or Social if you are uncomfortable with the word Spiritual)

What so much of this consists of is the obvious, common sense stuff. However, as my mentor Brendon Burchard says, *"common sense is not always common practice"*. (13)

Physical

- Sleep 7-9hrs a night. Good quality sleep not disturbed by blue light, caffeine or alcohol. As we have discussed, poor sleep inhibits a number of physical, cognitive and emotional functions.

- Eat smart. There is a lot of debate in the nutrition space but what everyone agrees on is that we should be eating less sugar and processed food and eating more vegetables (particularly leafy greens) and whole foods.

- Move every day. Whether that be walking, running, dancing, swimming, crossfit, yoga or tai chi, get that body moving for at least an hour each day.

Intellectual

- Learn something new each day. Whether that be reading, listening to podcasts or watching a TED talk, go to bed each evening with more knowledge than you had when you woke up.

- Express your creativity. We all have our own little ways of bringing new things into the world. For you that might be writing poetry or blogs; crafting pottery or robots; or composing music with an instrument or an audio program.

- Test your brain. Play brain training apps. Do puzzles such as crosswords and sudoku. Take part in quizzes at your local pub or as a family game.

Emotional

- Live with gratitude. Express thanks and appreciation whenever possible.

- Don't believe every thought you have! Question and reframe negative thinking.

- Meditate: it's the pill we can all benefit from.

Spiritual (or Social)

- Give time and attention to your interactions. We live in an age of hyper-distraction, where we are not really present with the people we are with.

- Work on a cause larger than yourself. We are all looking for meaning in our lives, this is how we find it.

- Give to others. Studies show that what we provide for others gives us more satisfaction and happiness than what we provide for ourselves. (14)

Masters look after their basic fundamentals on a consistent, disciplined basis. Arnold Schwarzenegger, throughout his years as an actor, businessman, politician and activist, has always stuck to the fundamental where he first achieved success: exercise. He cites exercise as the medium that taught him key principles that have allowed him to find success in multiple fields. (15) Masters understand that a building is only as strong as its foundations. In fact, if you want to know how tall a building is going to be before it is even built, look at how deep they are digging the foundations.

Specific

Whilst all masters have general fundamentals that they stick to, they also have fundamentals related directly to their craft or discipline that they are seeking mastery in. They look at the ultimate aim they want to achieve and break down what the component parts are which will allow them to build mastery in that area.

- Cal Newport, who has written five books and became a tenured professor by age thirty-four, tracks how many hours of "Deep Work" he does per day (we'll talk more about Deep Work in the next chapter) (16)

- Kobe Bryant, NBA Hall of Famer and the 3rd-highest scorer of all time, only left practice when he had successfully made four hundred shots. (17)

- Seth Godin, expert marketer and author of eighteen books, publishes a blog post every day. (18)

What are you looking to become highly proficient at? Is it tennis, the drums, website design, cooking, property law or parenting? What are the specific fundamentals required to build mastery in this area?

To illustrate with my more modest example, I am looking to achieve mastery in public speaking. I know if I can master public speaking then that allows me to communicate my message not just from a lectern or stage, but also from a video, a podcast and even this book. With this aim in mind, I have identified that I need to speak in public more. Makes sense right?

I run seminars and am a member of Toastmasters International, both of which help me, but aren't consistent enough to build mastery by themselves. To build real consistency, I have recorded videos. I have recorded a Youtube video, averaging at least ten minutes in length, every week since the age of twenty-two. When Instagram expanded its video feature, I started recording three sixty-second videos a week there as well. I also record live videos on Facebook that often last an hour. This practice has allowed me to bank hundreds of hours of "public speaking" regardless of whether I am stepping on a stage or not. I am by no means a master but I am building towards it.

When creating our specific fundamentals, there are two important processes to be aware of: deliberate practice, and incremental progress, which are the next two principles we will discuss.

Deliberate Practice

If there is one practice that unites all masters, it is deliberate practice. It's likely you will have heard of the 10,000 hour rule, whereby they say that it takes 10,000 hours of practice to become an expert in something. This number was quoted by Malcolm Gladwell in his book *Outliers,* who studied the research of Anders Ericsson into violin players.

Like most "facts" you hear in pop culture, this is off the mark. 10,000 hours is not where we become an expert…it is just the beginning.

Let's clear up the confusion. Anders Ericsson studied young violinists at the top music academies in Germany. He wanted to find out the difference between the good, the better, and the best. All of the students at the music academy were of a high calibre but what separated the best from the rest? He found that by the age of eighteen, the good violinists had practiced an average of 3,400 hours, the better violinists had practiced an average of 5,300 hours and the best had practiced an average of 7,400 hours. (19)

So the difference between the violinists was simple: the best violinists had practiced more...considerably more. However, where did 10,000 hours come from?

When Malcolm Gladwell conducted his research, he did not look at the practice recorded at age eighteen, he instead looked at the practice at age twenty. At age twenty, the best violinists had indeed accumulated an *average* of 10,000 hours of practice. Gladwell saw two nice round numbers — age 20, and 10,000 hours — and coined the 10,000 hour rule. However, as Anders Ericsson discusses in his book *"Peak"*, expertise and practice is far more nuanced than this. (20)

Firstly, 10,000 hours is not a concrete amount: it was an average number observed across the best students. As I shared with you at the beginning of the book, always be careful when you hear an average. Some of the students had practiced significantly less than 10,000 hours, some had practiced significantly more than this. 10,000 hours is not a hard and fast rule.

Secondly, these violinists were not historical figures; they were not filling stadiums and they were not breaking music records. They were still students. They were not masters of the craft, they were apprentices. 10,000 hours, average or no average, was not the end, it was the beginning.

Thirdly, and this is where we really get into Ericsson's work, not all practice is created equal. If you kicked a ball against a wall for 10,000 hours, do you think that would make you an expert football player? If you played the same song for 10,000 hours, do you think that would make you an expert pianist? If you built the same prototype for 10,000 hours, do you think that would make you an expert inventor?

Of course not. These examples might seem slightly facetious but actually they represent a real fallacy in our thinking. We assume that a doctor who has been working for twenty years is better than one who has been working for two. We assume that a friend who has been driving for twenty years is better than one who has been driving for two. Time spent doing something is no indication of excellence. Repetitive practice is not sufficient. The practice has to be *deliberate*.

This is what Ericsson has observed in his work, that excellence is not developed through 10,000 hours of mindless practice, but many more hours of what he calls "deliberate practice."

Deliberate practice requires the fulfilment of key criteria: (21)

1. Objective criteria for improvement (e.g. faster time, more widgets, higher income)

2. A clearly defined target (e.g. Complete 10km in under sixty minutes, not "run faster")

3. Feedback from a teacher or coach (this is someone who's expertise exceeds your own, so they can provide you a path to progress)

4. Repetition with refinement and improvement (not just mindlessly repeating something but doing so with specific improvements in mind)

Ericsson's research has focused significantly in musicians, where these criteria are easily fulfilled. Other good examples of where deliberate practice can be applied are sports, martial arts and chess.

However, deliberate practice does not transfer so well to other pursuits. What if excellence is judged on subjective criteria (e.g. painting or writing), your target is less certain (e.g. record sales or winning poker tournaments) or you don't have access to an expert to coach you? In this scenario, we might not be able to apply "pure" deliberate practice in the way Ericsson would like us to, but we can take the principles of his research and apply it to our chosen pursuit.

A particular evolution of deliberate practice that I like is Brendon Burchard's concept of "Progressive Mastery". Deliberate Ppactice, in Ericsson's form, is quite a "left-brain" endeavour. What Burchard does with Progressive Mastery is add an emotional element to it to make it more "right-brain". In the ten steps below, the steps in italics are the ones that add an emotional element to the process.

10 Steps of Progressive Mastery (22)

1. Determine a skill you want to master

2. Set specific stretch goals on your path to developing that skill

3. *Attach high levels of emotion and meaning to your journey and your results*

4. Identify the factors critical to your success, and develop your strengths in those areas (and fix your weaknesses with equal fervour)

5. *Develop visualisations that clearly imagine what success and failure look like*

6. Schedule challenging practices developed by experts or through careful thought

7. Measure your progress and get outside feedback

8. *Socialise your learning and efforts by practicing or competing with others*

9. Continue setting higher-level goals so that you keep improving

10. *Teach others what you are learning*

We are moved by emotion. What this framework does is charge the concept of deliberate practice with emotional energy in a way that I think is more accessible (yet possibly more effective) than Ericsson's original outline of deliberate practice.

I'll illustrate how I use the concept of Progressive Mastery to improve my key skill in my career: public speaking.

1. The skill I want to develop is public speaking.

2. I am aiming to increase the number of times I speak per year and the length I speak for in a single seminar.

3. What makes me step on stage is a desire to make my dad proud and to create an impact I will be happy with on my deathbed.

4. The factors that differentiate me from other speakers is my psychological education and scientific approach, combined with an ability to deliver academic material in a non-academic way.

5. In the lead-up to a speech, I visualise the audience in front of me. I focus on how I want to move across the stage, how I want to emphasise key points, and the energy that I want to give to my students.

6. I record a video training every week and have done since the middle of 2015. I do not speak with notes on camera or on stage. I don't rehearse and deliver speeches word for word. I push myself to speak from the heart and speak from a deep understanding of the material I am presenting, rather than trying to deliver a word-perfect speech.

7. For each of my events I record the number of people in the audience, the number of books I sell, and the number of people who sign up for additional training with me. I also collect testimonials and feedback from my guests whenever possible.

8. I am part of Toastmasters International, an organisation that arranges meetings around the world to help people become better public speakers. At these meetings I share my learning and journey with other mem-

bers and we push each other to be better.

9. At the time of writing, I am applying to deliver a TEDx talk, as well as run my first multi-day event.

10. Every time I get on stage, it helps me practice what I preach. When I deliver training, it further ingrains those principles and habits for me. I don't just teach for others, I also teach for me, as it helps me grow and progress more as a person.

Everything is trainable. Not just skills but also more abstract constructs. You could plug in "confidence", "wealth" or "marriage" into this framework, and start to create action steps as to how you advance in that domain. It might not be "pure" deliberate practice but we can take the principles from Ericsson's work to suit our own personal process of mastery. Understand that mastery takes an incredibly long time to build, far longer even than the 10,000 hour rule suggests. Also understand that just doing something does not constitute "practice". The practice needs to be targeted to a specific skill and it needs to be stretching your ability.

<u>Incremental Progress</u>

Our pursuit of mastery is an asymptote. What is an asymptote? An asymptote is a geometric term for a curved line and a straight line that never quite meet. The curved line bends closer and closer to the straight one and the change in distance becomes less and less as the lines continue.

We can see the straight line as mastery and ourselves as the asymptote. We can get close to mastery but never quite achieve it. There is always something more we can do or improve to get a little better. It is important therefore to see mastery as a journey, rather than a destination. (23)

We build towards mastery, we do not become masters. The great scientists through the eras — such as Newton, Einstein and Hawking — left uncompleted theories, gaps in their knowledge that they were not satisfied with, that they were working on in their final days. Masters are always seeking more answers, expertise and impact.

Whether you are a novice or an expert, you build towards mastery in the same way, through the principle of incremental progress.

Incremental progress is a slog. It is a marathon. There are no "hacks" involved. It is quite simply hard, consistent work. It's not what people want to hear but it's true. Thomas Edison took over ten thousand attempts to create the lightbulb. Ironically there was no "lightbulb" moment for Edison when the finished prototype suddenly popped into his head. He and his team made a prototype, learned from it, built another, learned some more, and repeated that process thousands of times until they completed the finished article.

What can be so discouraging for us in the world we live in now is that the overnight success is thrown in our face: the young singer, actor, athlete or entrepreneur who is "crushing it". Taylor Swift was the youngest winner of the Album of the Year award at nineteen years old. (24) Jennifer Lawrence was the second youngest winner of the Oscar for Best Actress at 22. (25) Usain Bolt broke the 100m world record (actually his own set a few months prior) at the 2008 Olympics at the age of 21. (26) Facebook hit one billion active users in 2012 when its founder, Mark Zuckerberg, was 28. (27)

What we don't see is the ten years of work behind these overnight successes. Taylor Swift was taking vocal lessons at age nine, (28) and submitting demo tapes at age eleven. (29) Jennifer Lawrence was starring in plays at age nine (30) and auditioning at age fourteen. (31) Usain Bolt was sprinting from the age of twelve (32) and competed in his first event at age fourteen. (33) Mark Zuckerberg was writing programs in middle school and helped build a digital music player in high school. (34) These young masters were putting in the work from an even younger age.

Incremental progress is like compound interest. If I give you a pound (or dollar, or euro) this month, and then one the next month, then two the next month, then four the next month, and keep doubling the amount I give you. How long will it take you to become a millionaire?

Month 1: £1
Month 2: £2
Month 3: £4
Month 4: £8
Month 5: £16
Month 6: £32
Month 7: £64
Month 8: £128
Month 9: £256
Month 10: £512
Month 11: £1,024
Month 12: £2,048
Month 13: £4,096
Month 14: £8,192
Month 15: £16,384
Month 16: £32,768
Month 17: £65,536
Month 18: £131,072
Month 19: £262,144
Month 20: £524,288

Month 21: £1,048,576

It would take you just short of two years to become a millionaire. Not bad huh? But what if I changed the rules? What if it wasn't doubling every month, but doubling every *year*.

Would you give up after ten years, when you'd earned "only" £512, and say "this isn't worth it".

Would you give up after fifteen years, when you'd earned "only" £16,382, and say "I'm never going to be a millionaire."

Would you give up after eighteen years, when you'd only earned 10% of your target, and say "I tried, this is good enough."

In this scenario, you wouldn't give up, because you know I'm going to keep doubling the output and that starts to hit staggering numbers at a certain point. Yet why do we give up on our dreams and desires when we feel "it isn't worth it", "I'm never going to make it" or the killer "this is good enough".

This is the part of the overnight success that we don't see. When the masters are building brick by brick; when even doubled progress represents little progress at all. But this is where *all* masters build from.

There is only one example I know of that is the closest representation of an overnight success. Justin Bieber hit the big time at age fifteen with a platinum album. (35) At age sixteen he had the most watched video of all time on Youtube, his song "Baby" (36). Justin Bieber was almost an overnight success.

Bieber found success at fifteen but he was uploading songs to Youtube by the age of twelve. (37) Even at that young age, he had still put in two years of work before he was discovered. His discovery was sheer luck, when music producer Scooter Braun clicked on one of his videos by mistake, and that is what accelerated his "overnight success". (38)

However, as we said earlier in the book: "The harder I work, the luckier I get."

There will be the anomaly in the process of mastery such as Justin Bieber but you can't count on being that anomaly. You have to respect and honour the journey.

Brian Johnson (who talked about "fun-dies" earlier) has a fantastic concept for explaining incremental growth. He observes that throughout the day, we have swathes of micro decisions and these decisions either give us a "+1" or "-1": we either take a step towards our goal, or a step away from it. (39) Let's look at some examples of micro decisions during your day.

1. When the alarm goes off do you...

A: Jump out of bed immediately (+1)
B: Hit the snooze button and roll over (-1)

2. When you get to work do you...

A: Identify your most important project for the day (+1)
B: Check your email (-1)

3. When you get back from work do you...

A: Pick up a book (+1)
B: Load Netflix (-1)

We make these micro decisions throughout the day and we accumulate a score. At the end of the day we have an aggregate score. We have either a net positive or a net negative. We have either advanced that day or languished.

Here's the thing about these micro-decisions. None of them matter.

In the morning, does hitting snooze instead of getting up drastically affect your life? No.

At work, does checking your email instead of identifying your key project drastically affect your life? No.

In the evening, does watching Netflix instead of reading a book drastically affect your life? No.

Taken in isolation, none of these micro decisions matter. Even collectively at the end of the day, none of them matter. They only matter when you zoom far out and look at them long term.

When you hit snooze every day you start to fall behind the person who is jumping out of bed at that time.

When you check your email every morning you start to fall behind the person who is working creatively at that time.

When you watch Netflix every night you start to fall behind the person who is reading at that time.

This is the nature of incremental progress. It is having the discipline to make a "+1" choice every time you are confronted with a micro decision. As you earn these points each day, they start to build capital and you start to earn interest. Eventually one day the scales tip and the exponential growth kicks into gear. This is the "overnight success" that you see documented so much in the media but that moment of critical mass takes a long time to generate.

Part 3: Flow

Have you ever had the experience where everything you touched seemed to turn to gold? You were playing a sport and you couldn't stop scoring. You were drawing and every pencil stroke seemed to fall in just the right place. You were at a party and every time you told a joke people roared with laughter.

This state is known by athletes as being "in the zone". Scientists call it "flow". This flow state is familiar to anyone who exercises, plays a musical instrument, engages in creative work, or likes to interact with others. I get it in sections of writing this book. It is where you are so engrossed in that one activity that you lose all perception of time, fatigue, hunger and thirst. You are utterly absorbed by and concentrated on the task at hand. This is the flow state.

Mihály Csíkszentmihályi has the honour of being the hardest name to pronounce in psychology (it's "cheeks-sent-me-high"); he is also the pioneering researcher into flow states. Csíkszentmihályi, along with his friend Martin Seligman, is one of the early changemakers in the positive psychology movement. Csíkszentmihályi's foundational studies into flow came from asking a simple question "when are we happiest"?

Take a moment to answer that question for yourself. Now you will have cheated a bit, as you've read the first section on Consciousness and have some idea of what your answer should be. However, most people when presented with this question will generally answer by talking about leisure time: they'll describe a holiday, relaxing and watching TV, hanging out with friends or something along these lines. However, this is not what Csíkszentmihályi and his team found.

Csíkszentmihályi used what was a novel approach at the time in psychology called "The Experience Sampling Method". He gave his research participants beepers that went off at random times during the day. When the beeper went off, the participant had to record what they were doing and how happy they were feeling. The participants therefore were not reporting what they thought or expected would make them happy, they were reporting what was actually making them feel the happiest. (40)

There was a clear winner. It wasn't leisure time when the participants felt happiest. It was when they were working.

Work was what brought engagement and meaning to the individual's lives. They might complain about it and find it challenging but that was actually what they enjoyed most.

Csíkszentmihályi was intrigued by this finding and he started to delve further into it. He started to ask people about the experiences at work when they felt happiest and he started to hear descriptions of this special state where participants felt intensely focused, immersed in their task, and highly productive and creative. One report described the "flow" between actions and so "flow states" was coined. (41)

As Csíkszentmihályi started to study flow states more he found that the frequency and intensity of flow states are a vital predictor of happiness, as they increase our sense of engagement and meaning in the world. (42)

One startling study revealed just how integral flow states are for our wellbeing. Csíkszentmihályi asked a set of participants to record all tasks they considered "non-instrumental": tasks that were carried out not out of obligation or to achieve a particular objective, but purely for the pleasure of doing the task.

Csíkszentmihályi then asked the participants to avoid doing any task that could be considered "play" or "non-instrumental". In just twelve hours, the participants reported feeling sluggish, complained of headaches, had difficulty concentrating, had trouble sleeping and felt agitated, tense, hostile, irritated and angry. (43)

Let's compare what the participants were feeling with what the Diagnostic and Statistical Manual of Mental Disorders (DSM-V) lists as common symptoms of generalised anxiety disorder (GAD). (44)

- Edginess or restlessness
- Tiring easily; more fatigued than usual
- Impaired concentration or feeling as though the mind goes blank
- Irritability (which may or may not be observable to others)
- Increased muscle aches or soreness
- Difficulty sleeping (due to trouble falling asleep or staying asleep, restlessness at night, or unsatisfying sleep)

Sound familiar? Depriving people of the opportunity to enter flow was creating symptoms of mental illness. Csíkszentmihályi pulled the plug on the experiment after forty-eight hours as it was unethical to continue putting the participants under such duress.

This study alone demonstrates the key role flow states play in our wellbeing. Csíkszentmihályi, however, hasn't just studied flow states, he's also examined how to create them.

He discovered that flow is a balance between skill and challenge: that we enter flow right on the threshold of our skill level. If the activity is too easy for us, we aren't fully taxed or stimulated, so don't enter flow. If it's too hard we get anxious and stressed, so don't enter flow. Further research by Steven Kotler has suggested a rule of 4% here, whereby a challenge that is between 1-4% above our skill level is optimal for creating flow. (45)

This can be a hard number to gauge; how do we determine what is 1% above our skill level in something? How do we actively create flow states for ourselves and not just fall into them randomly? There are three criteria that we can use to help direct us into a state of flow. These are:

1. Having clear goals throughout the process

2. Clear and immediate feedback

3. Balance between skill and challenge (46)

This is why musicians get into flow so frequently. They have clear goals throughout the process, for example finishing each verse of the piece. They get immediate and clear feedback, they either play the note right, or wrong. They can also match that skill and challenge, choosing pieces that match their level of playing ability.

The first part of flow comes from attention and focus. Steven Kotler has spent years measuring flow in extreme sport athletes. (47) When you are skiing a double black diamond, surfing a twenty-metre wave, or jumping out of space, you need to be 100% focused: anything less and you're dead. Circumstances are not so dramatic for us but the same principles hold. If we are seeking immersion and absorption, that can only be one activity at a time.

The second part comes from challenging yourself (which you'll love if you've developed a growth mindset). Flow is a state your body enters to perform at its absolute best. If you are coasting along with something that doesn't stretch you, then you aren't going to enter flow. You need to progressively, incrementally push yourself. This is easier to do in some pursuits than others (e.g. in the gym you lift a slightly heavier weight. Music has "grades" that get progressively harder).

However, if the natural progression isn't so obvious, there are always two factors that you can manipulate to create challenge: output and time. You challenge yourself by either aiming to do more output in the same amount of time, or the same output in less time. For example my average writing rate is about 1,000 words per hour. Therefore if I'm seeking to push myself, I could aim for 1,100 words in an hour, or 1,000 words in fifty minutes.

One special form of this I enjoy doing is the thirty-day challenge. Thirty days is both a short enough time to stay motivated and focused but also long enough to see a meaningful result. The thirty days provides a time constraint, then you challenge your output. For the first full-day seminar I ever did, I created and ran it in just thirty days.

I created a promotional video for the seminar, not actually knowing exactly what I was going to talk about. In those four weeks I collated what I knew into a structure and program for the day. During this time I also marketed and promoted the event. Up until that point, the longest I had spoken for was two hours, could I push myself to speak for about six? I know that might sound like I was pushing myself more than 1-4% (to be fair I probably was, but I was highly driven to make this happen and I had beginner's luck working in my favour). However, whilst the whole process might appear to be much more than an incremental growth, remember that this process breaks down into smaller chunks.

For example, I was following the first component of flow by having clear goals during the process. I had four weeks, and three sections to make. Therefore I spent a week creating each section, with one week to practice and refine it. Then each of those sections had sub-sections, and each of those sub-sections has smaller units. So on each unit, I was only pushing my challenge level a small bit. I could complete each unit relatively quickly, and thus I was working through each set of mini-goals. This activated dopamine and fuelled the chemical cocktail of flow.

Then I had clear and immediate feedback, the second component of flow. When I was typing up my notes and slides, each tap of the keyboard produced a tiny piece of content. That formed sentences and paragraphs, which I either liked or didn't like, but the feedback came quickly. Then when I was marketing the event, a Facebook post/ad might bring in a ticket sale or someone I spoke to at a networking event said they would come. Alternatively, the ad didn't generate a sale, or the person passed, either way I had quick feedback.

Now I'm not saying you have to set thirty-day challenges like this each month but I use this example merely to demonstrate what's possible when you harness the power of flow. There was no way I would've pulled off that seminar without hitting flow repeatedly during those thirty days and of course on the day itself, I was practically plugged into flow.

So what is a thirty-day challenge you could set yourself? What can you create in the next month using the power of flow? Not only will it lead to creation, success and achievement but if you are activating flow in the process, you will also feel happier and meaningful as you do it.

<u>Proficiency</u>

There is a process that all masters have honoured to develop their Proficiency. You will develop your own skill if you adopt and follow these same principles. When you do, you will be able to create the outcomes you desire, and we will explore how to do so in the following chapter on Performance.

In this chapter you have learned:

- That a combination of passion and perseverance predicts success
- To view success in any endeavour as a four year journey
- The importance of deliberate practice
- That progress is incremental
- How to get into a flow state

My biggest takeaway from this chapter is

_____.

Chapter 9: Performance

"The Power Plant doesn't have energy, it generates it." - **Brendon Burchard**

Where things can fall down in respects to Calling is the action. There are many dreamers and visionaries who never realised their Calling. They kept their great work in their head. In the Purpose chapter we examined identifying your "why": what your Calling is. In the Proficiency chapter we examined your "how": what will help you advance your Calling. What ultimately matters, however, is what you do. What action do you take on your Calling? How do you bring your Calling into reality? It's all about your Performance. In this chapter, you will learn how to set targets for your progress, how to manage your most important resource, and how to be more productive.

Part 1: Calling GPS

Goals are a big buzzword in the personal development field. You've got more acronyms thrown at you than you can shake a stick at: S.M.A.R.T. ; G.R.O.W. ; W.O.O.P. (I'll be throwing another one at you later). I'll use the word "target" rather than goal. I used to use the term "goal" until I spoke at an event with another speaker called Ben Ivey. He said he preferred the term "target".

A goal is a binary entity, you either score or you don't. You succeed or you fail. A target, on the other hand, is something you get closer and closer to. You can adjust your aim as circumstances develop. It is more organic and adaptive than a goal. As circumstances and priorities change in life, our targets can adapt, goals not so much. I agreed with Ivey's distinction here, I think the term target is a more useful description.

Targets are vitally important, if you don't type an address into the GPS, you won't be able to find your destination. However, many people only focus on this step, setting the end target. In addition, setting a target that is often arbitrary and vague e.g. "I want more money" or "I want to lose weight." This is like telling your GPS that you want to go to "Europe." If you're miles away, it might guide you a little bit of the way, but where in Europe do you *really want to go*, and *why* do you want to go there?

To continue with the GPS analogy, there are two other steps you need to take. First of all, the GPS needs to triangulate where you are *now*. If it doesn't know where you are, it can't tell you how to get from there to elsewhere. In order to set a target, you need to know where you are in your life right now.

With your start and end point determined, you can then begin to chart a journey between the two. We will explore and elaborate on how to do so in upcoming segments. First, let's get your Calling GPS configured.

Start Point

Where are you right now? A mistake a number of people make is chasing other people's targets. Do you want to be a doctor for you? Or because that was what your parents wanted you to be? Do you want to lose weight for you? Or is it for the faceless followers of social media? Do you want to get married and have children? Or is it just because your friends expect you to?

Determining whether these targets are aligned with who you are and what you want can require some exploration and self-awareness. I hope this is a process you have been going through as you read this book and continue to go through as you read it. For now we can do a basic self-assessment exercise to hone in on where you want to make improvements in your life.

I believe there is a "holy trinity" when it comes to creating a life we love: three primary needs. They are Health, Career and Relationships (which incidentally roughly correspond with the three principles we cover in this book: Consciousness, Calling and Connection). Pretty much every need or desire we have can be placed into one of these categories.

- Are you physically vibrant, psychologically clear and spiritually nourished?

• Are your skills developing, are your projects growing, is your contribution making an impact?

• Are you feeling love in your romantic relationship? Do you spend the time you want with your family? Are you engaged in exciting and enjoyable pursuits with friends?

What I'd like you to do is rate yourself on each of these factors, using a 0-10 scale. Each of these factors have contributing sub-factors (for example Health is comprised of physical, psychological and spiritual health). Write out your answers in the book or on a separate piece of paper. Rate each of the sub-factors first, then average these out to produce the overall rating for that main factor (e.g. if your scores were Physical = 8, Psychological = 6, Spiritual = 4 then your overall score for Health would be 6).

There's one additional rule I'm going to impose. You can't give any of your sub-factors a rating of 7. Why? Because seven is a number we settle for. It's a lazy answer we give when we don't want to apply real thought and intention to something. If something is seven out of ten, there is still room for improvement but we don't really push for it. It seems "okay".

However, there is noticeable difference between a six and an eight. If something is a six, we think to ourselves "that's not the best". If something is an eight, we think to ourselves, "that's pretty good." If something feels like a seven to you, I want you to decide whether it is a six or an eight. Most of the time, you will realise it's actually a six, which draws your attention to it and makes you realise there is work to be done.

With that caveat in mind, take some time now to rate each area of your life.

Health:

- Physical Health (exercise, nutrition, sleep, injuries, pain, energy):

- Psychological Health (mood, stress, concentration, decision-making):

- Spiritual Health ("me time", faith, appreciation, self-love, freedom, self-expression):

Career:

- Skills (meaningful work, growth and development, challenge and engagement, work environment):

- Projects (future prospects, sense of purpose, aspirations, financial stability, work/life balance):

- Contributions (job satisfaction, personal mission, service, charity, volunteering, passion):

Relationships:

- Romance (dating, sex, shared vision, quality time, intimacy):

- Family (grand/parenthood, family occasions, support, celebrations):

- Friends (shared experiences, get-togethers, helping and assistance, trust, encouragement):

When you complete these scores, you may see one of the three factors that is trailing behind the other by one, two or even more points on the scale. If you deep dive into this factor, there will likely be at least one of the sub factors that are pulling this score down for you.

Now this can relate to target-setting in one of two ways. The most obvious is to focus on your weak points and set targets that will improve this area of your life for you.

However, perhaps this score was low because it is not a priority or driver in your life. Perhaps you're not interested in romantic pursuits just now or you have no drive to start a new project. To create targets based on something that isn't important to you right now isn't going to advance your life.

The not so obvious approach, therefore, is to seek greatness in an aspect of your life that is *already high for you*. Are you feeling spiritually awakened? Then strive for extra enlightenment. Are you giving great value to your customers in your business? Then work out how to give them jaw-dropping service. Do you love the time you spend with your friends? Then seek to create a new, ambitious experience together.

Either choice is valid and both are approaches I have taken. My one disclaimer would be that if you have an area of health that is below a six, this is something you should seek to improve. Our health is one of our core, basic needs as humans. It is the springboard that propels us towards everything else. If you do not have good health, you will not be able to grow and thrive.

If you have a low score due to an exceptional life circumstance such as a physical disability, bereavement or even political oppression, there might be little you can do to solve that particular challenge. Instead, focus on how you can work around that issue to boost the score in other ways. For example, if an injury or disability is affecting your ability to exercise, then look at improvements you can make to your nutrition and sleep. If you are experiencing low mood or depression, then look towards removing stress and anxiety in your life. If you are in an environment where you feel you can't express yourself, then make sure you are boosting your self-care.

So now we've worked out our start point. The next step is to work out where we want to go.

End Point

Where are you going? As I said earlier, "Europe" is not a good enough answer. We need to form a clear idea of exactly where we want to be. This is when you might hear some practitioners shout the S.M.A.R.T. framework at you.

S.M.A.R.T. stands for *Specific*, *Measurable*, *Achievable*, *Realistic* and *Time-Bound*. These form important guidelines for setting targets, but I'm not a fan of the S.M.A.R.T. framework.

Why's that? First of all, because of that middle word "achievable". I think this makes people play small. If we only did things that we thought were achievable, we wouldn't get ahead in life. With the word "achievable", there is no room for dreaming. Dreaming allowed us to put a man on the moon. Dreaming created the iPhone. The speech was "I Have a Dream", not "I have a S.M.A.R.T. goal". Scrap that binding word "achievable" and dream big for yourself.

As well as not encouraging dreaming, the S.M.A.R.T. framework also doesn't prompt you to create targets based on your deep desires. It's possible to execute the S.M.A.R.T. process perfectly but not be satisfied with the result. As Stephen Covey told us, there's no point climbing the ladder quickly if it's placed against the wrong wall. (1) You can't just create a target with your head, you have to create it with your heart too. Your goal must be something that is emotionally and spiritually important to you.

My final criticism of the S.M.A.R.T. framework is that it doesn't prepare you for failure. The road to your targets is not a perfect one. There is going to be delay, distraction and defeat. This is natural, but it's something you need to think ahead and prepare for. There is nothing built into the S.M.A.R.T. framework that allows you to do that.

The S.M.A.R.T. framework does have some positives, however. What I have done in my work is take good aspects from a number of different frameworks and developed my own framework to address the criticisms I've just raised. It's called the **S.S. D.O.P.E.** framework: *Specific, Steps, Dates, Obstacles, Preparations, Excitement.*

Specific

What do you want exactly? For example, if your goal is to "get fitter" that might become "Be able to climb the stairs to my flat/apartment without being out of breath." "Be able to play football in the park with the kids for one to two hours" "Be able to cycle to work in less than thirty minutes".

What becomes clear is that when you study people who have enjoyed great accomplishments, they have often been super specific on what they wanted. Arnold Schwarzenegger left Austria with the desire to be the undisputed bodybuilding champion. (2) He did this by being crowned Mr. Olympia, the most coveted title in bodybuilding, seven times. Nelson Mandela started his political activity with the dream of black people earning democratic participation of "one man, one vote": (3) a right they used for the first time to elect him President in 1994. John F. Kennedy promised to put a man on the moon within the decade, (4) and seven years after that promise, Neil Armstrong and Buzz Aldrin walked on the moon.

If you are clear on what you want, it becomes much easier to plan how you are going to achieve it.

Steps

What are the steps required to reach your target? These steps should be challenging and stretch you just out of your comfort zone. Remember my yoga practice? Stretch, don't snap. When we set targets, we don't want to aim low and not be ambitious. Equally, we don't want to set ourselves unrealistic steps that will cause us distress, frustration and burnout trying to achieve.

I've already said that I encourage ambitious goals. I encourage mastery, creation and contribution...but you need to honour the process. Schwarzenegger did not try to build the Mr. Olympia body in a single gym session. Mandela did not march people into a polling station and try to put paper in the ballot boxes. Armstrong and Aldrin didn't jump in the first rocket that was built and hope for the best. Each of their achievements came in stages; stages where they stretched themselves and pushed just beyond what they thought might be possible, and found the possibilities existed.

To continue with an exercise example, as I feel these are relatable and tangible, if you feel comfortable exercising twice a week, can you push yourself to three times a week?

Dates

Setting a time frame gives you a sense of urgency and commitment to your target. To do so, set a starting date and completion date.

John F. Kennedy said there would be a man on the moon in a decade. Jim Carrey said he would receive a payment of $10M by 1995. Imposing that time limit can generate the focus and drive required to succeed. I gave myself sixteen months for this book.

You can use a thirty-day challenge as a useful increment to focus on. If we created a thirty-day challenge for exercise, this might be "Run sixty kilometres in the next thirty days". This is an average of fifteen kilometres a week, or two kilometres a day.

Obstacles

What is likely to stop you from achieving your goal? What internal variables (fear, willpower etc) and external variables (work commitment, travel etc) are there?

An internal variable preventing you from sticking to an exercise regime might be willpower. By the time you come home from work, you can't be bothered going to the gym or out for a run. You wake up with the best of intention, but after eight hours of work you come back home and you just want to curl up on the couch.

An external variable might be weather. If you frequently experience ice and snow in the winter, you might not be able to run outside. Your desired exercise might be seasonal, such as skiing.

Be honest with yourself about internal obstacles. Don't pretend you are a Navy SEAL when it comes to discipline if you're not. Don't pretend you're Hercules when it comes to strength if you're not.

Think deeply about external obstacles, try not to be flippant and obvious. What would different types of injuries mean for your health goal? What about if you get ill? What if the gym raises its membership fee? What if the gym has a water leak and closes? (this has happened to me!)

Preparations

When you've preempted the potential roadblocks, how can you plan ahead to avoid or minimise them? This is the sign of someone who is far more likely to achieve their targets. It is not the "positive thinker" who believes they can stick up a vision board and everything is going to happen for them. It is the pragmatic optimist who recognises there will be obstacles but believes in their ability to overcome them.

Internal variables are something we have a reasonable amount of control over. It might feel that your fear or indiscipline is in control but you have the ability to take action to assert more control. Take the example of lacking willpower. By the time you get home from work, you can't summon the will to go out again to exercise.

In that case, you need to put some systems in place to avoid that moment of relying on depleted willpower. Instead of driving home after work, drive straight to the gym or running path and start exercising despite how you feel (remember the twenty minute rule from the last chapter?).

Alternatively you could commit to exercising before work, when your willpower levels are highest. Put your workout clothes in front of your bedroom door so you can't leave without falling over them. Stick them on, and you will "feel" more like heading to the gym or out for a run at this point.

External variables can be a bit less controllable. You can't be expected to control weather conditions, a financial crash or election result. All you can do is control *for* them. Scientists do this in experiments to remove or reduce the effect of other variables that they don't wish to measure. Apply some of this scientific rigour to your potential external variables. If you like to run outside, what are you going to do on a day when it's pouring down? If money suddenly got tight and you needed to cancel your gym and club memberships, how could you still maintain your regime in a cheaper or free form?

Excitement

Why is your target important to you? Where does your passion for this target come from? What is going to make you want to stick at this target when the going gets tough? This is the motivation part of your targets. You could have all the previous components down to a tee, but if you don't have this, you don't have a worthwhile target.

Any target you set should excite you. It should speak to values deep within you. It should be based upon intrinsic motivation.

Exercise goals are a great analogy for this, because so many people pursue exercise goals for the wrong reasons. They do it because they want to lose weight, be more muscly, or even to fit in with their friends. These are superficial reasons. Of course being a healthy weight with reasonable athletic ability is useful and beneficial for us but make sure you are seeking that end for the right reasons.

Don't fall into the trap of thinking that losing weight or having more muscles will make you happy. There are plenty of people with big biceps and six packs out there who are miserable. What happens when you lose weight? How does that really change your life? The target is a means, not an end.

If you want to lose weight to improve self-esteem, or to look as good as some of your friends, this is not a strong motivator. This is not going to get you out of bed at 6am to go for a run. It's not going to help you walk past McDonalds even when you're starving. It's not going to help you order a glass of water when everyone around you is ordering alcohol and snacks.

Instead, if you want to lose weight so that you can engage more in your children's activities; so that you can run a marathon to raise money for a cause you're passionate about; so that you have more energy to commit to your life's mission; that is a whole different type of motivation. It is something bigger than yourself. It's something to get excited about.

When you've built your targets into this framework, you then have the end point in the GPS. With a start point and an end point, you then have a clearer idea of the type of journey you need to make. In the rest of this chapter we are going to explore some of the concepts and strategies that are going to help you advance along this journey.

Part 2: Your Most Precious Resource

Time. Our most precious resource. It cannot be bought, borrowed or stolen. It is one of the few commonalities that unite us all. We are all going to die. We all have a finite time on Earth to live out our story. As I have stressed a couple of times in this book. What are you going to do with your time? Are you going to spend it in an unfulfilling job? Are you going to spend it in a toxic relationship? Are you going to spend it scrolling social media feeds? If you want to Author Your Life then you need to get serious about how you spend your time.

Urgency vs Importance

Stephen Covey's book *"The Seven Habits of Highly Effective People"* is one of the most profound books I have ever read. Some of the strategies he presents are somewhat outdated, or too geared towards the corporate setting to be applicable in other domains of life, but one concept that I believe still stands strong is Covey's time management matrix. (5)

The matrix outlines how everything in our lives can be defined on two spectrums "Urgent" and "Important".

"Urgent" indicates how quickly something demands a response. If it demands an immediate or quick response, it is urgent. If it demands a slow or no response, it is not urgent.

"Important" indicates how necessary it is to carry out a task. If a task generates fast or high growth, it is important. If it produces little or no growth, it is not important. With these two markers, we then create four different categories, which form the quadrant, which I will describe below.

Quadrant One: Urgent and Important

Tasks in Quadrant One require immediate action, as they are both urgent and important. These are the real emergencies in life. If the fire alarm goes off, that goes straight into Quadrant One. If you hear gunshots in the street, that is Quadrant One. If you get pains in your chest, that is Quadrant One. Such things require an immediate response and it is also vital that you respond to them.

Quadrant One is also home to slightly less drastic tasks. If you have a big exam tomorrow and you don't feel you have revised enough, that is Quadrant One. If your child is poorly and needs care and attention, that is Quadrant One. If you and your partner have had a big argument and you need to clear the air, that is Quadrant One.

Quadrant One can often be the things in life that blindside us and we have little control over. However, sometimes they are emergencies of our own making. If you haven't revised for that exam because you've spent the past week partying and watching Netflix, that is your own poor time management that has made it a Quadrant One issue. If you caused the argument because you have not been giving your partner enough love and attention, that is your own poor time management that has made it a Quadrant One issue.

If something is in Quadrant One, then it gets first priority, but it is key to remember that with effective time management we can prevent a task becoming a Quadrant One concern.

Quadrant Three: Urgent, but not Important

I'm going to go out of order and skip ahead to Quadrant Three, as I feel this is an important one to highlight. This is where the difference between urgency and importance becomes apparent. Tasks in Quadrant Three demand a response but it is not necessary to respond to them. This is where so much of our communication falls under. If the phone rings, it demands a response. When the email hits our inbox, it demands a response. When the notification lingers on our social media feed, it demands a response.

But know that we rarely need to respond in that moment. If the phone call is important, they will leave a message. If the person needs you right now, they won't be sending an email. Notifications on social media are highlights of superficiality. However, even though they do not require a response, we spend so much of our time stuck in this quadrant.

We are in an eternal struggle to reach "inbox zero". We respond to each notification that pings through on our phone (did you know the average person checks their phone eighty times a day? That's roughly once every twelve minutes (6)). We allow other people to dump tasks and chores on us that have little relevance or impact.

Do you find hours or even days have gone by and you wonder what you've actually achieved? You've been busy but what has been the real output of that busyness? You've been ticking things off the to-do list; you've been typing away; you've been running from place to place; but what has that work really done or changed?

These are the feelings of someone stuck in Quadrant Three and it is not a good place to be. This is where we feel stressed and that our life and work lacks meaning. We must shrink this quadrant by learning to say no, learning to ignore the notifications and digital noise and by evaluating what tasks and activities will really move us forward in life.

Quadrant Four: Not Urgent and not Important

Quadrant One and Quadrant Three are stressful quadrants to spend our time in. They demand our energy and attention and after a long time it becomes exhausting. When we are able to free ourselves from their clutches in a lunch break or weekend evening, then we often compensate by spending time in Quadrant Four. Quadrant Four is where we truly waste our time. This is where we do things that are neither urgent nor important. They don't demand a response, nor should we entertain responding.

When we endlessly refresh our Facebook feeds, we are in Quadrant Four. When we bounce from suggested video to suggested video on Youtube, we are in Quadrant Four. When we binge watch an entire season in one day on Netflix, we are in Quadrant Four.

We sink into Quadrant Four because we seek the opposite extreme of the stress and urgency of our regular life: passive escapism. We want to laze about. We want decisions made for us. We want a lack of responsibility.

Now, I am not suggesting we should never switch off, nor even that we should never have a bit of passive escapism. In the final round of the Six Nations rugby tournament, all six teams play on the same day, one match after another, on the day dubbed "Super Saturday". That equates to seven to eight hours of consecutive rugby coverage and I won't move from the sofa until I have finished watching it all. However, what you won't catch me doing is having a "Super Saturday" every week, wasting away an entire day each week consuming rather than creating.

Free time is important, but quality free time is more important. In fact you won't actually find free time in this quadrant. Quadrant Four is for things that aren't urgent, and aren't important. Free time *is* important and so it is classified in Covey's final quadrant.

Quadrant Two: Not Urgent and Important

Quadrant Two is where the magic happens. It is where we classify all the meaningful things in life. Is getting married urgent? Is travelling the world urgent? Is meditation urgent? The sky isn't going to fall in if we don't do these things but we know they are important. However, that is precisely why we often don't prioritise them.

When we get sucked into the urgency of Quadrant One and Three, we lose the time to invest in Quadrant Two activities. Quadrant Two is where everything we have talked about in this book so far resides. Exercise is Quadrant Two. Working on meaningful projects is Quadrant Two. Spending time with the kids is Quadrant Two.

The reason why you feel you don't have enough time for these things is not a lack of time, it is a lack of prioritisation. Because these things are not screaming at us like the fire alarm or taunting us like the unread email we don't allocate time to them. Then, when we have finally put out the fires of the day and attended to everyone else's agendas, then what do we want to do with our free time? Our energy and willpower is at a level for nothing more than the passive escapism of Quadrant Four.

To be master of our time, we must prioritise Quadrant Two activities first. For example, our morning routine might allow us to meditate and exercise before the urgency of the day arrives. Booking the weekend away resolves us to clear our work schedule. Reading with the children at night allows you to find out about their worries and concerns.

Everything I talk about in this book is a Quadrant Two activity. You don't have to do it. But if you don't prioritise what you learn in this book (and the other books you read), then you will never create the change you desire in your life.

To prioritise effectively, you are going to need to be ruthless at times. You will need to make tough decisions. You will need to be proactive and plan ahead months in advance. It's not easy but change is not easy. Mae West told us: *"I never said it would be easy. I only said it would be worth it."*

Time is not something you can mess around with or take for granted, because for all of us, we have that timer tick-tick-ticking away. One day your time is going to be up. When you look back on your life, will you be proud of all the fires you put out? Will you be proud of all the emails you answered? Will you be proud of all the Netflix seasons you watched? Or will you be proud of the person you became, the impact you made, and the love you created?

<u>Deep Work</u>

The age of the machine is upon us. No, I'm not talking about the next Terminator film. I'm talking about your job.

There are two big threats posed by the machine in the workplace. The first is the culture of connectivity. Email, social media and instant messenger command huge swathes of our attention and effort, often to the detriment of our productivity. A 2012 McKinsey study found that the average knowledge worker now spends 60% of the work week engaged in electronic communication and internet searching, with close to 30% of a worker's time dedicated to reading and answering email alone. (7)

The second is even more insidious. Logistical, repetitive tasks are being done by machines rather than people. As artificial intelligence improves, it is able to do more of our jobs better and at a lower cost. The machines aren't just stealing your productivity, they will eventually steal your job. Four and a half million truck drivers' jobs are under threat in Europe alone from the introduction of self-driving trucks. (8) To put that into perspective, that is almost the entire population of my home country of Scotland.

Is it time to panic and prepare the Resistance? Not at all. The age of the machine does not mean humans are redundant. What it means is that we have to commit to more Deep Work.

"Deep Work" is a phrase coined by Cal Newport in his book of the same name. Newport defines Deep Work as: *"Professional activities performed in a state of distraction-free concentration that push your cognitive capacities to the limit. These efforts create new value, improve your skill and are hard to replicate."* (9)

Deep Work is where our unique creative expression shines through. It is where we develop and share our expertise in a unique (and human!) manner. Deep Work has been employed by the geniuses of prior centuries and will allow us to continue to thrive in the centuries to come.

What we do have to worry about, is Shallow Work, which Newport defines as: *"Non-cognitively demanding, logistical style tasks, often performed while distracted. These efforts tend to not create much new value in the world and are easy to replicate."* (10)

There is a vicious cycle in our workplaces. As the McKinsey report noted, we are increasing being distracted by non-cognitively demanding tasks, which is hampering our productivity. As this continues, there will come a time where you are dispensable, because the majority of your work is easy to replicate and systemise.

So we want to get away from doing Shallow Work as much as possible and instead focus our efforts on Deep Work. Looking at Newport's definition of Deep Work, let's break down the individual components of how you can start increasing the amount of Deep Work you are doing.

Attention

"Time without attention is worthless, so value attention over time." Tim Ferriss notes. Yes, time is a finite resource but it is attention that helps you extract the value from that finite resource. In the Deep Work context, Newport articulates this through an equation:

High-Quality Work Produced = Time Spent x Intensity of Focus (11)

Productivity is not just about how much time you dedicate to something, it is about how much attention you dedicate to it. Let's plug in some simple numbers to demonstrate this.

Let's say you spend an hour doing something, but you're only giving it half your intensity. The equation would read:

Time Spent: 1 x Intensity of Focus: 0.5 = 0.5

However, lets swap those numbers round. Let's say you only work for half an hour, but at full intensity.

Time Spent: 0.5 x Intensity of Focus: 1 = 0.5

It's the same amount of output, but in the second scenario, you have done it twice as quick. That is the power of attention. It is multiplying the outcome of whatever time you are dedicating to a task.

How do we harness the power of attention? Just like time, attention is a finite resource, so we have to allocate it wisely. Neuroscientists have observed that we only have a certain number of "attention units" that we can allocate at any one time. (12) Furthermore, when we allocate these units to different stimuli, the power of our attention shrinks dramatically. Despite the common myth, humans can't multitask (even you lovely ladies). When you are switching between two tasks at once, you lose about 40% productivity (13).

Research has identified that we have an "attention residue". When we pay attention to one task, then switch our attention to another task, we don't take all our "attention units" with us. Some of our attention stays with the previous task for another 15-20 minutes. (14) If we keep switching between tasks throughout the day, we have never actually given anything our full attention.

So to cultivate attention you focus on ONE task. No television on in the background, no card deck of browser tabs, no phone pinging notifications at you. One of the best productivity hacks I use is a little button on your phone called "Airplane Mode". This helps you get 35,000 feet away from the agendas and distractions of others and focus on what you need to do. My phone goes onto Airplane Mode at 9pm each night and stays that way until at least 9am the next morning. The longer I keep that Airplane Mode on, the more I can get done. I love days when I can keep it on until three or four in the afternoon, as it gives me an amazing stretch of focused attention.

Keep your focus on one task until completion, then move onto the next task. You will get through tasks far faster this way than trying to multitask them. Remember the acronym FOCUS: Follow One Course Until Successful.

Scheduling

As we covered in the previous formula, we have two finite resources. One is attention, the other is time. You must manage both equally well to enter Deep Work.

Firstly, I recommend you schedule "Block Time". These are hour-long sections of your day that you set aside to work on particular tasks. If you are stepping up your exercise regime, where in your timetable are there going to be hour blocks dedicated to exercise? If you are working on a book, where in your timetable are there going to be hour blocks dedicated to writing? If you are looking to expand your social circle, where in your timetable are there going to be hour blocks dedicated to attending social events? There's a fairly common heuristic: if it isn't scheduled, it isn't happening.

In this block time, I like to use the Pomodoro method to make effective use of the block. The technique applies mainly to work but the principle and concept behind it is one to consider and adapt to your personal life and relationships too.

The Pomodoro method entails taking an hour and dividing it into a "work" period, and "rest" period. Some people like to do twenty-five minutes of work, followed by a five minute break, and then repeat. Others prefer forty-five minutes of work followed by a fifteen minute break. I personally prefer fifty-five/five. When you arrive at your work station, make a note of the time, or even set a timer for your allocated work time.

As we covered in the segment on attention, you FOCUS. Work on one task until it is either completed or you reach the end of the work period. If you complete it within the work period, then you can move onto another task. If you reach the end of the work period, then you take your break: walk, stretch, make a cup of tea.

After your break, you then move onto your next work period, and if necessary, your next task. After every 2-3 Pomodoro blocks, you then take an extended break of 20-30 minutes. This gives you a period of focus, interspersed with short periods of rest to recharge your energy and attention. Deep Work is demanding and cognitively draining, it is not something you can sustain for hours on end.

Development

Deep Work involves the careful cultivation of two variables: attention and time. This careful cultivation is a skill and like any skill it can be developed and improved. You might have read this part of the chapter on Deep Work and (much like I did when I first read Newport's work) say "that's it, I'm going full-hermit and embracing this Deep Work philosophy full-time".

However, if you have been used to Shallow Work and distraction, this will not be a seamless transition. It's like the person who gets on the treadmill on January 1st and, ten minutes in, realises "Woah, this is not going to be as easy as I thought.".

Don't worry if you feel the same the first time you try to concentrate and enter Deep Work. You will get better the more times you commit to the practice. With that in mind, here are a few tips that are going to help you develop your Deep Work ability.

The first technique is the "Just five more minutes" technique. When you are trying to concentrate, you will get distracted. You can bat away distraction a couple of times but sometimes a particular distraction will keep looping. Something is bothering you. You realise you haven't sent an email, you haven't made a bank transfer, you haven't booked a table for dinner. This might be bothering you right in the middle of a time block. It's affecting your ability to concentrate.

When this happens, tell the thought "Just five more minutes!". Don't give into it immediately, as you are training yourself to give into distraction. Instead stay in Deep Work for five more minutes, then, if it is still bothering you, you can leave Deep Work to sort it out.

This isn't encouraging you to break Deep Work every time you decide you would like to check Facebook or play Candy Crush. Instead what you are doing is training yourself to resist distraction. As time goes on, you may find the temptation fades after five minutes, or you are able to resist for longer. This is training your brain's ability to focus and concentrate.

Another training method you can use is something called the Roosevelt Sprint. This technique is named after President Teddy Roosevelt and accounts how he used to work in college.

Roosevelt was a multi-passionate individual whose interests varied from boxing to dance to poetry to bird watching. As such, much of Roosevelt's time at university was not spent studying. However, what Roosevelt lacked in time, he made up for in intensity (remember the formula). In the scattered periods of time he had throughout the day, he would set himself challenging targets as to how much work he could complete in a set period of time. (15)

Cal Newport calls this "interval training for your brain". (16) It is giving your brain short, sharp bursts of sustained effort motivated by an artificial deadline. This technique is effective for inducing a flow state as it ramps up the challenge level. If you activate flow for yourself, then you are releasing a chemical cocktail that not only helps you perform better but makes you feel good as well.

With these techniques, you can train your brain to be a better Deep Worker, and that is the best way to fight the rise of the machines.

Part 3: Increase Output

Whole books are written on productivity, and productivity is a bit of a "buzzword" in the success literature nowadays. It's the low hanging fruit; the easy sell; the — dare I say it — get-rich-quick scheme. I'm not saying it's not important, but I have waited until the end of the Calling section to mention it for a reason. If you don't have the foundational work of Purpose and Proficiency first, no "hack", "strategy" or "accelerator" is going to help you get what you want. That said, productivity is one of just six habits that are significantly correlated with long term, sustained success. (17) So if you can learn in the final part of this chapter some methods to increase your productivity, then you will be able to Author Your Life with increased detail.

Our drive for creativity is one of our strongest intrinsic drivers. For a long time I neglected the importance of creativity, as I associated it with specific practices such as art, design, music. I didn't consider myself a creative person, as I wasn't proficient in one of these categories. Even when I published my first book I didn't think of myself as creative.

Over time, however, I came to realise that everything we do in life is creative. If we break creativity down to its root meaning, it is simply to bring into existence something that wasn't there before. We are doing this all the time. We do it with our hairstyle, we do it with our clothes, we do it with work projects, we do it in our relationships, and yes we also do it with hobbies and pastimes.

For me, our most important expression of creativity is the impact we make and the legacy we leave. One day we will all be dust and bones, but what will remain is what we created. To stimulate our creativity, we must increase our output. The more we create, the more impact we make. What follows are some simple techniques that will allow you to increase your output, spark your creativity, and leave your impact.

3x3

The 3x3 is a simple planner that I use to organise my daily tasks. What this involves, unsurprisingly, is writing down three priorities. These are your most important projects in the area of health, career or relationships.

The second part of the 3x3, is under your three priorities, list three steps to move them forward. These can be activities to do, things to plan, or people to meet. If you get these three things done by the end of the day, you can consider the day a success.

I have found this to be a more useful and realistic tool than many other planners if you have multiple commitments: such as combining an exercise regime, business or family with a full-time job.

To apply the 3x3 model to my day, it would look something like this:

1. Finish Productivity Segment

- Brainstorm productivity strategies
- Create categories
- Write section

2. Podcast

- Record weekly episode
- Upload and schedule episode
- Reach out to potential guests

3. Seminar

- Promote to social media and email list
- Confirm room booking
- Create curriculum framework.

The 3x3 helps you focus in on what is important and what you can do that day to move each project forward.

By themselves, these tasks might seem to create little or no progress, but when performed consistently, they start to accumulate. If you do three small things every day to move towards your target, by the time a year has passed, you will have taken over a thousand steps towards your target. Would you be more likely to achieve your goal if you were a thousand steps closer? Absolutely.

What many people try to do with their targets is take the thousand steps in one go. They want to lose a quarter of their bodyweight; build a business from scratch; find the love of their life; and try to create that outcome in one go. When they inevitably fail, they get discouraged and abandon the target completely. However, rather than trying to take a thousand steps in one go, we break it down and put in the consistent, disciplined effort. Through this, we create momentum, which creates results. The next strategy takes this momentum building a step further.

McCrae's Momentum Method

For decades, I had a dream of writing a book, but never built the consistency to get beyond more than a few chapters at a time. Eventually I decided that I needed a method to build the consistency and actually get a book completed.

Therefore, when I wrote my first book, I set a target of writing 1,000 words a day. My writing rate at the time was 500 words per hour, so writing 1,000 words would take me roughly two hours (through deliberate practice and activating flow, it now just takes one hour). As soon as I had accumulated those 1,000 words, I would consider that a success. It didn't matter if those 1,000 words were particularly good, it didn't matter if they made the final draft. All that mattered was getting those words on the page.

Because what I'd find is that I would rarely shut down the writing as soon as I hit 1,000. I would start to creep further, completing 1,200, or 1,500. On a good day that would go up to 2000-3000. My record in a single day was 6,000, which is twelve hours of my (conservative) output!

However, I couldn't just produce a 3,000 word day from a standing start. To hit those higher numbers, I needed to have built up the graft work. I needed to have done a couple of days of the 1,000 word stutters to get into the 3,000 word blasts. That 6,000 word day came after a couple of weeks of sustained writing.

Furthermore, the words I wrote during a 2,000 or 3,000 word session were more likely to make the final draft. The words I created in a 1,000 word session were more likely to be cut or edited. This is because I was building creative momentum for myself.

We've all heard the story of the apple falling on Isaac Newton's head and from this incident he "invented" gravity. We fall into the false belief that creativity emerges from such "lightbulb" moments. We do have moments of realisation, but even when we do, we then have to work further to expand upon that realisation. The apple made Isaac Newton ask an important question "what made this apple fall to the ground?", but he still had to build upon his observations and theories. I had waited eighteen years to be "inspired" to write a book. What I needed to do was build creative momentum.

This is what the McCrae Momentum Method (MMM) allows you to do. Every day you work to a target and you persevere until you have reached it. Through this commitment, you then awaken your creative genius.

By the way, sometimes you won't reach your daily target. There were some days when I just couldn't get the words together and I'd fall flat at 700 or 800 words. On these days, I was genuinely "uninspired". But I didn't use that as an excuse to stop me before I'd even begun. Additionally, sometimes life gets in the way, and you will miss a day. The key thing is to not miss two days in a row. If you miss two, you break your chain of momentum, and have to start again.

The MMM doesn't just apply to creative endeavours. Want to get fitter? Commit to thirty minutes of running a day. Want to earn more money? Commit to five sales calls a day. Want to make more friends? Commit to saying hello to three new people each day. As you build momentum, you won't stop at thirty minutes, five sales calls or three people, you will build momentum, and your output will grow as a result.

Performance

When you are able to put your dreams into action, you have mastered an art that so many don't. We can all dream, but with the concepts outlined in this chapter, you now know how to bring those dreams into reality. When you are able to bring your dreams into reality, you have answered your Calling. You have accomplished your heroic quest. You have taken important steps along the Author Your Life journey.

In this chapter you have learned:

- **How to assess areas of your life for improvement**
- **How to effectively set targets**
- **How to prioritise through urgency and importance**
- **How to enter Deep Work**
- **How to increase output with the 3x3 and MMM**

My biggest takeaway from this chapter is

_____.

Section 4: Deepen Your Connection

"No one is born hating another person because of the colour of his skin, or his background, or his religion. People must learn to hate, and if they can learn to hate, they can be taught to love, for love comes more naturally to the human heart than its opposite." - Nelson Mandela

Author Your Life is about more than just you. So far that is largely what we have looked at: we have looked at how you develop yourself as the protagonist and the quest you embark on. But a story is never about one character. There are multiple other supporting characters in the cast. You never become the Hero of Your Story in isolation. Connection is all about finding alignment with the other characters in your story. This section will introduce you to the final three part framework that will allow you to deepen connection in all your relationships.

The first step is INTEGRATE. The first type of character in your story are those that you look up to, people who are further along the path you wish to go down. These are your teachers, parents, bosses, coaches and mentors. Who you choose to learn from, and how you learn from them, are key aspects of your journey. In life most people are making poor choices about who they are spending time with and what people they are looking to as role models. One of the most fundamental truisms of life is that you are a product of the people around you. To take your life in a new direction, you must INTEGRATE with people who are going to support you along that journey.

The second step is INFLUENCE. The second type of character in your story are those you stand shoulder to shoulder with. These are your colleagues, siblings, friends, lovers. These are the people we spend most time with, the people who make your life tick. Sadly, many people in life do not feel they have many deep relationships. A study by the relationship charity Relate found that one in ten people report that they have no close friends, and one in five rarely or never felt loved in the two week period preceding the survey. (1) The deeper the relationships you can build with your peers, the more joy and adventure you will experience in life. With these skills, you will be a person of INFLUENCE who employs fundamental principles and practices for successful relationships.

The third step is IMPACT. The third type of character in your story are those who look up to you. These are your employees, children, students and secret admirers. It is the interactions with these characters that often provide the most meaning and fulfilment in our lives. Yet most of us are not serving to the degree of which we are capable of, we are not spreading kindness and we are not embracing our capacity for leadership. You have more to give to the world than you ever thought possible. When you begin to share this with the world, you will live a life of meaning and IMPACT.

Perhaps relationships have not been great for you up until this point. It is not your fault if not. Relationships are something we are simply not educated sufficiently on. We interact and communicate on a daily basis, but when were we taught the skills of relationships? This is a valuable lesson that was missed out of the curriculum at school. We assume that relationships are just something that comes "naturally" to us. I disagree. We have the natural capacity for speech, but unless we have guidance and education, we won't learn how to speak properly. We wouldn't leave a toddler to their own devices to try and learn how to speak, so why do we leave our children to their own devices to learn how to interact?

Clearly this approach is not working, given the divorce rates, broken homes, interpersonal violence and workplace hostility. Many people are brought up with a script of dysfunction, conflict and intolerance, so is it any wonder they repeat this same script later in life?

Even for those who are brought up with functional and supportive relationships, sometimes there is struggle here too. The digital age is a threat to our intimacy. Our fast paced lifestyles can cause us to get swept away in our own worlds and not take time for others. We interact more often than at any other point in human history, yet we seem less connected than ever before. The problem is that we are living in ISOLATION. Just because we are not stuck on a desert island, doesn't mean we are not isolated. Living in this isolation will prevent us from moving through the framework of Integrate, Influence and Impact.

The first isolation we find ourselves in is ISOLATION FROM MENTORS. This can be a problem from the moment we enter the world, if we have poor family relations, but it's often a problem we become aware of when we first make a decision to change; when we have taken the first steps on the Author Your Life journey. Just because we have made the decision to change, doesn't mean we know how to make that change happen. We look around for guidance and support and realise there is none coming. This can be an incredibly lonely experience and it often prevents us from moving forward.

However, just because you don't see any mentors, doesn't mean there are none available to you. You will be surprised at who there is in your social circle who can be an inspiring influence. You will be surprised at who is accessible to you that can provide you the mentorship you desire. You will be amazed that as you spend time with different people, the quality of your life will change. You can overcome this isolation by submerging yourself in a positive community.

The second isolation we can experience is ISOLATION FROM PEERS. This is where we feel the presence of peers but we struggle to interact with them. This ultimately stems from an inability to express our true self. We might be socially anxious or awkward. We might struggle to hold and develop conversation. Perhaps we freeze and fumble on dates. We are scared of judgement and conflict.

We can also experience this isolation because we have drifted away from old colleagues or friends. With the changes we make we can lose the rapport and affinity we once had. Moving on from certain people is a natural process of life but this does not mean it can't be painful at the time. This is another scenario that can cause you to feel lonely and lost.

Remember, however, that at one time you started from scratch with relationships. You met new people and had to develop relationships with them…and you did. Your ability to do that has not disappeared. If you are looking to find new peers, or redefine the relationships you currently have, you have the ability to do so.

It is not a case of being an "extravert", a "people person", or "charismatic". It's simply understanding and applying natural tools of communication. When you learn some simple skills it will help you flow through conversations with ease, allow you to show up in your relationships as yourself, and find people who accept and appreciate that.

The third isolation we can experience is ISOLATION FROM FOLLOWERS. No, I'm not talking about your Social Media audience. This is an isolation that can exist under the radar, something that unsettles us, but we're not entirely sure what it is that doesn't feel "right". We can sometimes be so focused on what's going on in our lives, that we forget about focusing on others. This can be from a noble place of looking to improve ourselves but nonetheless it can cause us to have a narrow focus.

Alternatively, it can be something that is a very apparent frustration. Because we are not being of service to people, we don't feel like an integral part of a social group or workforce. We may find ourselves acting falsely to try to earn status and recognition. If we are not serving others (or feel like we're not), we lack a feeling of meaning and impact in our lives.

What I hope you have learned so far in this book is that you have wonderful qualities, qualities that can serve others. You don't have to give in a way that drains you or does not provide meaning. You don't need rank or status to serve. We all have our place in the world. You can find your place of service, live with meaning, and ultimately leave a legacy.

It's time to remove yourself from Isolation. When you learn how to Integrate, Influence and Impact, you will deepen your Connection.

Chapter 10: Integrate

"You are the sum of the five people you spend most time with" - **Jim Rohn**

The Author Your Life journey is not one to be undertaken alone. There are a number of other key characters you will encounter in your narrative. Some of the important characters will be those you learn from: the teachers and mentors you meet along the path. They will help you discover your own wisdom and provide strength and support along your path. In this chapter, you will learn how incredibly receptive you are to the influence of others. You will learn how to find role models and emulate their qualities as your own. You will learn how to gather a powerful tribe of like-minded individuals who will work together with you on your journey.

Part 1: Social Sponge

In this book, I hope you have learned a number of valuable concepts and strategies. However, do you realise that your biggest source of learning is actually the people around you? I don't just mean your teachers, parents and bosses. I mean *everyone*. As humans we often like to think we are independent, autonomous beings. In reality we are massive copycats and are shaped to a large degree by the people around us. This can often work to our detriment if we are not careful about who we allow to be in our circle of influence. On the other hand, it can cause us to grow and progress far further and faster than we ever could under our own devices. This is where social learning comes in, to recognise the strengths and values in others, and to integrate them into our own consciousness. This is where Connection begins.

Social Contagion

The second half of the 20th century was when psychologists first started getting really interested in how we influence each other as humans. This was born largely out of the horrors of World War Two and the Holocaust. At the Nuremberg Trials, many of the Nazis used the defence that they were "just following orders" in regards to the war crimes they had committed. It was not a moral defence, but psychologists did consider whether it was a psychological explanation for their actions.

One of the first landmark studies into social influence was conducted by Solomon Asch in 1951. In this study, a group of students were shown a line on one card and had to pick a line that was the same length from a choice of three on another card. The lines were obviously different, so it was not a difficult cognitive task.

What was difficult was that only one of the eight group members was a real participant. The rest were "stooges", people "in" on the experiment who deliberately and consistently gave wrong answers to pressure the lone participant. What Asch found was that a high percentage of participants cracked under this pressure. Three out of four participants gave at least one answer they knew was wrong to conform to the rest of the group, even though the right answer was obvious. (1)

This study showed that people conformed on a simple cognitive test. That was not on the same level as "following orders" and putting people into gas chambers...or was it?

Stanley Milgram took Asch's work one step further in the 1960s, with his infamous "electric shock" experiment. In this study, participants were invited to what they thought was a learning experiment. They sat in a room with the experimenter and were assigned the role of "teacher". Another participant, a "learner", sat in another room. The experimenter explained that the teacher was going to ask questions through an intercom. If the learner got an answer wrong, the teacher was to administer an electric shock. The teacher was told that this was to test if punishment improved memory. Each time they administered a shock, they increased the current by fifteen volts.

The participant thought they were shocking another participant. Actually the learner was another stooge, an actor who deliberately got answers wrong. As the voltage increased, the actor would scream in pain, complain of a heart condition and say that he couldn't take anymore. The real participants started to get uncomfortable with this process. They would argue with the experimenter; they would inquire about the learner's safety; they would hesitate and delay in administering the shocks.

However, with minimal prompting from the experimenter, the participants would proceed. Over two thirds of the participants continued until they were delivering "shocks" that were four hundred and fifty volts, a shock that can be fatal. (2)

When Milgram first pitched this experiment, the top psychologists predicted that less than 1% of the participants would proceed to this level. (3) They thought that only the most psychotic and twisted individuals could knowingly inflict such harm on another human being. The final results were utterly unexpected. It demonstrated that we didn't have the moral high ground we thought we had over the Nazis. If we had been in the same position, would we have really done any different? We might have had our reservations and conflict but we would likely have also "followed orders".

What social psychology experiments such as these began to demonstrate was how susceptible we are to the influence of others, even for tasks we find easy or actions we find reprehensible.

These findings were taken in a different direction by a psychologist called Albert Bandura. Bandura didn't just want to see how other people could influence our behaviour, he wanted to investigate how it influenced our learning.

In 1961, Bandura ran an experiment called the "bobo doll" experiment. (4) In the experiment, Bandura assembled two groups of children. Each child was taken into a room with an adult.

In the room was a "bobo doll". A bobo doll is a big inflatable figure that is weighted at the bottom, so no matter how you throw, push, or generally mistreat or assault it, it will always return to an upright position.

One group of children watched the adult playing nicely with the doll; carrying it carefully, playing gently, and speaking to it nicely. The other group watched the adult playing aggressively with the doll; punching, kicking and throwing it as well as calling it names.

After ten minutes of observing this behaviour, the child was then given the opportunity to play with the Bobo doll. The group of children who had seen the gentle adult model copied their example. They treated the doll with care and consideration.

The group who had seen the aggressive adult model also copied the example they had been shown. They assaulted the doll physically and verbally. What was interesting was that there were toy guns in the room, and although the adult role model hadn't picked up a gun, some of these children picked one up and used it in their aggression towards the doll (6) (You can watch the footage on Youtube by searching "bobo doll experiment").

What this demonstrates is that we model those around us. We like the idea of having free will and personal responsibility but if we are not conscious and aware, we will copy the bad example of others around us.

This effect has been dubbed "social contagion" and is evident across multiple arenas in our lives. The people around us affect how much you sleep, (6) your eating habits (7) and how much money you spend or save (8). A variety of negative outcomes such as smoking, (9) obesity, (10) depression, (11) divorce (12) and drug use (13) have been found to be socially contagious. Astonishingly, this effect is evident up to three degrees of separation, meaning your friend's friend's friend could be influencing your smoking, drinking or overeating. (14)

It may seem that we are programmed to make decisions we know are incorrect, violate our morals and hurt others based purely on the influence of others. But what I want to impart is that while we are hugely influenced by the people around us, this works both ways.

The children with the friendly role model copied their behaviour. One third of Milgram's participants refused to proceed beyond their moral dilemma. One quarter of Asch's participants never let themselves be tricked. Whilst negative behaviours and outcomes are socially contagious, so are positive ones. Happiness (15) and even expert performance in fields such as sport and music have been found to be socially contagious. (16) If we surround ourselves with bad role models, it brings out the worst in us. However, if we surround ourselves with good role models, it brings out the best in us.

Imagine a time when your personal responsibility won. Think of a time when you had a minority viewpoint, you stuck to it in the face of social pressure, and were proven correct. Think of a time when you felt forced to carry out an action that violated your moral principles and you stood your ground and maintained your integrity. Think of a time when you saw two contrasting models of behaviour and you chose to follow the example of the good model.

In these examples, you rose above social pressure. You stepped to a higher level of consciousness. This is an example of what is available to you on a frequent basis when you surround yourself with positive role models: people who guide you to the right answer; who respect your principles; who model outstanding behaviour. In this chapter, you will learn how to develop these positive relationships. First let's start with the people in your life who might not be such a great influence.

Burning The Fields

Farmers know that sometimes, to garner the best crop, they have to burn what they currently have. The act of burning is restorative. It cleanses any disease, it puts fresh nutrients into the soil and it ultimately creates space for something new.

Sometimes we must also burn some fields. We may have a crop that is not creating the yield we want it to. It is becoming a nuisance to tend.

Perhaps it is even spreading disease to the other crops. Instead of wheat, rye and barley, our crops are our friends, family and colleagues.

What we have examined up until this point is the incredibly pervasive effect the people around us have. If we have negative people around us, then they will be a negative influence on us. We can do all the personal development we like but ultimately we will be held back by someone who is not aligned with our life and mission.

What I have learned during my journey is to be highly selective about who I choose to allow into my social space. How we spend our time is precious and life is too short to spend with people who aren't right for us. Conversely, the quality of our time will be enhanced when we spend it with people who are right for us. I think it's important to monitor who we spend time with in our lives and determine if we are spending it with the best people we know.

The first step to performing this analysis is to take an inventory of the people who closely influence you. I recommend writing down a list of the twenty people you spend most time with. At the top of your list put the people you spend most time with and towards the bottom the people you spend less time with. This isn't a strict procedure; I'm not asking you to count up the minutes to make a distinction between person number eight and number nine. However, you will have a rough gauge about who is closer to number one and who is closer to number twenty.

When you have written these names down, I'd like you to simply put a "+" or a "-" next to their name. When you weigh everything up, is that person generally speaking a positive influence for you and your life or a negative one?

If you have a list of twenty people with a "+" next to their name, amazing! You are truly blessed with the company you have. However, I'm going to assume that is not the case for you. As you look down that list, those "-" may be frowning at you from the page. First of all count them up. Is it a quarter of your list? Is it half? Is it pretty much all of them?

Next, look at where in your list those negative people are positioned. Are they languishing in your bottom ten or have they infiltrated your top five? Depending on where they are, we can consider different approaches.

Let's face it; we are always going to meet negative people in our lives. Having twenty positive superstars is a nice ideal to aim for but it's a high target to reach. If you have some negative people in your bottom ten, this is not necessarily something to worry about. The time you spend with such an individual may not be large or their negative effect is small. They are probably someone that you factor out and don't get bothered by already.

However, what might be of more concern is if there is a high number of negative people on your list and they all come from the same source. For example, you might have eight colleagues in your bottom ten who aren't highly negative individually but collectively throughout the day they are hard work. Alternatively you might have one person who doesn't feature often, but really upsets you (a boss for example).

In the case of a high number of negative people from the same source, you can look at how you factor out that source from your life. Perhaps that means leaving a club or society you are a part of. Perhaps that means trying to transfer departments at work. Perhaps that means choosing a different set of people to go to the bar with on a Friday night. If you have a large group of people bringing you down in a specific environment, then you've got to ask yourself whether it's worth spending time in that particular environment.

What about the one highly negative person? The first step is always diplomacy. You can raise the issues you have with them and work on creating new standards or setting clear and firm boundaries with them. If this is not working, then you can take steps to phase them out of your social circle. You don't need to return their messages. You don't need to meet with them. You don't need to feel any sense of obligation or duty to have a relationship with them. It's great to want to give people a fair chance and be kind to them but don't pour your good will into a black hole.

It's certainly easier to be selective with the people on the perimeter of our social group. But what happens when those individuals are in the top ten or the top five? In our top ten, there will be two sets of people: friends, or family. It's unlikely that we spend that much time with a colleague unless they are also our friend, so we can make these two clear categorisations. Friends, we choose, family we don't.

Let's look at the people we choose first. If you have a negative friend near the top of the list, ultimately you have chosen them. You choose to spend time with them. You choose to return their messages. You choose to tolerate and accept whatever behaviour has caused you to put a negative sign next to their name.

The first course of action you can take is to repair the situation. To have a frank discussion about your values and expectations and state there is certain negativity that you are unhappy about and do not wish to tolerate. You might be surprised by the outcome of this discussion. If your friend is a genuine friend, they will be thankful that you pointed out something they might not have been aware of and resolve to fix it. As the cliché goes, you have turned a negative into a positive.

However, if this does not work and you believe that you will never be able to address this rift in the relationship, you then have a much tougher decision to make. If this friend is a negative influence, and you believe always will be, why are they a part of your life? You may have ancient loyalty to them or mutual bonds but what are you remaining loyal and bonded to? If that person came into your life right now, without the history and shared connection, would you welcome them into your life?

If the answer is no, then it's time to bring that relationship to a close. You explain to them the reasons why you feel the relationship is not working and move on. You begin to disconnect from them. You unsubscribe from them on social media. You ignore their messages if they pester you. You distance yourself from them if you have to be in the same room as them. If they are part of the same social group, you might not be able to sever ties completely, but you can phase out interactions as much as possible. This does not mean being unpleasant to the person or wishing them ill, it simply means you have created space between the two of you.

Depending on what has caused them to be a negative influence, you may feel the need to sever ties completely. There are two people so far in my life whose actions have warranted this response from me. They were both in my top five. I had a deep history and a number of mutual connections with them. However, their actions violated my values and there was no remorse or redemption from either of them.

They are blocked on social media. I have made it clear to my mutual friends that I don't wish to be in the same room as them. It is unfortunate that it has come to such extreme measures but if you compromise your values, what do you have left? If someone will not walk the road with you, then you must walk on different roads.

Ultimately, with our friends we always have that choice. At one point we chose to let them be a part of our life and we have the right to choose to no longer have them as a part of our life. But what about people we don't choose? What about our family?

Well actually, we can work through the same process with family as we do with friends. Firstly, you seek to repair the situation. If they are a loving family member, then they will likely be glad you pointed out the issue and work to improve on it.

If this does not work, then you look to disconnect with them. Just as with friends, this might be difficult; sometimes even more so. Parents (and in-laws), siblings and children can be particularly tough ones. But ultimately as an adult, you have the responsibility to make your own choices. You can set firm boundaries with invasive parents, establish a no-man's land with a volatile sibling or show tough love to a dependent child.

Also remember that loyalty is more than flesh and blood. Nobody has a right to loyalty just because they share genetic relatedness to you. Loyalty has to be earned through values and behaviour. If someone is not earning loyalty, then you have no reason to give it to them. If it goes as far as severing ties with a particular family member, that is sad, but you can't keep putting up with bad behaviour.

We are going to continue talking about difficult decisions sadly. Up to this point, we have discussed negative relationships and what we do about individuals or groups who are pulling us down. But what about a more challenging scenario? Where individuals or groups are not doing anything wrong; they are people we like and love but ultimately they are on a journey we are not; they are in a different place in their lives to where we are in ours.

This is one of the hardest challenges I have ever faced on my journey. Speaking on stage and writing books is nothing compared with distancing myself from people I love.

During my final year of university, I started to feel myself drifting from my friends. I had become interested in entrepreneurship and I was stepping up my commitment to health and wellbeing. Throughout the years of school and university, my friends and I had bonded over shared activities of video gaming, partying, watching sports and chasing ladies; all the usual stuff young men like doing.

In this final year though, I was starting to make changes. I was attending networking events and workshops rather than parties. I was reading rather than gaming. I abstained from alcohol. But my friends were all doing the same stuff.

In the evenings, I stayed in my bedroom doing yoga, while my flatmates shouted at *Grand Theft Auto*. When we hung out, they ate pizza and drank beer while I sipped a green tea and munched on a salad. I was finding it difficult to hang out with them without compromising some of the new habits and values I was wishing to build for myself, just so I felt like I was still fitting in with them.

This disconnect was developing when my dad got ill and eventually passed. As you know I stood at the door of that hospice room and resolved to change everything about the way I was living. One of these changes included the people I was spending time with.

I made the decision to step out of my group of friends. I realised that I was about to walk a different path from them, to go on a journey that they weren't going to follow at this point in time, if not at all.

I would politely decline invitations to parties. If it was an important event such as a birthday, I would show up a little earlier, drink some tea or water and leave when the alcohol started kicking in for everyone else. I would meet up for dinner, provided I could eat something healthy, and leave when my friends wanted to move to a bar or stay in a pub and drink. I didn't go round to their places and play video games or smoke weed with them all day.

I continued to make an effort with them but on my terms. Rather than coming together as a group and jumping on the game console and cracking open the bottles, I would meet with them one-to-one for coffee or a meal. I tried to ensure that I never went too long without seeing them. For periods of time we were living in different places and I'd make the effort to see them if we ended up in the same city.

I never stopped being friends with them. I never stopped loving them. They are good people, and as long as they remain good people, they will always be my friends. The names that you will read in the acknowledgements at the back of this book are these same friends. I'm sure they noticed my actions and I hope they understand them.

This was something that was vital for me to do but it was not at all easy. I separated myself from one group but that didn't mean I had another waiting for me to jump into. I pretty much wiped the slate clean. I had new values, interests and passions that I was looking for in friends. I was also still finding out about myself and what I wanted. Gradually, one by one, I started to meet new people and join new circles. My list of twenty people changed and new names began to climb up the rankings.

For about twelve months or so, this was a big challenge, but as time went on, an interesting thing started to happen. My old friends integrated with my new direction. I remember I met them for bowling one day. I arrived slightly late and they had already loaded the game. I've had a variety of different nicknames and monikers over the years but when I arrived I found they had given me a new one for the game: "The Coach". They had noticed what I was working on and had integrated that into our relationship.

When they invited me places they would say things like: "I know you won't be drinking" or "I know you will want something healthy to eat". Sometimes as I was ordering water they'd say: "you know what, I'll just have water too."

On occasion, they will ask me about the changes I've made e.g. "what kind of foods do you eat?" or "how can I start a business?". They have seen the positive effects of some of my changes and would like to find out how they can make those changes too.

Here's the key distinction though. I never tried to change them. When I removed myself from the group dynamic, I did so with an acceptance that I would never get back in. I did so with the vision of joining a new group and having occasional nostalgic get-togethers with my old friends. I still don't see my old friends as much as I did in the past but I'm at peace with that.

At the end of *Harry Potter and The Philosophers Stone*, Dumbledore tells the Great Hall: "It takes a great deal of bravery to stand up to our enemies, but just as much to stand up to our friends". (17) It is a tough decision to cut negative people out of our lives, but it is sometimes even tougher to separate ourselves from people who haven't done anything wrong. There are difficult choices to be made on the Author Your Life journey, and this can be the toughest.

Part 2: Mirror, Mirror on the Wall

What was illustrated to you in the previous section is how strong an influence the people around us are on the way we behave, think and feel. We examined some shocking findings about human behaviour but it's not all doom and gloom. You are not destined to a life of conformity and unhealthy habits because of the people you have in your life. You don't have to ditch every friend and family member you have because they're not supportive enough of your personal development.

From this point on in the chapter, it is less about the unhealthy influence of others and instead looking at the ability of others to empower, educate and enliven us. As we saw in the Bobo doll experiment, the children who saw a good role model displayed good behaviour. You are exactly the same. If you surround yourself with positive role models, this will have a positive effect on how you show up in your life.

I'd like you to begin by thinking of your top three role models; people who you find inspiring; who you look to when you need answers; whose example you seek to follow in your life. These people can be people you know personally or don't. They can be alive or dead. Who are your top three?

Next, I'd like you to write down the name of your first role model and write down the qualities you admire in them: not what they achieved, but who they were/are as a person.

I'll illustrate with an example of my first role model: Nelson Mandela. I admire Mandela for his utter dedication to his cause, his ability to forgive and for his wisdom. These are things that I would be writing under his name. I also admire Mandela for his political and social achievements but I wouldn't write these down. I'm focusing on what enabled him to create those outcomes, rather than the outcomes themselves.

Here's why. We can't always associate ourselves with someone's achievements. Quite frankly I am not prepared to go to prison for twenty-seven years (that is longer than I have been alive at the time of writing). I don't anticipate that I will free a country from political oppression. If I start comparing myself to Mandela's achievements, I could feel quite daunted.

However, when I compare myself to Mandela's qualities, something different occurs. I feel inspired. I feel connected to Mandela. The reason is that when I look at Mandela qualities, I start to see those qualities in myself.

This is the key part. We cannot see in others what we do not already have within us. If you look at your role model and see compassion, courage or creativity, you can only see that because you are already familiar with that quality. A racist person cannot see Mandela's qualities, because they do not share the values and perspective of Mandela.

To illustrate with a personal example, I must admit that I have never been able to resonate with Steve Jobs; not because I don't appreciate and respect his achievements, but merely because I don't possess the visionary creativity he possessed. I cannot see in Steve Jobs what I do not possess in myself.

When I look at Mandela though, I admire his wisdom because I too am wise. That is a difficult sentence to write without appearing conceited but it is merely recognition of a quality and a gift I'm blessed to have. From a young age I've always been called an "old head on young shoulders"; throughout my life I've frequently been mistaken to be several years older than my actual age because of how I think and interact.

I'd give advice and mentorship to people even before I started my business; now I work with people who are sometimes twice my age. We all have our gifts: wisdom and perspective happen to be mine. Do I claim to be as wise as Mandela? Certainly not. That is why he is my role model; because he inspires me to become a better version of who I currently am.

Repeat this process for your remaining two role models. All of these qualities that you find yourself writing are qualities that exist within you. You might not feel you have these qualities, but know that purely through your ability to recognise them, you have them. This is the reason why you are attracted to these people as your role models and not others. One of the most foundational rules of social psychology is that we like people like us. (18) You like your role models because they are like you.

However, it is one thing to recognise the qualities of our role models, it is another thing to emulate them. We can spend our lives looking up with admiration and wishful thinking at the great people of the world or we can seek to join them and become great people ourselves. We can keep them as models or we can *model them*.

Social psychology is not about lines, shocks and dolls. It is about taking the same principles that have led to the darkness of human behaviour and using it to amplify the light within. We look at our role models and use their example to improve who we are.

One of the nice and humbling things that people tell me is that I have a calm, warm manner of speaking, particularly on stage. It is lovely to hear this but it isn't really surprising. One of my earliest models, as I shared with you in the beginning of this book, was Wayne Dyer. Dyer had a wonderful quality to the way he talked and taught and following his example has helped me unlock more of that quality within myself.

Another flattering compliment I sometimes receive is how positive and engaging I am. Again nice to hear but no surprise. I have watched hundreds of hours of Brendon Burchard on Youtube. I have spent four days watching him on stage. Burchard shows up for people with joy and enthusiasm and that is what I aspire to replicate in my interactions.

What has allowed me to awaken these qualities within me is my study of my role models. In fact, there is a specific technique called "modelling" that has helped me do so.

"Modelling" is a Neurolinguistic Programming (NLP) technique (19) that we have used since birth, but somehow seem to forget as we get older. When we are growing up we use models for learning. We listen to how people speak and we try to replicate the sounds they make. We observe how people walk and we try to copy their movements. In fact, we have mirror neurons in our brain that are primed to copy the behaviour of others around us, not just as an infant, but across our lives. (20) Our brains are wired to replicate the example of others. "Modelling" is a simple three-step process that accelerates our learning and growth.

Step One is to find someone who is where you want to be. If you want to be a rugby player, who is the best player in your position? If you want to own a business, who is the most successful person in your industry? If you want to raise your children well, who is the best parent you know of? This person is going to be your model of excellence. Daniel Amen, the psychiatrist who we talked about in the Consciousness section, gives the advice that if you want to be healthy, spend as much time as possible with the healthiest person you can stand. (21)

Step Two is observation. Observe the person's habits and behaviour to see what separates them from others. How does the rugby player pass the ball and how do they run? How does the businessman write marketing copy and how do they present on stage? How does the parent speak to their children and how often do they cuddle and hold hands with their children?

Step Three is replication. Seek to reproduce their behaviour. When you pass the rugby ball, have your hands in the same position as your model. When you sell your products, use the same marketing as your model. When you speak with your children, use the same phrases as your model.

This three-step process is a basic one but it is hugely effective. One prominent example of this process is Kobe Bryant, the NBA's third highest scorer of all time. When you look at Bryant, much of his style was reminiscent of Michael Jordan, whose place Bryant took on the scoring charts. Bryant saw a role model who was achieving success, looked at what he was doing, and how he could replicate Jordan's techniques to emulate his success.

That is where the NLP technique of modelling stops, but that is not where I want you to stop. I don't want you to become a clone of someone else. The problem with wanting to be the next Serena Williams, the next Oprah Winfrey, the next Angelina Jolie, is that you are not them. No one is better at being them than they are. We have seen a number of poor imitations in the world of sport, acting and music, I don't want you to join that list.

NLP lists three steps in the modelling process, but I believe there is a fourth: *evolve*. When you have followed your role model's example, develop it. When you have learned how to follow someone's recipe, you start experimenting with different ingredients. When you have learned how to play other people's music on an instrument, you start composing your own. When you have learned how to structure a novel, you start writing your own story.

This is where you stand on the shoulders of giants, building on the work before you and ultimately advancing the process of humanity as a species. That might sound outlandish but that is the narrative of our history.

One day, one human discovered how to walk upright and the rest copied them; one human learned how to make fire and the rest copied them; one human learned how to make a tool and the rest copied them.

Our evolution is more advanced now, as we pass on athletic feats, artistic genius and technological wizardry rather than survival tips, but it's the same principle. You can experience your own evolution when you embrace the technique of modelling.

Part 3: C5

As the Jim Rohn quote at the beginning of the chapter highlighted, we are the sum of the five people we spend most time with. I call these people your core five, or C5 for short. These are the five most inspiring people you know, who you surround yourself with on a consistent basis. What we're going to examine in this part of the chapter is how to build this inner circle, so you can create an awesome tribe of supporters and mentors who are with you every step of the way. To examine this further, I'd like to share three perspectives on the different levels of relationships.

Eternal Teachers

Marianne Williamson in *"A Return to Love: Reflections on the Principles of A Course in Miracles"* (22) talks about three levels of learning; three progressively deeper interactions that teach us valuable things about ourselves.

The first I call "the casual encounter". This is the fleeting encounters we have on a day-to-day basis: the shop assistant, the bus driver, the courier. These encounters might seem insignificant but they provide important clues about ourselves, because how we do anything is how we do everything. Irritations, judgements and insecurities that come out in these types of interactions will definitely manifest themselves in deeper relationships. If we are unable to have empathy, presence and compassion in these interactions, then how do we expect to possess these traits in deeper relationships?

The second I call "the bringing together". This is when we are brought together with another person for both individuals to learn specific lessons. This relationship is destined to end, in order for us to learn the lessons. This is the business partner who cheats us (or you cheat), the friend who betrays us (or you betray), the lover who leaves us (or you leave). Often we can view these endings as failures but an end does not mean a failure. If both people learned the lesson they were supposed to learn, then the relationship was a success. The only failure is if one or both of them do not learn the lesson, because then the relationship will be repeated. This is why people find themselves continually being taken advantage of in business, falling in with the wrong crowd, or arguing with partner after partner. Until they can learn the lesson and grow, the cycle will repeat itself.

The third I call "the eternal teacher". These are the people who are a continuous source of learning in our lives. These relationships can be positive; the empowering parent; the wise friend; the compassionate lover: equally they can be negative; someone who is a constant thorn in your side; someone who sucks you dry; even an arch enemy.

An interesting example of this type of relationship is Batman and the Joker. The Joker is always planning his latest scheme to create anarchy and chaos and Batman is ever vigilant against him. Yet despite their consistent conflict, Batman always shows mercy to his opponent and the Joker never intends to kill Batman. The two need each other to survive. The Joker gives Batman a focus for his heroics and Batman gives the Joker a challenge for his cunning. Batman and the Joker are two eternal teachers for each other.

The first part of creating your C5 is to recognise the different levels of learning that exist in your relationships and to be aware of our gaps in relationships. If a certain dysfunction exists in your fleeting encounters, this will sour the vibe of your C5. If a certain pattern is not being recognised in your bringing together relationships, this will pop up again in your C5. The C5 is not a council of perfect individuals, but you must be mindful of potential gaps in your learning and development and form your C5 accordingly.

Growth Friends

Brendon Burchard has another perspective on differing levels of relationships. He focused on the depth of connection and the allocation of time to individuals in his book: *"The Charge: Activating the 10 Human Drives That Make You Feel Alive"*. (23)

The first level of relationships, as Burchard sees it, is old friends. I prefer the term "acquaintances". These aren't the fleeting encounters that Marianne Williamson talks about. These are the people you begin to build rapport and shared experiences with. These are the people you lived with at university, someone at the desk next to you at work, or that holiday romance you had. These are people we liked and still get on with but ultimately are not a part of our lives. These are the people you care enough about to send them a birthday message on Facebook but don't speak to them the other 364 days of the year. These are the people you stop and say hi to if you meet them in the street but don't schedule a follow-up coffee with them.

There's nothing wrong with acquaintances. They were nice people to have in our lives, we have good shared memories with them, but now both of you have moved on. Occasionally an acquaintance does pop up again in your life as a more permanent figure but this is a rarity. What is important is to be mindful of the time you allocate to them. Don't keep messaging someone for coffee who is just an acquaintance. Don't travel to another city to visit someone who is just an acquaintance. Accept that your relationship is not as deep as that and be content with the memories and experiences you created with them.

The second level of relationships is "maintenance friends". These are people that you have built consistent connections with. These are the people you studied with, worked with, or travelled with for an extended period of time. These are the people who were part of the "gang"; who would be in the group messages, the party invites and the wedding photos. However, perhaps you were not that close with them, or you were close but have drifted apart on different life journeys. Despite this, they are still someone you enjoy spending time with and keeping in touch with.

The time allocation here is a little different. You might catch up with them at hen/stag dos, weddings and naming ceremonies. You might get together for dinner/coffee/drinks every couple of months. You might take the time to travel to their city and visit them. This is enjoyable and worthwhile but this is the limit. You do not have closeness beyond this. In the priorities of your life, they don't score higher than this. Again this is okay. We should not try to make relationships more than they are. Your best friend as an eighteen year old is not necessarily your best friend at thirty years old. Who you hang out with when you're single is different to who you hang out with when you're changing nappies.

Your maintenance friends are *not* your C5 and this can be a difficult distinction to make. Your maintenance friends can be some of your oldest and dearest friends but they are not your C5. They are not your C5 because you no longer have the closeness, same priorities or even the shared values you once had. If you try to make a maintenance friend into something more, it won't work.

Your C5 will be made up of "growth friends", the third and deepest level of connection. Growth friends are rare; you will not meet many of them in your life. You may meet some people who you think are a growth friend but they fall a little short of the mark. Burchard estimates that there will be somewhere between six and ten people across your lifetime who are a growth friend. (24)

Growth friends are people who energise you, inspire you and bring you joy. When you know they are coming to a party, electricity tingles in your fingers. When they get the same holidays as you, you start scribbling ideas down for the things you can do. When they have an idea, you pump the air in joy. It is a totally different feeling that you get compared to the rest of your friends.

Growth friends are those who you don't just see on a frequent basis, you design your life to see them on a frequent basis. Contact with growth friends is at least once a month, if not once a week or more. The question is, who makes you feel this way? Who lights you up? Who do you eagerly anticipate seeing again?

Your growth friends are the first people in your C5. They are people who not just bring you joy but also help you grow as well. They push you to be more adventurous, help you gain new insights and build upon your creative sparks. These are the people who actively improve your life not just through the time you spend with them but through active contribution to your life.

Risers

Vanessa Van Edwards provides the third perspective on relationships in her book *"Captivate: The Science of Succeeding With People"*. (25) She talks about "risers", people you want to integrate into your circle of influence. You might have fleeting encounters or acquaintances who you want to develop into something more. In life we will meet people of inquiry and interest. Don't lose touch with these people. Don't let them slip down your list of priorities simply because you don't have a relationship with them yet. You never know who you're going to meet who's going to make a dramatic shift in your life.

Be mindful of the relationships you have and the relationships you develop as time goes on. Observe when someone you meet has an "essence" or "quality" about them. This person may be an eternal teacher, a growth friend or a riser. That person may be someone who forms one of your C5.

When it comes to crafting your C5, this is not something that is going to happen by accident. You must be intentional about the type of person you want in your outer social circle and in particular your inner circle. In your inner circle, there are three types of relationship: friends, family and lovers. For each of these relationships, ask yourself two key questions:

1. What defines a deeply connected relationship to you?
2. What would you have to do to deepen the relationships in this area?

From this, you can identify a set of values, principles and practices that you wish to foster in your C5. You can also make an assessment of what you would like to do to improve your current relationships and start deciding who you want in your C5.

Making Time

You may remember at the beginning of the book I talked about Nelson Mandela, the Lonely Visionary. Mandela had reached excellence in the two areas we have covered so far in the book: Consciousness and Calling.

However, where he was lacking was Connection. I don't want you to have the same regrets as Mandela did. There's no point creating your C5 and then never spending time with them. I believe you can be a Visionary *and* enjoy Connection. But to do so, you have to be strategic. Time can be sucked away from you if you are not careful, so you need to learn how to make time.

The way you make time, is to schedule it. The reality of our fast-paced lifestyles nowadays if that if it isn't scheduled, it doesn't happen. You want to start going to the gym? You want to start writing a book? You want to learn a second language? I'm sure you've had a new project that fell by the wayside because you didn't develop consistency and routine with it. Don't let your relationships fall the same way.

You schedule important things like doctor and dentist appointments right? What does that scheduling really mean?

It means that at that specific time, you have prioritised that activity over anything except a genuine emergency. If you have a dentist appointment at 2:30pm and a friend asks you if you want to go for lunch, you say "I can't, I've got a dentist appointment". You don't call up your dentist and say: "I need to reschedule, I've decided to go for lunch with my friend instead."

Why do we only employ this strict prioritisation for medical procedures? Why don't you create appointments for the other important areas of your life? I was only able to write this book because I scheduled time that was devoted to writing. You will only be able to deepen your relationships if you schedule time that is going to be devoted to the most important people in your life.

Schedule your social time well in advance. I schedule with friends and family about six months in advance, I schedule parties 2-3 months in advance. I want important social occasions to be the first thing in my calendar, then the rest of my life fits around my social commitments, not the reverse.

I would also recommend having a fortnightly tradition where you get together with people in your C5. This could be a dinner at someone's house; going out for drinks; hikes in the country, whatever best suits your preferences. This creates a default to meet up. You might not be able to get everyone together each fortnight — people will have important deadlines, family commitments and other things that cause them to opt out from time to time — but it means that you develop the consistency of seeing most of your C5 most of the time.

As well as scheduling when you can see your C5 collectively, also consider when and how you see them individually. Write down the names of each of your C5, and next to their name write down a rough schedule for them. Do they work 9-5? Do they travel often? Are they more of a morning person or a night person? Start to identify time that you can schedule with them.

In addition to this, write down the shared interests and activities you have with that person. For example, my friends know there's little point inviting me to the bar on a Friday night, because I don't drink alcohol and I wake up early. However, they know that I love a cup of tea. Therefore, my friends know that the best time to schedule time with me is in the morning in a coffee shop, rather than at night in a bar.

Your C5 will have preferences that are different from each other, so consider how to cater to them individually as well as collectively. Your arty friends aren't going to want to go and watch the game every weekend. Your sporty friends aren't going to want to go to get pizzas every Thursday evening. Plan out how you can meet each of your C5 individually according to their needs and preferences.

To help establish the routine of regular contact with your C5, you may want to consider using the phone alarm strategy we discussed in the Consciousness section to consistently remind you to schedule time with them and keep in contact. This is especially useful in the beginning when you are trying to create the new habit of consistent contact. It's easy for a week or two to slip by and you realise you haven't spoken to one of the people you share the closest relationship with. Even as I write this, I've remembered I haven't heard from one of my C5 for about a month as they are currently traveling. I've just sent them a message to check in and see how they're doing. You could set a weekly reminder to message any of your C5 that you haven't heard from in the course of that week, or even better, schedule face-to-face time with them.

Like any practice in this book, you need to build the habit. Maintaining good relationships is no different. As you start to assemble your C5, build the habit of consistently communicating with them. If you do so, then you avoid the trap of the Lonely Visionary.

Integrate

We are shaped by the people around us. In this chapter you have learned how to control and even harness the power of those around you to effectively Integrate with others. Through this you begin to deepen your Connection. In the next chapter, you will learn how to enhance and deepen the relationships around you by increasing your Influence.

In this chapter you have learned:

- That everyone around you is an influence
- That you will need to make some tough decisions about who you will allow to influence you
- How to replicate the excellence of your role models
- The different categories of relationship
- How to select your C5

My biggest takeaway from this chapter is

_____.

Chapter 11: Influence

"Be the change you wish to see in the world"
- Mahatma Gandhi

Along the Author Your Life journey, you will meet many fellow travellers and seekers: people who are on the same level as you; with the same aspirations and values as you. These are our peers: friends, colleagues and lovers. All relationships bring value but through different channels. It is with our peers that we are likely to have our most pleasurable and joyful experiences: the parties, holidays and weddings. However, do not suppose that these experiences come by chance. You must be intentional about how you approach these relationships. There are certain principles and practices that will help you develop and deepen the relationships with your peers. When you employ these, you can become a person of influence in your social circle. In this chapter, you will learn the secrets of non-verbal communication, the principles of developing rapport and likability and how to resolve conflicts.

Part 1: Your Body Speaks

Depending on who you ask, anywhere between 65-93% of our communication is non-verbal. (1) The research differs slightly, (2) and does carry a number of limitations, (3) but it all agrees that a significant amount of our communication does not come out of our mouths. So why does most communication training focus on words?

In school, we are taught how to say *words* but not how to communicate with our bodies. Psychotherapy practices largely focus on what someone — the patient or practitioner — is *saying*. Spin doctors give politicians a *script* to explain the recent mishap. We know body language is a large part of communication, yet we focus our efforts on changing just one dimension of communication: what we are saying. What follows are ridiculously simple changes we can all make to improve our interactions without saying a thing.

Eye, Eye

The eyes are the windows to the soul, as they say. If you access someone's soul, then you have the deepest connection that can possibly be made with them. Making eye contact with someone is a simple action but something we find difficult to do. Can we look our parent in the eye as they scold us? Can we look a friend in the eye as we point out a flaw? Can we look our partner in the eye as we make love to them?

Eye contact is a sign of vulnerability and trust. When we make eye contact with someone, we are showing our vulnerability and showing that we trust someone. It's a powerful gesture. If reciprocated, it displays an open, accepting interaction.

Activist Jae West and her team at Liberators International produced a video called: "The World's Biggest Eye Contact Experiment." They got over 100,000 individuals from 156 cities across the world to hold eye contact with a stranger for one minute. This simple act moved people to laugh, cry and hug someone they had known for just that single minute. (4) This displays that power of connection we can develop through eye contact.

Yet in our interactions, we don't make as much eye contact as we could. Research shows that we make eye contact just 61% of the time in our interactions. (5) Put another way, that means that nearly half the time, we aren't properly looking at each other as we talk. That's a bit weird, isn't it?

One characteristic of autism is the reduced ability to successfully identify emotion. Autistic children are 13% less successful at identifying the emotion on faces than non-autistic children. What has been observed in these children, using eye tracking technology, is that they also spend 20% less time looking people in the eye than non-autistic children. (6) This research suggests that eye contact allows us to better understand and empathise with people as we have a clear idea of their emotional state.

So how can you take the step to make better eye contact? A simple strategy I use is when I meet someone I try to find out their eye colour. In order to find out their eye colour, guess where you'll need to look? In the eye.

Moreover, you can't stare, because that's a nice creepy way to end the interaction. You need to look, and if you perhaps don't see properly the first time, you'll need to look again. By this time, you might be struggling to distinguish between a hazel or brown, or a blue or turquoise, so you require another glance to confirm. Through learning another person's eye colour, you have established a habit of looking them in the eyes, hopefully one that you will continue throughout the rest of the interaction.

This isn't just an exercise for meeting new people. Out of your group of friends, how many can you say you know the eye colour of? If you think back to the list of the twenty people you spend the most time with, whose name could you confidently write down "blue", "green" or "brown" next to? If you can't say for sure, then you could also do with engaging in more eye contact with the people closest to you.

Handyman

Have you got a good set of "jazz hands"? Good, because our hands are another key part of our interactions. If you look at people as they speak, we use our hands to communicate — some more so than others. If you watch me on stage or on YouTube, I use my hands a lot. I'm a visual person, and I will draw out what I'm speaking about with my hands. My partner tells me this can be quite distracting at times!

Just like our eyes, hands are a sign of trust. In our caveman days, the way we would determine if another human was dangerous was to look at their hands. This was to check if they had a weapon in their grasp. If we could see their hands were empty, then we could trust them. (7)

However, if their hand was behind their back, then we didn't know what they might be concealing in their grasp. As humans grew more sophisticated and we developed clothes, we then started to shake each other's hand; this allowed us to check that the other person wasn't hiding a dagger up their sleeve.

Our hands are a powerful extension of our natural expression. This was demonstrated in a study of TED speakers. All people who are invited onto a TED stage are experts in their field with a message worth listening to, but some TED talks and speakers are much more powerful than others. One of the key distinctions between the two turns out to be the way they use their hands.

The least popular TED talkers use an average of 272 hand gestures in their eighteen-minute presentations: the most popular use an average of 465 gestures — nearly twice as many. (8) If you look at a speaker like Simon Sinek, who I consider to be a particularly accomplished speaker, he used over 600 hand gestures in his hugely successful TED talk "Start With Why: How Great Leaders Inspire Action". (9)

So if you want to communicate with intention and confidence, as well as build trust with someone, show them your hands. Keep your hands out from behind your back and in your pockets. Also initiate touch with the hands. Once again not in a creepy way and not even just for flirting either. Physical touch stimulates our chemical oxytocin, which is associated with trust and bonding. Friendly pats on the back, hair tussles and hugs help activate this chemical for us.

Hugs in particular are something that I try to initiate whenever I can. A group of students at Pennsylvania University were instructed to give a minimum of five hugs a day for four weeks. The recipients of those hugs couldn't just be romantic partners, close friends and family, they had to try and find new people to embrace. These students managed, impressively, an average of forty-nine hugs over that period and reported a significant increase in happiness compared to a control group who were asked to increase their reading. (10) Hugs make everyone feel good, give them more often.

Poser

How we hold ourselves is a key part of how people will react to us. If you struggle with confidence and social anxiety, then changing your posture may have some surprising results for you. In particular, adopting something called the "power pose" is going to dramatically affect how you feel in interactions and how positive the outcomes are in those interactions.

To explain the power pose, let's take an evolutionary perspective again. Our ancestors lived in small social groups with a defined hierarchy (you could actually argue that little has changed since). In these social groups there was an alpha male at the top of the chain and he got first pick of the food and females. (11) If anyone else wanted to become the alpha male, they would have to show that they were more dominant.

You can see this all over the world in mating rituals. One of the key signs of dominance is an open body posture: the gorilla beating its chest; the bear standing on its hind legs; the peacock spreading its plumage wide. These rituals are all designed to display possession over their surroundings and dominance over their rivals.

Us humans, for all our claims of sophistication, do exactly the same. What does a runner do when they cross the finish line? They spread their arms and open their posture to display their dominance and triumph. In studies it has been found that when people who have been blind from birth are asked to imagine winning a race, they do exactly the same posture, even though they have no social model. (12) This action is hardwired within us.

On the flip side, when an animal is confronted by a more dominant individual, they shrink as a sign of deference. Think of the dog that whimpers and cowers in the basket after it's been told off. They close their posture and take up less space. This is a sign of submission.

These postures aren't just for show; they represent physiological changes in our body. Harvard psychologist Amy Cuddy has conducted extensive research into body language, in particular "power poses". (13) Power poses are the open, dominant postures that animals and humans adopt when feeling superior.

Cuddy has found that opening our posture and adopting a power pose raises our hormone testosterone by an average of 25%. (14) Testosterone isn't about muscles and ego as we usually think, it is our hormone related to dominance, competitiveness and confidence. It allows both men and women to get ahead and be more successful.

Power poses also cause the levels of cortisol to fall by 20%. (15) You may remember that cortisol is our so called "stress hormone". When we enter a power pose, we feel more confident and less stressed; not because of some woo-woo, motivational hype, but because our biochemistry has literally changed to make us feel this way.

Cuddy has conducted experiments getting participants to do mock job interviews. The participants were split into two groups. One group did a power pose for two minutes before the interview, the other group did nothing. They were then judged by people who were completely blind to which group the participants were in. These judges overwhelming rated the individuals who had done power poses as more competent candidates. (16) Therefore, just two minutes of standing in a power pose can be the difference between you getting a job and not getting one.

Looking at the flip side of this, shrinking into a submissive posture raises our cortisol. Moving into this posture actually puts us into a fight-or-flight mode because by adopting this position our body thinks it's under attack. Pretty much all of us do this several times a day. Whenever we hunch over our phones or a keyboard we are raising our stress levels. People with depression are more likely to adopt a hunched standing position than people who don't suffer from depression. (17) Adopting what is affectionately termed the "iHunch" can make you more likely to be stressed and depressed.

Just by changing our posture, we can lower our stress and depression, and increase our confidence and performance in interactions. How are you sitting right now? Are you rolled up into a ball at the edge of the sofa? Are you bent over nearly double on the subway?

Cuddy has observed a number of different power poses you can adopt such as "The Winner", "Wonder Woman" and "The CEO". There are two adaptions I particularly like and I feel are realistic to incorporate naturally into your posture.

If you are standing, I like to adopt the "Wonder Woman". This involves putting your hands on your hips and rolling your shoulders back. Now it's easy to exaggerate this position, puffing your chest out like a bird during mating season and standing like you've got a stick up your butt. If you exaggerate in this way, it looks forced and inauthentic.

When I first started learning about body language as a teenager, I overcompensated in this way. I would strut around the corridors at school swinging my arms like pistons and looking around like I owned the place. As one of my (now) close friends revealed to me after we'd left school: "I didn't talk to you for the first five years of school because you walked around like were trying to hold in a s***."

That's not the impression you want to give off! Instead, just place your hands gently on your hips; keep your arms loose and relaxed; and just roll your shoulders back in their sockets. This pulls you up out of a potential "iHunch" and also keeps your hands visible to the other person to help build trust. I have found it the best blend between looking powerful and relaxed.

If you are sitting, I aim to stick to the "one cross" rule. That means I can only have one limb crossed in front of my body. This can be one arm or one leg, but not two arms, or an arm and a leg. So if my leg is crossed, I want to have my arms away from my torso. If I have a hand resting in my lap, then I want my feet resting on the floor. As soon as I cross two limbs, I find myself in a closed and subversive position. My favourite default position is to have both feet on the floor, one hand on my knee and the other arm resting on the chair/couch behind me. This displays openness without cockiness, balancing power and relaxation in the same manner as the "Wonder Woman".

If you feel uncertain in interactions, then give yourself a stable position using a power pose. This will give you the foundations to communicate with confidence.

Part 2: The Currency of Interactions

There is a driving force behind all our interactions. When you understand how to harness this driving force, the depth and engagement of your interactions will increase substantially. This driving force is interest.

It doesn't matter how "charismatic" or "confident" you are in interactions. If you cannot generate interest, your interactions will suffer. As with so many results in life, generating interest in interactions begins with us.

We often want people to be interested in us, but if you want people to be interested in you, you must be interested in them first. If interest is the currency of interactions, then you should think of it as you do money. You must make a deposit in an account before you can withdraw. You must invest before you can make returns. Let's look at how you can accumulate the currency of interactions.

The Sweetest Sound

I don't get irritated by too many things, but I have one thing that has consistently irritated me throughout my life. It's an irritation I won't escape. The irritation is people spelling my name wrong.

"McCrae" is not the most common of surnames. As I write it just now in this word document a squiggly red line has just appeared under it. In Scotland, "Mac"s and "Mc"s are common, but you will far more often find a Mackenzie or a McDonald than a McCrae. In fact, McCrae is not even the most common way of spelling the surname. The original spelling is "MacRae", with additional spellings including "McRae", "MacRay",

"McRay" as well as my "McCrae". To further complicate it, there is also the almost identical "McRea" and "McCrea" surnames.

Suffice to say, my name is nearly always spelt wrong. On the phone, despite telling people "M-C-C, R-A-E. That's Roger, Alpha, Echo", I frequently find further correspondence to me spelt incorrectly. One of my real bugbears is when I have sent an email containing "davidmccrae" in the address and signed "David McCrae", I still find the name spelt wrong in a reply.

The reason why this irritates me is not just the consistency of the error, but because I am proud of my name. My name has history.

The MacRae clan was one of the smaller Scottish clans and we were allied with the larger MacKenzie clan. As a result of this alliance, the MacRae clan were granted guardianship of Eilean Donan Castle, one of Scotland's most popular landmarks. One of my favourite stories comes from this stewardship.

In a famous battle, most of the garrison were out hunting when the castle was attacked by a force of 1500. There were just two MacRaes left to defend the castle. One of the MacRae's shot the opposing chieftain in the eye with an arrow. The invaders, demoralised by the death of their leader, retreated, not knowing they faced a defence force of just two men.

We have our own family tartan and I own a kilt with that tartan. We have our own family motto, which I have tattooed on my leg. My surname means a lot to me and it irritates me that people do not even pay it enough attention to spell it correctly.

In my life so far, I think only two or three people have spelt my surname right first time. I was astonished when they did so and I instantly liked them more because of it. Such a simple act, yet it meant a lot to me because of the pride I associate with my surname.

My first name, on the other hand, is much more common. David is one of the most common names in the English speaking world (plus its variants in other languages). Yet people still manage to get it wrong. I always introduce myself as "David", yet every now and then, people will decide to take it upon themselves to shorten it to "Dave". I don't like "Dave" which is why I don't call myself "Dave" or introduce myself as "Dave". This annoys me because I have given them my name how I like it, but the person has decided they like it better their way.

Now I haven't described this to you just to rant and get this off my chest. I have shared this with you to demonstrate an important fact about people.

Names have power. I just have to say the name "Hitler" and you immediately have emotional associations with that word. Conversely, if I say the name "Mandela", you will have a different emotional association.

We all hold our names in higher esteem than the names of others. The sound of our name is one of the sweetest sounds we know. We like the sound of our name and even like to hear someone else with the same name.

If you want an easy way to connect with someone, use their name. When you meet me, if you call me David and spell my surname right, then you have earned my full attention. It's an easy way to develop rapport with someone.

The first step is to learn someone's name. How often do you get introduced to someone and forget their name? Take a little more care at the beginning of an interaction, and the rest of your interactions can be much more fruitful.

The first technique to use is to try and link that person's name to something you recognise. Maybe this person shares the name of one of your close friends. Perhaps they have the same name as someone famous. Maybe you can link the first letter of their name with something distinctive about them e.g. "Ryan with the Red shirt" or "Erica with the large Earrings".

One of my most successful examples of this was with one of my seminar students. At most of my seminars there's at least 50% of the audience who I've never met before, so I try to learn some names to build a connection with them. I still remember one of my students "Esther". I remembered her name because she looked like Esther Perel, a relationship therapist and author who's work I admire. I have forgotten most of the names from that seminar, but I still remember Esther because I was able to create a strong emotional connection with her name.

The second technique is repetition. When the person tells you their name, use the phrase: "Nice to meet you <insert name>". Firstly, this gives you the opportunity to check pronunciation if it is a trickier name. Secondly, it kickstarts the process of integrating their name into the conversation. After the initial greeting, look to say their name in the next few sentences of conversation. Often a good way to do so is to ask them a question, for example "So <name>, what brings you here tonight?" or "Who do you know in the room, <name>?". Another winner is in a compliment (I notice ladies are skilled at doing this, men not so much!). For example: "I love your earrings <name>." or "<name>, you have a really relaxing voice to listen to.".

Don't panic if it is an unusual name, because you can actually use that as a conversation starter. You might say "Kayode, how do you spell that?" or "Stylianos, does that name mean anything in your native language?". You also get more time to adapt to and reinforce an unusual name. It's easy to say "I just want to check I'm pronouncing Tsvetelina right" than "I just want to check I'm pronouncing John right". If you're lucky, there will be some story connected to their name that you can expand upon and use to kickstart the interaction. If there isn't, you can create one yourself. I once met a Finnish lady named "Siiri" and I immediately thought of Siri on the iPhone, and the name stuck in my head.

Just to warn you, like all things, this is something you can overdo. If you are starting or finishing every second sentence with someone's name, then they know you're just using a strategy on them and will resist it. However, just the occasional sprinkle works wonders. Using someone's name takes little additional effort but it captures their interest so much more. If you meet someone as pedantic about their name as I am, then you can quickly win their affection through correct usage.

Make People Feel Important

If we want people to like us, then we need to develop a fascination for finding out more about them. This isn't superficial details such as job, relationship status, or where they live. This is wanting to know a person's passions, opinions, values, beliefs and hopes. When we are interested in others, others find that dead interesting. They find that interesting because it makes them feel important.

This is based on the simple fact that people love talking about themselves. Brain scans have shown that people's dopamine centres light up when they are talking about themselves. (18) Even the most humble and gracious or shy and guarded person can't wait to tell people about themselves. I'm sure even the Dalai Lama, modest as he is, enjoys being asked to give his opinion on something. The easiest way to get another person to talk about themselves, and therefore to like you, is to ask them questions. Asking questions shows that we value and respect what someone has to say.

Now this isn't just any old question. We don't ask boring questions and we don't ask intrusive questions. We don't ask "How old are you? I'm really fascinated to know more about you" or "What colour of underwear do you have on? I'm really fascinated to know more about you". We ask interesting questions. If we ask interesting questions — surprise, surprise — we get interesting answers.

I've got an example fresh in my mind. It happened about two hours ago. I'm writing this on the train home from a networking event and at this event I was speaking with a lady who told me she was an architect.

Uh oh. I don't know anything about architecture. Now I can choose to talk over her and change the subject to something I'm comfortable with. Or I can show an interest in her interest.

"What type of architecture do you do?" I ask her. She tells me she does commercial offices (this wasn't really an interesting question; I could've done better here to be honest).

"What made you want to be an architect?" I ask her. She tells me about her mum the art teacher, who was always drawing with her (Much better question. This is the one I should've actually asked first. Now we're talking about something meaningful, the fond memories of her mum nurturing her creative expression).

"What's the most exciting project you've worked on?" I ask again. She tells me about working on the UN embassy in Turkey (Great question. By asking her about an exciting project, I'm likely to get an exciting answer).

"If you could work on any project, what would it be?" I ask once more. She tells me about designing a hostel or a bed and breakfast, creating every intimate touch for an amazing user experience from the blueprints up (This question has put her in her passion zone. She's enthusiastic, engaged and happy; sharing her dream with someone else).

At this point, sadly, an old white dude in a suit thrusts his business card into our conversation and kills the vibe (Tip on how to be likeable: don't lead with your business card. Why do people still think this works?

It's like asking someone if they'll sleep with you before you've even gone on a date).

I glance down and see "real estate developer" on the card and decide to make a tactical retreat.

"I'll leave you with a thought," I say, "If your dream project is designing a B&B, why are you making offices for corporations?"

Now *that*, is an interesting question.

How can you ask interesting questions? A study by Vanessa Van Edwards has identified questions that people find more interesting than others. She ran a study that randomly partnered over 300 participants in a three minute speed-networking scenario. Each partnership was given a list of different conversation starters, and then the participants ranked how interesting they found the resulting conversation. From this study, the top three conversation starters were:

1. What was the highlight of your day?
2. What personal passion project are you working on?
3. Have anything exciting coming up in your life? (19)

These questions work because they are open-ended, rather than closed. Closed questions are questions asked in such a way that they elicit a Yes/No answer or some other limited choice of response (for example "what is your favourite city?"). An open-ended question has no expected answer or limited choice (for example "can you tell me about your favourite city?"). When you ask someone an open-ended question you give them the opportunity to give an elaborative and unique answer, rather than a fixed and generic answer.

They also trigger an emotional response in the person you are asking the question to. A closed question generally elicits a logical response ("this is the answer") whereas an open-ended question generally elicits an emotional response ("this is how I feel about the answer"). When you move people emotionally, you are influencing them, and they will feel more connected to you as a result.

You can use the questions above to start good conversations, and to inject fresh life into a faltering conversation too. Throughout a conversation, I also like to use what I call "curiosity cues".

Since launching my podcast, I have learned a different skill in communication. Through interviewing people on the podcast, I have learned to ask better questions. I aim to make my interviews as relaxed and conversational as I can, but ultimately there is an onus on me to ask good questions and allow the interviewee to do most of the talking. You can't rely on a stock list of prepared questions, because sometimes the conversation takes new tangents and you want to adapt and delve deeper into this new tangent. You need adaptable interviewing skills to keep up.

As I'm listening to someone I'm interviewing, I make little mental bookmarks as they're talking. They might mention something and move on, or talk about something I don't fully understand, and I make a little bookmark next to that point. When they finish speaking, I then have a set of mental bookmarks that I can then use to formulate my next question. These are the curiosity cues, and you can open up these cues with simple statements such as:

- "You mentioned…"
- "I noticed…"
- "I was curious about…"
- "I was wondering if you could explain more about…"

These are cues that you can use in your conversations too. As someone is speaking, make bookmarks next to parts of their account that interest you, just like you would bookmark webpages you'd like to come back to. With your curiosity cues, you can then open up these bookmarks and continue to take the conversation in interesting directions.

Oldest Form of Communication

Let me ask you a question. What is Microsoft? Can you tell me where I can find Microsoft?

If you're pointing to a computer, you're wrong. That isn't Microsoft: it's a Microsoft computer. Try again.

If you're pointing to Microsoft's headquarters, you're wrong. That isn't Microsoft: it is Microsoft's offices, digital hub and recreational campus. Try again.

If you're pointing to Bill Gates, you're wrong. That isn't Microsoft: that is Microsoft's founder.

So what is Microsoft? It is something made-up. We cannot point to anything material as "being" Microsoft. Yet we would all argue that it exists. Why? Because we have created the *story* of Microsoft.

Creating stories is one of the most powerful things we as humans do. It is how we have created our current society. (20) There is no such thing as a company — Microsoft, Apple, Starbucks, Uber — we have just created the story that it exists, therefore it does.

Money has no value. There is nothing useful about pieces of paper or numbers on a computer. However, because we have created the story of money, it holds high value for us. Money only exists because when I give you a coin, and you take it, we both believe the same story about what the coin means.

How about happiness? You cannot give me happiness. You cannot point to happiness. You can't even say what it is for you. However, it is completely real. Why? Because you have created a story about what happiness is and how you find it. It exists because you believe the story that it does.

Stories are a hugely important part of what makes us human and no less so in the way we communicate. Stories are our oldest form of communication. When we sat around campfires, we would pass on lessons and knowledge through stories. Before perhaps we could even use language, we were painting stories on cave walls. You may have noticed I have been sharing stories with you in this book. This is no accident. I have used stories to enhance your learning and retention.

Do you think it is a coincidence that some of the most impactful books in human history are the Bible, the Quran and the Bhagavad Gita? How are these books written? As a textbook? As a list of instructions? As marketing copy? No. The holy books are written as stories because that is how we create and understand meaning in the world.

If it worked for Jesus, Muhammed (PBUH) and Krishna, don't you think it might work for you? When you start to communicate using stories, you will start to access the deepest form of communication we have.

When humans share stories, some interesting reactions occur in our brain. A 2010 study found that when someone is telling a story, the part of their brain related to emotion is activated. Nothing particularly surprising there. However, in the person listening to the story, the exact same regions are activated in their brain. When we share stories, we are literally synchronising our brains with other people. (21) That is why stories have been a part of our communication for so long. We have always felt this connection and affinity when we tell each other stories and now science has caught up to tell us why.

This doesn't mean that you go up to people and start telling them all about yourself just to "tell a story". Story telling is not about narcissism.

The first part of unlocking the power of stories is actually to get the other person to tell you a story.

How do you get them to do so? It's back to questions again. You're not going to ask just any question, however. We're not talking about boring demographic questions. When you ask a question about someone's age, occupation, marital status, number of children or residence, you are going to receive a fact in response. We don't want facts, we want stories.

You can use open-ended questions such as the ones listed earlier in the chapter to encourage people to start telling a story. You can also use the curiosity cues. Sometimes even just asking "what's the story behind that tattoo/scar/etc" will obviously result in someone telling you a story.

Of course, stories are not a one-way street. You can also tell people stories yourself but I always encourage you to get the other person talking first. As we know, people love talking about themselves and people will like you if you give them an opportunity to do so.

I encourage you to have a "bank" of stories that you can bring into conversations to tag onto different subjects. Whether the conversation moves from travel, to politics, to books, to work, to dating, to sport, you have a relevant story that will entertain, educate, or empower the person you are speaking to.

I have a number of stories that are reliable "winners" for me in conversation, some I have already shared with you in this book. Others I have shared in videos online. When I was younger and had lower emotional intelligence, I learned that telling stories was a great way to get people to be interested in you at parties (i.e. ladies). However, my problem was that I didn't realise there was a second step to this process. So all I would do was tell stories, and talk about myself. It was no surprise then that I came across as arrogant (which wasn't helped by that awkward walking I did!).

What I've learned in more recent years is to use what Vanessa Van Edwards calls the "boomerang" technique. (22) By all means, raconteur people with your story, but when you've hit the punchline, try to refer it back to them and open up an opportunity for them to respond with a story of their own. Use phrases such as "have you ever found yourself in that situation?", or "have you ever felt like that?", or "what do you think you would do in that scenario?" to give them an opening to tell a story of their own. You only need to share a couple of stories with someone to feel like you have a strong bond with them.

Part 3: White Flag

Whilst you might be equipped with all the smooth moves of building rapport and understand all the social psychology factors that help you build a relationship with someone, you will, eventually, make a mistake. At some point, conflict will arise. It is inevitable.

Some people try to go through their lives avoiding conflict, however, all you end up doing is creating an unhealthy passive-aggressive environment. Other people, however, seek out conflict, and they escalate conflict to levels where it creates permanent rifts and wounds. Instead of fearing or enticing conflict, we must instead approach it with maturity. We must learn how to wave the white flag and make peace. Managing conflict is a vital part of having successful relationships and, if navigated correctly, actually makes your relationships stronger.

Avoid

Whilst I just told you that trying to avoid conflict is unhealthy, the first stage I'm going to walk you through is avoiding conflict. Don't worry, there is a nuance. What I mean here is avoiding unnecessary conflict. How many stupid arguments have you had with people? How many times have you wound up and been wound up for no good reason? How many times have you stepped in it and made a massive faux pas?

We don't have to deal with a conflict that doesn't exist; neither do we have to deescalate something that hasn't escalated. In my experience you can deal with most conflict in a calm and systematic manner, despite what the politicians on television would have you believe.

The biggest cause of all conflict is a lack of perspective. It is the inability to see the other person's side or even to see any side apart from your own. The fact of the matter is that we don't see the world as it is, we see it as we are. When two people are shown an optical illusion, they will report seeing different images, even though the lines are in the same place. Give two people a different newspaper and they will form different opinions of the same event. The adverts that stalk you across the internet are designed to give you more of what you like and confirm more of what you believe.

One of the reasons we argue and disagree with people is because we perceive them to be wrong, rather than seeing them as having a different version of the truth: an important distinction. The Left and Right are at each other's throats in politics, when actually both of them are largely trying to achieve the same thing: a growing economy, increased opportunities and reduced poverty. Christians and Muslims have slaughtered each other even though both of their religions are far more similar than different: teaching virtues of compassion, charity and mercy. Only in a select few areas, such as maths, is right and wrong a binary distinction.

Therefore, it is important to remember that any conflict comes from two interpretations of the same event, experience or circumstance. Both of you can have a correct interpretation and both of you can have an incorrect one. If you start arguing over these different interpretations, then conflict will ensue. If you can learn to recognise these differences, then you can avoid the conflict. Not in a passive-aggressive way, but a mature, accepting way.

For example, I have strong spiritual beliefs. I have never attached myself to a particular religion (as I have suggested, I believe they are different interpretations of the same truth), but I believe in spiritual ideas such as there being a creative force behind everything in the universe; that as individuals we each have a purpose in our time on earth; and that there is life after death.

My partner, on the other hand, thinks this is a heap of rubbish. Now I can take offence at this or I can recognise this as her interpretation of the truth. Because I have no basis for my beliefs: they are just that…beliefs. From the evidence I have experienced, I have come to spiritual conclusions. From the evidence she has experienced, she has come to non-spiritual conclusions. From our perspective, we are both right.

I think a big part of avoiding conflict is to stop trying to be right all the time. Theodore Roosevelt said that if he managed to be right 75% of the time, he would consider his leadership a successful one. (23) If you can be right 51% percent of the time, you can head to Vegas and earn yourself a fortune. So why aren't you heading to Vegas this second? Because you don't believe you can be right 51% percent of the time, do you? So if you don't believe that is the case on the tables, why would you believe that is the case in relationships?

We can destroy relationships through our urge to be right. It satisfies the ego to be right but not much else. If you dogmatically pursue the need to be right, you will break others down, sour your relationships and create rifts that never fully heal. You will feel triumphant for a moment but quickly grow moody as the other person distances themselves from you. In your desire to bring them closer, you will try to assert once again that you are right but just drive them further away.

Instead, avoiding conflict takes real humility. The ego is not good at humility because it puts it at risk. It opens it up to rejection. By admitting you were, or may have been wrong, you damage the ego's credibility. If the ego isn't right, then why does it even exist? However, who are you trying to form a relationship with? Your ego? Or another person?

These two ingredients — perspective and humility — are vital not just in avoiding conflict, but also resolving it too, which is what we are going to move onto now.

Alleviate

While I would argue that a lot of conflict is avoidable, or can be resolved at a low level of tension, we are not going to eradicate it. We are not clones with identical programming. Our differences make us special but they also create conflict. When a conflict has occurred, don't get wound up and frustrated by it. There is a systematic approach that you can use to resolve it and move on. However, it requires embracing a lot of perspective, empathy and humility, and many people simply aren't willing to do that. Most conflict that festers and escalates does so not because the problem is unsolvable but because one or both sides have not developed the maturity to embrace these key principles.

The first step, is to take a self-distanced perspective. The reason for this is that a conflict is rarely one-sided. Rarely will it be entirely the other person's fault. You will have had some part to play in a conflict. This does not mean what you did was malicious, or even intentional. Sometimes we will have unknowingly triggered someone or touched a wound. This is why it's especially important to get out of our own head. Because it's easy for us to throw our hands up and say "I've no idea what I did" or "That came out of the blue". It might appear that way at first glance but that's taking the easy way out. If we want to become more emotionally intelligent, and write a better story for our relationships, then we need to be more proactive than that.

When cameras were first invented, they were huge, bulky contraptions. They could only take a picture of what was straight in front of them. It was grainy and it was slow. This is like us when we are at a low level of emotional intelligence. We have very little idea of what is actually going on and we are slow to pick up new insights. We just have our personal snapshot.

Then personal cameras were invented. They were small and simple to use. They could take a picture quickly and at good quality. This is us as we improve our emotional intelligence. We can pick up cues in conversations quickly and realise when the tone has suddenly changed. However, just like the personal cameras, we have limitations. We can only see the picture where we are looking. We can only operate on the information available to us in a single snapshot.

However, videography has advanced to the point where we can now take panoramic pictures, and do 360 filming. Cameras can now see the whole picture, and with exceptional quality. That is the emotional intelligence we should aspire to. To be able to see the whole picture of what is going on in an interaction, and in particular for the other person or people in the interaction, which is usually our biggest blindspot.

There's a visualisation technique you can use to gain more perspective on a conflict you had. I call it the Panorama Perspective. Just like modern day cameras, it is designed to help us see the whole picture in exceptional quality.

When we view a situation, or replay it in our mind, we generally focus on how something happened. We focus on actions and reactions and we replay these again and again in our heads when we look back. This is especially true if we were involved in the situation. We see everything from a first person perspective.

So instead what we want to ask is "why?": *why* things are happening or have happened in the situation. By asking "why" we widen our scope of thinking to consider the larger implications of what is going on. Research has found that asking people to reconstruct an event from a "why" perspective not only gives people a greater understanding of an event, it also lowers their stress response and activation in the cardiovascular system caused by the event. (24) With this combination of calmness and clarity, we can then resolve the situation more effectively.

The Panorama Perspective takes you through this perspective of asking "why". I have written out the instructions to the exercise in the following paragraphs. As done previously in the book, you can record yourself reading the exercise and listen back to it. Alternatively, you can listen to and download the exercise in the book resources at:

http://davidmccrae.thinkific.com/courses/author-your-life-book-resources

I want you to close your eyes and think back to a situation that has created some conflict or hurt during the last month. It doesn't have to be big, but pick something you feel wasn't truly resolved.

Recall the opening snapshot of the scene. See yourself in the situation. Not through your own eyes, but from a third person perspective, like you are on camera. Now zoom out slightly. What do you see? What do you sense? What do you feel?

Zoom out a little further. Now ask yourself, why are things happening as they are? What is going on in other people's lives? What is there in the environment that could've triggered them? What are you doing to provoke the situation? Are there any new explanations you can think of for this event?

Allow the scene to play out from this wider perspective. Keep asking these questions as the mental tape plays. What do you see? What do you sense? What do you feel? Consider what others may be thinking. Observe how they are interacting with the environment. Analyse your actions.

The really key part of this process is to keep asking yourself what is going on for the other person. You know what was going on for you. You know that you came home after a hard day at work. You know you have trust issues because of your last breakup. You know you're easily upset by rude or aggressive people. But, unlike the general theme of this book, I'm saying this isn't about your story...it's about theirs.

Think of all the complexity that makes you act and react the way that you do. That person who cut you off in the morning rush-hour can still be irritating you at lunch. Being turned over for promotion at the start of the month has left you seething even at the end of the month. The expectations that were placed on you as a six-year-old are still dictating your life decisions at sixty-six years old. If you have that complexity, then so does the other person.

Start thinking about what might have annoyed the other person that morning. Start thinking about who they have in their life who is treating them unfairly. Start thinking about how they might feel about their four younger siblings all being married and they're not. Because we bring all these stories into our interactions. That is what really fuels the conflict.

Is Ireland divided because Protestants and Catholics like to worship God in slightly different ways? Do white police officers shoot black civilians because they make an error in a split-second judgement? Do Republicans and Democrats chastise each other because they don't agree on policy?

In each case, the conflict is not in the moment, it is in the stories that have built up. The messages that have been fed to an individual or group. The narrative that has been woven for them as long as they can remember. If we want to pick apart these conflicts, then we need to pick apart the stories that have been fuelling them.

If we want to resolve our personal conflicts, then we must also tease apart the stories that have led us to that point. You might not get to the truth, or even very deep at all with the other person; but by at least considering what stories are running their lives, you have taken the first step.

Once you have done this and distanced yourself from the conflict, you have not only increased your perspective but dampened your emotions. You see conflict is not an intellectual, rational construct; it is an emotional, irrational construct. As Einstein said: "We cannot solve problems at the same level of thinking that created them". Neither can we solve conflict if we remain in the emotional state in which we created it. Once we have settled our emotions, we are then ready to work through the problem with the other party.

A framework that you can use to approach this problem is the G.U.C.E. framework. It is a four step process that can create the right energy for resolution and open the other person up to working constructively on the problem. The responsibility for this process begins with you and requires more of that perspective and humility we've been talking about.

Growth

The first step is to see conflict as an opportunity for growth. We are not just resolving conflict to be rid of the stress and pain it causes but because there can be an improved outcome on the other side of it. If we see conflict as a learning opportunity, it changes our attitude to it from one of dread to one of exploration. There are answers to find, if we take the time and effort to engage properly in the process.

I think Europe provides a great example of how conflict ultimately leads to something better. For centuries, countries in Europe waged war against each other. It was the central theatre of two world wars. After the second of those wars, it started to restructure and seek to find collaboration rather than conflict. It first created a common market, then a common political and economic organisation in the form of the European Union. Nearly every country in Europe is now a democracy, when monarchy, fascism and communism used to run many of them. When you look at the indexes for happiness, health and education, the top 30 countries on each index are predominantly European.

I'm not suggesting for a moment that the death and suffering experienced on this continent was "worth it" for the conditions that now exist. But what I am saying is that out of those terrible conditions, a better world was created. Much work is still required but progress has been made.

This is not to overdramatise your conflicts at all, but to provide a larger example of how your smaller conflict can lead to something better. Your conflict, if approached in the right way, can lead to growth. It might help you develop better communication, cooperation or confidence. When you approach a conflict with this mentality, you are already in a much better position to resolve it before a word is said.

Before you talk with the other person, begin with the end in mind. What do you want from this conversation? How do you want you and the other person to feel after it? What outcomes would you like to work towards? We take these steps to plan in the workplace but we seem to completely disregard this strategy when it comes to relationships. Start to think about what growth can be created from this encounter.

Understand

The second stage is to understand. The key distinction here is that you're not trying to make the other person understand you; you're seeking to understand them. This is not a fact proving mission; it's a fact finding mission.

What this means is little talking from you and much more listening. Listen to their side of the story and begin to understand where their disagreement is coming from.

When they have done so, run through your understanding of how they saw things. It doesn't matter if you don't agree with this version; you just outline their version of events to make sure you understand it.

Next, convey how that person felt. You might say "I can see you're angry" or "I can hear you're disappointed". This "convey" part is vital, this shows your empathy and helps show the other person you understand them.

Finally, you swallow some ego. You acknowledge that the other person's feelings are justified. Remember this isn't from your perspective. It's from theirs. And from their perspective, their feelings are justified. You can't argue with a feeling, so don't try.

Through these steps, you have demonstrated your understanding of the situation. If you are getting positive, affirming responses from the other person, this is going to make the next stage easier.

Common Ground

When two parties disagree, you have to begin to build the bridge using planks of common agreement. Look for the small things. There's a small piece of common ground that both can start to work from.

Start with broad statements such as: "we both want what is best for the kids" or "we both want this project to succeed". Then start to narrow it down, reinforcing agreement as much as you can. For example "we both agree that their education is a priority just now" or "we both agree that we need to diversify in this market."

Keep on narrowing down until you hit the point of disagreement. That is something you can start to work through when you've completed the GUCE process, but there's still one step to complete first.

Error

This is where humility comes in. You look for areas where you can admit error and admit you didn't get things right. This is the power of vulnerability. When you do this, you reduce the other party's defensiveness and you open the door to consideration and compromise.

A big part of admitting error is apologising. Mastering the art of a good apology is key to the process of resolving conflict, in particular, because this is where so many people screw up the process. Your apology needs to be full and sincere; otherwise it will never be accepted. An insincere apology can actually make the situation worse. So, here are the steps for apologising.

- Say the words "I am sorry". So many people apologise without using the word "sorry". Sorry is a word with a specific meaning, and thus a specific magic...use it.

- Say sorry for every single transgression. You say "I am sorry" for each of the actions you did wrong. You say "I am sorry" for all the negative feelings you gave the other person. You say "I am sorry" for any expectations or rules that you broke.

• Do not attempt to justify your actions. You are not defending yourself in a court of law: you are apologising to someone. Attempting to justify your actions removes the sincerity and power of your apology. Regardless of whether you shouted at someone because you were stressed at work, or because you just fancied being cruel, they are hurt just the same. The reasons behind your actions don't matter to them.

If you have worked through the GUCE process effectively, you have done everything in your power to apologise. If the other person recognises that, your apology will often be accepted.

The GUCE framework creates a congenial atmosphere in which an agreement can start to be reached. It may not happen immediately, so be patient. If one discussion doesn't create those outcomes you desired, then take a break. Give each side time to think over the problem some more. There may be some lingering emotion in the mix that needs time to dissipate.

John Gottman, psychologist and marriage counsellor, warns against "flooding". (25) Flooding is when our emotions start to run riot and our physiology changes; we start to drop into fight-or-flight mode. As soon as this happens, an attempt at a level, rational discussion is nearly impossible. When one person starts to feel flooding occur, it is vital that they announce this and you take a break from the discussion. If you catch it in time, a twenty-minute break can be enough to cool down and restart the discussion. Daniel Amen recommends "the bathroom break" at this point. (26)

The important part of the GUCE framework is that you are making the effort. You are walking 60% of the way across a bridge to someone. You are approaching the conflict with a growth-minded attitude: trying to understand their position; looking for shared views; and admitting your own faults. In my experience, if you approach someone 60% of the way, most people are willing to come the other 40% to meet you.

When you give someone the respect of the GUCE process, you can sometimes find yourself being GUCE'd back. That is when it is the time to possibly start looking at mitigating circumstances, to try and identify what caused the situation. However, you can only engage in that process with two rational minds. You need to defuse the emotion in the situation. With this framework, you can diffuse the emotion and create the conditions to resolve and grow from conflict.

Influence

Through understanding some basic principles about successful communication, you can vastly enhance the quality of your relationships, and your ability to Influence others. However, there is a step beyond Influence. It is the final component of the Author Your Life journey: your ability to Impact others. That is what we will cover in the next chapter.

In this chapter you have learned:

- How to effectively communicate without saying a word through good eye contact, use of hands, and your posture
- The importance of names, questions and stories for building the currency of interactions
- How to avoid conflict
- How to resolve conflict when it arises

My biggest takeaway from this chapter is

_____.

Chapter 12: Impact

"Service is the rent we pay for living on this Earth."- Nathan Eldon Tanner

This is where the Author Your Life journey has been leading you. The journey up until this point has been largely self-centred. It has focused on *your* happiness, *your* purpose, *your* relationships. However, if you stop the journey here, you will not be a complete individual. You will not live a life of fulfilment. As long as you serve yourself, you will always feel like there is something missing. This chapter is the longest in this book because of one fundamental truth. When you have changed your story, you then need to change someone else's. In this chapter, you are going to learn how to do that.

Part 1: The Secret to Living

Tony Robbins, the famous seminar leader and life coach (did you know Robbins was the person who invented the term "life coach"? (1)) describes a difficult time in his life when he was struggling to make ends meet. He didn't have money for food, fuel or rent.

Robbins had loaned a friend $1200 and he was desperately calling his friend, telling him he needed the money back, but his friend wasn't returning Robbins' calls.

Robbins finds himself with just $25 left. He takes this money to an all-you-can-eat to get as much food as he can. As Robbins is eating, he sees a little boy about eight years old come in wearing a suit. He opens the door behind him for his mother and pulls out her seat to let her sit down. There was something about the boy's demeanour that really captured Robbins' attention. He was moved by the young man so he went and paid $7 for his all-you-can-eat and walked up to the little boy.

"Excuse me," Robbins says, "I just want to acknowledge you for being such an extraordinary gentleman. I saw the way you treated your lady; how you opened the door; how you pulled the chair out. That's class. My name's Tony, what's yours?" They shake hands and the boy introduces himself.

"That's amazing," Robbins continues, "taking your date out for a lunch like this."

"Actually," the boy says, "that's my mom. I'm not taking her to lunch, I'm only eight."

"Yes you are," Robbins said. Before he could even think about it, he reached into his pocket and gave the boy all the money he had left. "You're taking her to lunch." The boy's eyes lit up and Robbins turned and walked away.

Robbins flew out of the restaurant, even though he had just given away all the money he had left. He flew because he had given even when he had so little to give.

The next day, when Robbins has no idea where his next meal is going to come from, a letter arrives in the mail. It's from the friend he loaned money to. The friend apologises for avoiding Robbins, thanks him for the generosity, and encloses the $1200, plus an extra $100 for the bother.

From that experience, a phrase came to Robbins: "The Secret to Living is Giving". (2)

What Robbins understood in that moment was a fundamental truth about life. Life lacks meaning if we make it just about us. We will not experience true fulfilment unless we give to others.

From that moment on, Robbins aimed to give, even when it felt like he had nothing to give. He realised that we never lose anything we give away. With this shift in mentality, suddenly his life started to turn around. His financial situation improved and so did his impact. This trend continued over the decades until he reached the heights he has today.

The first way we can change someone's story is through giving: we can give things, time, information, expertise and experience. There are many different ways we can enrich the life of someone else. In this part of the chapter, we are going to explore some of the principles of giving and some of the surprising results you may find yourself creating through giving.

Scratch my back and...

Consider a scenario. You're struggling with a project at work. One of your colleagues sees your distress and provides you with a key piece of information that helps you not only complete the project but also earns praise from your boss. In what way do you view your colleague's help?

A) Phew, my colleague's information was really useful there. I'll have to find out what else they can help me with.

B) Man, they really got me out of a pickle there. I owe them a big one.

C) Wow, with the right information, you can really make a difference to someone's project. I'm going to see if I can help someone out in the department in the same way.

Your answer to this question points to your giving value.

If you answered A, you are a *Taker*. You like to get more than you give. You put your own needs ahead of others. You likely believe that the world is a competitive place and you need to do whatever you can to get ahead. You have to prove you're better than others. This doesn't necessarily mean you don't care about others (although at the extreme end of the spectrum, it does) rather you are cautious and self-protective. Takers do help others, but only strategically, when the benefits of helping outweigh the costs.

If you answered B, you are a *Matcher*. I suspect many of you reading this will have answered B. In our society, we have a value of fairness and reciprocity. If someone does a good turn for us, we see ourselves as indebted to them. We try to repay this favour if we can. That is the essence of being a Matcher: you try to "match" the good deeds of others, to make sure you are always even with others. Matchers keep score. They don't like to be in debt to someone. Equally, when they help someone, they will expect something in return.

If you answered C, you are a *Giver*. A Giver tries to pay it forward. If a good deed is done for them, they try to pass on the benefit of that good deed to someone else. This isn't to say that they don't appreciate the favour that's been done for them but they don't feel guilty about passing on that good deed to another person rather than back to the original individual. In the Matcher relationship, the good deeds are contained between two people. With the Giver mentality, the goodness ripples out to many more people. Givers give when the benefits to the other person outweigh the personal costs.

These three attitudes come from the work of Adam Grant, a professor at Wharton Business school. (3) In his work, he has examined how the wealthiest, most powerful people have reached the top of their fields.

How do you think they got there? Do you think they accumulated great wealth by taking it from others or by giving it to others? Do you think they got to the top by pushing people down or lifting people up?

The answers are obvious aren't they? They couldn't acquire all that wealth by giving it away. You can't add by subtracting. Therefore they have to make sure they're always getting more than they're giving.

You also can't get to the top by putting more people above you, by increasing the competition for yourself. You can't get to the top of the staircase by building more steps. Therefore, they have to be stepping around, over and on people in order to rise up.

For that reason, Givers appear on the bottom of the success ladder. Grant's research has found that they are less productive (4) and less wealthy (5) than Matchers and Takers. The Givers literally give away their success, whilst the Matchers and Takers accumulate it, and rise to the top.

An obvious, clear-cut conclusion isn't it? Which is why, like most myths, this conclusion is wrong. There aren't many things that are clear cut and obvious in the world and Grant's research demonstrates this.

Although the research found that Givers were at the bottom of the success ladder, it was not Matchers or Takers who were at the top. *It was actually Givers again.* (6) Givers were at the bottom and the top of the ladder. How does this work?

The difference is whether they are a selfless giver, or an "otherish" giver. Selfless Givers give with no thought to their own wellbeing. They say yes to everything. They are people pleasers and they burn themselves out. Barbara Oakley has described this as "pathological altruism" which is "an unhealthy focus on others to the detriment of one's own needs." (7) It is these Givers who are exploited, overworked and overwhelmed at the bottom of the success ladder.

"Otherish" Givers, however, do look after their own needs. They do have self-interest and personal ambitions. Additionally, they have an equal desire to help and serve others. The best expression that I've heard to describe otherish giving come from a conversation I had with a student at one of my seminars.

They said: "When you pour from your own cup, your cup quickly becomes empty, and you have no more to give. However, when you keep pouring into your cup, your cup overflows and fills the cup of others."

Otherish Givers know that to be of greatest service, they also have to look after themselves. They intertwine self-interest and other-interest. When you ask an Otherish Giver what their goals are, they will list nearly twice as many goals related to others than a comparison group. However, they will also list 20% more goals related to themselves than the comparison group. (8) Otherish Givers are ambitious and strive for excellence for themselves as well as others. It is these individuals who rise to the top of the success ladder.

We'll cover how to avoid being a selfless Giver and evolve into an otherish Giver later in the chapter. First let's dig a little deeper into the myth of Taking. We hear all these expressions: "Nice guys finish last", "You've got to look out for number one" and "It's a dog-eat-dog world" that suggests that the only way to survive and get ahead is to be a Taker. Why don't Takers end up on top?

Adam Grant did find prominent examples of Takers who had risen to the top. He found that developing proficiency in being a Taker, under the guise of a Matcher or Giver, can generate big success. However, such success is often volatile and fleeting.

Take for example, Ken Lay. Lay's company, Enron, was one of the most respected companies in America. That was until leaks of widespread corporate malpractice emerged, stock prices plummeted, and the company went bankrupt, all under Lay's watch.

Ken Lay pretended to be a Giver, he enlisted in the Navy and won the National Defence Service Medal, he set up a charitable family foundation that gave over $2.5 million to 250 organisations and made political donations to both George Bush senior and junior.

However, at Enron, Ken Lay had taken personal loans out of the company, used corporate jets for family trips and used political donations and bribes to seek energy deregulation laws. (9) When George W. Bush was running for governor of Texas in 1994, he asked Lay to chair his finance campaign. At this point, Bush was the underdog in the polls and Lay declined, instead serving for the Democratic incumbent Ann Richards. He made a donation of $12,500 "just in case" to Bush. When the polls shifted, and it looked like Bush was now going to win, Lay made another donation of $12,500, seeking political favour with the future governor. (10)

Speaking of American Presidents, a more contemporary example of a successful Taker would be Donald Trump. In 2007, Donald Trump came to my hometown of Aberdeen, Scotland to build a Trump Golf Resort. The area he chose was Balmedie Beach, an area of conservation and protected wildlife. The Scottish government, the Scottish National Party (SNP), were eager to accommodate him. They saw Trump as a marquee name to bring to Scotland, an enterprising businessman who recognised Scotland's potential as an up and coming nation (The SNP were pushing for an independence referendum for Scotland to leave the United Kingdom. This vote occurred in September 2014, a narrow 55% to 45% decision to remain in the UK).

Less than a decade later, Trump won a shock election to become President of the USA. This was an election characterised by a number of extreme Taker behaviours: misogynistic comments, exploitation of social media and suspected collaboration with a foreign government.

Scotland's government, still the SNP, widely condemned Trump's policies and behaviour. Trump became the president of America but has overseen the biggest downturn in foreign relations (11) and the lowest approval rating of any president. (12)

So you can get to the top by taking, conniving and bulldozing. However, can you stay there? Grant's research has found that if you want sustained success, then it is the Givers who last over the long term. Consider Bill Gates, often ranking as the world's richest person despite his huge philanthropic efforts. Think of Muhammed Ali, who risked his athletic career to protest against war. Picture Nelson Mandela, who offered the Afrikaners who had overseen his oppression seats in his government.

As alluded to earlier, giving may be the path to success, but it can also be the path to failure if you're not careful.

The Empty Cup

As Grant's research has found — and as I'm sure you've found — over-giving can be tiring. When you're a Giver, or aspiring to be one, there is a temptation to throw yourself into giving. You end up helping everyone with everything and running around like a headless chicken. That isn't helping anyone. It's not helping you, because you're stressed out and will end up resentful of the help you're giving. It also isn't helping the people you are serving, because you are not giving them your full attention and energy to help them to your fullest capacity.

How can you avoid over-helping and being a selfless rather than an otherish Giver? One way is to quantify the amount of time and energy you devote to yourself and the amount you devote to others. One strategy you can use is the 50/50 rule. You spend half of your time doing things for yourself: career advancement, self-care, hobbies and recreation. The other half you spend doing things for other people: mentoring, volunteering and taking part in the recreational choices of your friends and family.

This can be a broad-brush stroke strategy to readdress an imbalance you might have in your life, either extreme self-focus or extreme-other focus. However, not all things can be so easily quantified as "self" or "other".

I'm writing this book for you but I also enjoy the writing process. This might appear to be an "other" activity but I'm choosing to write this particular part of the chapter on a Saturday morning, suggesting this is a "self" activity.

Alternatively, I consider my morning exercise routine to be something I do for my own health and wellbeing. However, I also notice that

I'm more productive and serve to a higher level during the day after I've exercised. This is a "self" activity that has "other" benefits.

So avoiding Giver burnout is not as simple as a 50/50 split. Where is the nuance? Again Adam Grant's research is suggesting that it is why and how we give that matters.

One way we get burned out is if we don't receive recognition for our giving. When you have a giving mentality, you do so because you are motivated by the change you create in people. If you can't see that change, it makes you feel like you are giving into a vacuum. You are expending the effort but aren't seeing the reward.

This is a reason why there is a high level of burnout in two service-driven industries: education (13) and medicine (14). The effect that teachers have on the development of students might not be apparent for many years. Additionally, with some students, it may seem like nothing is sinking in for them at all. A similar phenomenon can be observed in medical professionals. They too may not see the effects of their care in the short term, nor be able to see any apparent effect of their treatment.

There are two methods to combat such giving fatigue. The first is to make the effects of your giving more obvious. Researchers in Israel achieved this in a simple way. They found that they could improve the diagnostic accuracy of radiologists by 46% simply by attaching a photograph of the patient to the report. The radiologists' reports were 29% longer when the photograph was included. (15) When the radiologists could see the photograph, they could see who they were fighting for. This enhanced their motivation and reason for giving.

A simple study was carried out by Adam Grant in a university call centre. The callers were required to call university alumni and ask for donations. Grant measured each worker to see if they had a Taker, Matcher or Giver mentality and found that the Givers were the worst performers. Takers were securing three times as many donations as Givers.

That was until Grant got each worker to read letters from students who had received scholarships that had been funded by the callers' work. Just like the radiologists, the callers now had an idea of who they were fighting for. The Givers' donations tripled as a result of these letters. When Grant arranged for the callers to meet a scholarship recipient in person, those donations quintupled. (16)

As these results demonstrate, fatigue decreases and performance increases simply by rekindling the prime motivation for giving: the results on the beneficiary of the giving. To reduce giving fatigue for yourself, think how you can make the results of your work more visible. That could be having photographs of the people you're fighting for in view. That could be following up with clients you've helped. That could be collating a journal of every statement of gratitude and appreciation you've received and rereading them when you feel demotivated.

How we give is also important. When looking at Givers who are the least productive and least happy, they usually give in a "sprinkling" fashion: giving little and often. When looking at Givers who are the most productive and happy, they give in a "chunking" fashion: giving substantially but less frequently. (17) Sprinklers often tend to give in to the demands of others, allowing themselves to become reactive to the needs of others at the expense of their own needs. Chunkers, on the other hand, proactively plan their helping so that they can create a greater impact.

The first step to being a good chunker is to find one cause you are passionate about. Don't raise money for an animal charity if that is not a cause you are passionate about. Equally, don't try to save the world. There are many things we may want to change in the world but we can't fight every fire. Pick one cause that you can really invest your time and resources into.

Secondly, block out time to work on this cause, even if it is just an hour a week. For that hour, that cause gets your full attention (as we discussed in the chapter on Performance). Reduce the minor but consistent commitments you perform during the week for your family, your friends and your community. If you are going to give to these areas, give in larger, less frequent chunks.

You may find this second part difficult as other people attempt to fill up your agenda with their agenda. Effective giving is not just about managing your own agenda, it is also about learning to moderate the agendas of other people. There's a difference between being a Giver and a sucker and that is what we will explore more in the next segment.

How to not be a Sucker

What we have observed in Adam Grant's research is that whilst some Givers rise to the top of the ladder, it is also Givers that languish at the bottom. These are the selfless givers who do not look after their own needs too. They give compulsively whenever it is demanded of them. This quickly leads to fatigue and burnout as we've discussed.

Another key reason that Givers can sink to the bottom is if they allow themselves to be exploited. We've all been stung in the past by chancers, manipulators, and the ignorant. You may remember earlier in the book I shared how I loaned £2000 to a friend and never got paid back. I got exploited by a Taker and didn't take the steps I could've to protect myself. This can be a big barrier to our giving behaviour. We ask "why would I give when I'm just going to be taken advantage of?" and rightly so.

When we give on demand we are not being generous, we're being a sucker. In this part of the chapter, we're going to look at how you can still be a Giver but not get burned out or stung in the process.

Burnout is likely to occur when we feel compelled or obligated to give. We are not giving through our own motivations, so we are out of alignment. If we are doing a job because we need the money rather than because we genuinely enjoy the service we are providing, we are more likely to get burned out. If we are loaded with extra tasks by our boss that we don't enjoy, we are more likely to get burned out.

Earlier I gave the example of writing this book and how it was something I was doing both for myself and others. The key nuance is that I am choosing to write this book. I can do anything I want this Saturday morning and it is my choice to spend it writing. Writing this book is aligned with my values, motivation and desires. That is why it is simultaneously a "self" and "other" activity. When we are engaged in giving that is aligned in this way, we are much less likely to get burned out.

One way to protect against burnout is to avoid obligated giving as much as possible. We set boundaries in our relationships as to how much we are going to do for people. We don't just become a doormat for people's agendas and needs. We learn how to say no politely and firmly. One great strategy I've learned from Cal Newport is to make your "No" definite, and your reasons vague. (18) For example, look at a typical no we might give:

"I can't do that sorry. I'm too busy preparing the presentation for next week, and I'm going to my sister's wedding at the weekend."

When you say no in this manner, you give the other person specific targets to argue against. They might say in response:

"It will only take half an hour or so. The presentation's not until next week. You could do it before the wedding's started, or not drink too much at the wedding and you can do it the next day."

So begins a back and forth debate where you get more guilty and the other person gets more resentful. This usually ends with you caving to the request. If you keep on caving to requests in this manner, you are in a state of obligated giving.

Instead, consider this response: *"I can't do that sorry, my schedule is full."*

With this type of response, you kill the topic dead. It's a definite no and the other person hasn't really got anything to pick apart. They can't debate your schedule being full without outright accusing you of lying. One or two obnoxious people will try their luck in this regard but most people will admit defeat and accept your No.

As a Giver, we often try to appease people when we are letting them down so that we don't hurt their feelings. However, what often happens is instead we provide the opportunity for the other person to guilt trip us into turning our "no" into a "yes". You have to be able to protect your giving so you don't burn yourself out.

With this in mind, a second important point Newport adds is to not get guilt-tripped into offering a consolation prize that is going to take away nearly as much time and effort as the original request. For example: "I won't have time to work on the presentation with you but feel free to send me over the final draft and I'll look over it for you." No means no.

Learning how to say no can be a real challenge for a Giver. It clashes with both your conditioning to be polite and your morality of being help- ful. Despite this, the research shows that otherish Givers are good at decid- ing when not to give. They have a keen warning system against people who are trying to exploit them.

Generally speaking, we are poor judges of a person's intentions. A key mistake we often make is to confuse politeness with trustworthiness. If someone is a smooth talker, well-mannered and shows an interest in us, we assume we can trust them. However, that is the exact front that someone who wants to exploit us will present.

There are a couple of signs that can help you see through the veneer, however, what I call "peacocking". When peacocks are looking to attract a mate, they spread their tails wide, trying to attract as much attention and admiration as they can. Takers cannot help but do their own "peacocking".

If someone is looking to promote their own interests, they will struggle to fully hide their sense of self-importance.

The first way you can spot a Taker is through their use of pronouns. Takers will make it much more about "I" and "me" than "you" and "we". They will take unrelated tangents in conversations to talk about themselves. A study of CEO interviews in the computer industry found that the CEOs of computer companies used first person pronouns 21% of the time on average. However, CEOs who displayed Taker tendencies used such pronouns 39% of the time. (19)

A second way you can spot a Taker is though the types of questions they ask. If they ask questions related to themselves, that is evidence they are a Taker, rather than asking questions about others. It is not necessarily what they ask, but the way they ask it. Consider these two questions:

1. "Do you have any suggestions for how I could improve my marketing copy so I can get more money?"

2. "Do you have any suggestions for how I could improve my marketing copy to reach more people?"

The questions are asking for the same information. In fact both use the pronoun "I". However, I'm sure you know which one a Taker would be more likely to ask. In the first question, the person is implying they care more about money than service. Their primary motivation is their bottom line. In the second question, they are implying they care more about service than money. Their primary motivation is making an impact. The type of answer someone is looking for when they ask you a question can provide a clue as to their intentions.

The third way you can spot a Taker is how they treat people they consider to be superiors compared to how they treat people they consider to be inferiors. Takers will often be ingratiating and engaged with people they can get something from, but dismissive and rude to those who can't do anything for them.

Observe the way that people treat shopkeepers, waiting staff and drivers on public transport. Observe how they treat employees under their management. Observe their reaction if they find out there is something you can't help them with. When a Taker feels in the "one-up" position, they will display subtle changes in their behaviour and reactions that you can pick up on.

What can you do if you spot a peacocker? Someone who you are cautious about trusting. What successful Givers are able to do is adapt their giving behaviour. They will move into strategic matching if they smell trouble. (20) They will repay a good deed or favour if it comes their way but will not jump into making the first move. They are willing to be proven wrong, if someone looks like they are genuine and are actually a Matcher or a Giver, then they will switch back into giving. However, they will stay cautious and guarded, especially if Taker tendencies are confirmed. When you feel under threat, or have suspicions about someone, use matching as a defence mechanism to protect yourself.

In this part of the chapter, you have learned about the importance of giving. When you look at the top, you find Givers, not Takers. However, if you look to the bottom, you will also find Givers. That is where you can end up if you do not give effectively, if you allow yourself to become burned out and exploited. Successful Givers also look out for themselves as well as others, that is what allows them to be more effective. If you want to be an effective Giver, you must do the same.

Part 2: The Strongest Passion

Creating an Impact does not have to be about giving things or opportunities to people. Neither does it have to mean inspiring and motivating others to greater things. Consider individuals such as Mother Theresa and the Dalai Lama. The tangible results of their impact are not on the scale of a global business or revolutionary social change but most people would agree that they are hugely impactful individuals. This is because their method of Impact is compassion. It is bringing love, kindness and forgiveness into the world. In a world that is experiencing strife, anger and bitterness, you can do a lot to impact it in this way. That is why I say the strongest form of passion is compassion.

Day of Kindness

There are many things we can give, and embrace the Giver mentality. However, sometimes we don't have the expertise, information, resources or time that could really benefit someone. What can we give then? What is always available is to share part of our inner goodness with them. To give them the power of kindness.

Kindness is frequently viewed through a moral, ethical, or spiritual lens. It is seen as something we should do because it is the right thing to do. "Treat others as you'd want to be treated", "Love thy neighbour", "What would happen if everyone did it" are common mantras in this regard. I don't disagree here at all. Our world could sure use a lot more kindness right now. But why aren't more people doing it? Perhaps they could be encouraged to begin by realising what's in it for them.

You see, the kinder we are, the happier we become. Kindness is one of twelve scientifically-backed practices identified by Sonja Lyubomirsky as increasing our happiness. (21) Kindness is not just great for the other person, it is great for us too. When you perform acts of kindness, you begin to view yourself as an altruistic and compassionate person. This new identity can promote a sense of confidence, optimism and usefulness. (22)

As we covered earlier in the chapter, we must be smart with our giving. Lyubomirsky has found that kind acts can make us happier...but only when done in a certain way. She ran a study with two groups. One group were told to perform five kind acts over the course of the next week. The second group were asked to perform five kind acts but they had to choose a single day to do it on.

What Lyubomirsky found was that performing kind acts did increase happiness but only for the group who performed those five acts on a single day. The group who had spread them throughout the week did not display any increases in happiness. (23)

This research adds evidence that "chunking" our giving is better than "sprinkling" it. When the kind acts were performed throughout the week, they got lost in the other activities during the day. However, when performed in the one day, they had an accumulative effect where the results of that kindness were felt more strongly.

Lyubomirsky and her team have found another important nuance to kindness. They ran another study which again used two groups. One group were asked to pick three kind acts and perform those acts each week for ten weeks. The second group performed three kind acts for ten weeks but could vary and change what those three acts were. The first group actually reported a dip in their happiness during the study. Doing the same acts over and over was not rewarding, it was tedious. (24)

From Lyubomirsky's research we can see that we should concentrate our kindness, rather than scatter it randomly. Additionally, we should vary this happiness rather than repeat the same acts.

Therefore, what I recommend is picking a "kindness day". One day of the week you designate for kind acts, small or large. Buy a coffee for the person behind you in the queue. Buy another hot drink and give it to someone sleeping on the streets. Take time during your lunch break to mentor a young colleague. Give a lonely member of the family a phone call. Keep an eye and an ear out for every opportunity during the day to be kind to someone.

If you are aiming to be kinder, what sounds like an easier change to make? Being kinder on one day of the week, or seven? The former right? It is a smaller commitment, making it more manageable and feasible. You are more likely to follow through on it and stick to it. That is why I recommend setting a designated day. It creates a sense of fun and novelty to your kindness, as you think up and plan new ways to be kind on that day.

Let's examine some more ways that you can expand your kindness practice.

Volunteer

One particularly effective way of maximising your kindness day is to volunteer. Surveys of volunteers show that volunteering is associated with diminished depressive symptoms and enhanced feelings of happiness, self-worth, mastery and personal control — a "helper's high". (25)

Furthermore, volunteering might also make you smarter. You want to be around volunteers because they tend to be more educated and successful people. In the US, almost 40% of those over the age of twenty-five who have a bachelor's degree or higher volunteer. That compares with 15.6% of high school graduates and 8.1% who have less than a high school diploma. (26)

Volunteering fulfils the "chunking" giving that characterises fulfilled Givers. Individuals who volunteer between 100 and 800 hours per year are happier and more satisfied than those who volunteer less than 100 or more than 800. (27) However, no extra benefit has been found beyond 100 hours. (28) This suggests that there is a "sweet spot" at 100 hours per year, which is just two hours a week. This can easily be chunked into your "kindness day". Research shows that volunteering two hours a week increases self-esteem and life satisfaction. (29)

Leave your comfort zone

To expand your kindness, try a kind act that doesn't come naturally. For example if you are normally shy and reserved, try speaking to a homeless person. If you are the opposite and can never keep your mouth shut, take the time to listen to someone's problems without offering commentary and advice.

I also recommend doing a kind deed where you don't tell anyone and don't expect anything in return. Yes there is self-interest in kindness but can you really move past that and give purely for the other person? To seek no reward or recognition for the act but just to make the world a better place? Although we have focused on the effect of kindness for personal happiness, it is important to remember that kindness has an effect that extends far beyond us.

The Ripple Effect

Research has found that when someone is the recipient of a kind act, then levels of their chemical oxytocin rises (remember oxytocin is a chemical linked to trust and connection, that "warm fuzzy feeling"). It's not too surprising to think that when someone is kind to us, we feel more trust and connection towards them. (30)

It's also not hugely surprising that in the person performing the kind act, their oxytocin also increases. You know you get a warm fuzzy feeling when you do something nice for someone. To be kind to someone is us showing that we feel connected to them in some way, it's unsurprising our neurochemicals agree. (31)

However, what research has found is that in someone watching the act, neither giving or receiving, levels of their oxytocin also increase. (32) After someone has witnessed a kind act, the good feeling they get makes them want to go and perform one themselves. (33) This is the ripple effect being scientifically observed. In fact, kindness is highly contagious, and its effect can spread up to three degrees of separation away from us. (34)

Metta

"Metta" is Sanskrit for "loving kindness". In Buddhism metta is the wish for all sentient beings to have happiness and its causes. To cultivate this, Buddhists have a special "loving kindness" meditation that they perform.

In this meditation, the meditator focuses on someone they care about, such as a parent, sibling or partner. You send this person wishes of well-being and to be freed from suffering. The meditator allows their mind to be filled with this feeling and lets it spread to all sentient beings.

If you remember earlier in the book we talked about the study into expert meditators and how they recorded gamma activity that was off the charts. The type of meditation they performed to generate this was loving kindness meditation. As well as this high gamma activity, activity in the insula and temporoparietal junction was also noticeably high. The insula is involved in bodily signals associated with emotion and the temporoparietal junction is important for empathy. Not only this, there was a long-term training effect observed in the monks. Doing this meditation repeatedly was making them more kind and empathic. (35) Loving kindness meditation helps us to get in touch with our own emotions more and to get in touch more with the emotions of others.

You might infer from this that loving kindness makes us more sensitive and thus more vulnerable. However, the scans revealed the opposite. The study found that this meditation dampens down amygdala activation in response to seeing images of suffering. What this suggests is that the meditation helps you connect more with a person who is suffering but the negative effects of that suffering do not transfer onto you.

I like to practice Metta in a lighter form. As I'm going about my day I pick two people who I see out and about and I take 30-60 seconds to send them good thoughts. This is my adaption of a practice Tim Ferriss outlines in his book *"Tools of Titans"*, where he recommends secretly wishing two other people to be happy for ten seconds, then repeating that eight times. (36) It is randomly sending people kind thoughts for no good reason. You are not necessarily wishing them well because you feel some kind of sympathy for them, an affinity with them, or a liking for them. You're doing it purely to operate from a place of kindness.

This practice might seem highly "woo-woo" but it seems to have some tangible results. Sonja Lyubomirsky has shown us that even when we perceive ourselves as being kinder, we are happier. (37) Ferriss reports some feedback he received from teaching this exercise:

"I attended your talk on Monday, and did the homework on Tuesday, and Tuesday was my happiest day in seven years." (38)

As Ferriss says, achieving a peak experience like this with a practice that takes eighty seconds total is pretty phenomenal. I'm always interested to see what practices and principles have stood the test of time, and the Buddhist concept of "Metta" has been going strong for thousands of years. Bring a bit of Metta into your life and you may be surprised at the peak experiences you enjoy.

Part 3: The Everyday Leader

As soon as you saw the word "Leader", some of you reading this would have recoiled. "I'm not a leader, why are we talking about leadership?" Some of you may have glazed over: "I'm not a leader, this doesn't apply to me."

Well that is why the title is "The Everyday Leader". Because we are all leaders in life. A leader is someone who inspires others. A leader is someone who others look up to. Yep, that makes you a leader. You might not think you inspire others, but you certainly can, if you aren't already (and you probably are, you just don't know it). You might not think others look up to you, but they certainly can, again if they aren't already.

Robin Sharma calls this "The Leader Who Had No Title." (39) You see we have a myth in our society that leadership comes with a mark of rank. You need to be a team captain, a department manager or even an "alpha male" to be considered a leader. Well, when you help your friend through a challenging time, you are a leader. When you provide guidance on a work project, you are a leader. When you have a child, you are a leader.

Rank has nothing to do with being a leader. Did you have a team captain on a school sports team who's idea of "leadership" was chastising and belittling others? Did you have a manager who couldn't lead a party in a brewery? Did you have a parent who was absent and unhelpful? Just because they had a title, this did not give them leadership qualities.

You can choose to be a leader at any time. When someone is in need of leadership, you provide service by being a leader for them. Numerous experts and scientists have provided frameworks for leadership. Some of these frameworks are applied in the business sphere, some in athletics, some in politics. These frameworks might have limited transferability out-side of these domains, but what is apparent are certain common principles that are applicable to everyday leadership. These principles I outline be-low.

<u>Responsibility</u>

One of the core tenets of a leader is how they take responsibility. It is not just taking charge of their actions, it is an unshakeable realisation that they have influence over everything in their life. If there is something they don't like; something that has gone wrong; someone who has screwed up; then they don't blame, they don't vent and they don't make excuses. They take what Jocko Willink calls "Extreme Ownership." (40)

Willink is a former Navy SEAL commander who served in Iraq in 2006. His squad were located in Ramadi, at the time the most volatile city in Iraq with a ruthless and co-ordinated guerrilla insurgent force. Willink learned a number of leadership principles in this theatre, but the foremost was Extreme Ownership. In such a volatile and unpredictable environment, Willink recognised that he could allow himself to be dictated by external circumstances very easily: to blame squad members; get angry at cowardly enemy tactics; or curse the nature of the warfare.

Instead, he took Extreme Ownership. If a squad member had not car-ried out an order, it was Willink's fault for not communicating it effective-ly. If an IED caused damage and death, it was Willink's fault for not being more cautious. If his soldiers were struggling to adapt to urban, guerrilla warfare, then Willink had not devised appropriate tactics.

Willink realised that no good comes of pointing fingers and making excuses. He might not have full control over all the variables but he still had the ability to influence them. This is how we can view responsibility: having the ability to respond.

This is what great leaders do. They always trust and believe in their ability to improve circumstances. They still have faith when the faith of people around them runs out.

Linked to this sense of personal responsibility is a deep humility. You might think that believing you have control over everything demands a swollen ego but in fact it is the opposite. If you are to take responsibility for all the errors and mistakes, that is something someone with a large ego cannot handle. It is in fact the individuals with ego who cannot embrace Extreme Ownership, as they refuse to accept anything that makes them look inadequate or fallible.

One example of this humility that sticks in my mind is Nelson Mandela. In 2000, Nelson was invited onto the Oprah Winfrey Show. When he arrived into the studio, Mandela asked the producer: "Could you tell me please, what is the subject of today's show?". The producer looked at him in disbelief: "Mr Mandela, you are the subject of today's show." (41) Nelson was so detached from his ego that he could not see why anyone would want to base a television show around him.

It is this detachment that allows leaders to do their work. Leadership is a selfless task. We often see leadership as a boon, bringing accolades and status, but leadership is about duty and sacrifice. Leadership, Simon Sinek tells us: "is not a license to do less; it is a responsibility to do more." (42)

Leadership does bring benefits but these benefits are necessary for the responsibility, not surplus to it. If we look to ancestral hierarchy (and to the hierarchy still practiced in the animal kingdom) there was an "alpha" in the group. The alpha enjoyed the best pick of food and first choice of mates. But this was not for the alpha's selfish gains: it was for the benefit of the group.

The alpha, who was stronger and better fed, was expected by the group to be the first to rush into danger to protect the tribe (responsibility: "the ability to respond"). They were granted first choice of mates because it was beneficial for the group to have the alpha's strong genes being reproduced. (43)

Ultimately, leadership is about being a role model. Would you hire a personal trainer who was overweight? I doubt it. You'd look at them and say: "If you can't do it for yourself, how can you possibly do it for me?".

A key lesson that I learned about being a role model comes from my work with children. One truth that I have observed over and over again is that children don't do as you say, they do as you do. Children in this sense understand leadership far better than we do.

Have you tried telling a child to eat healthy? *Eat more fruit and veg. Don't drink sugary drinks.* Our doctors and schools are constantly banging this message home. How is that working? Our childhood obesity statistics are a disgrace, because the children are not having healthy eating modelled for them. They don't care about statistics: they care about example.

When I was working in a school, I sat in the wellbeing base with the pupils during lunchtime. Whilst they were buying burgers and chips from the school canteen, I was bringing in a packed lunch of a salad; grilled fish and vegetables; or a homemade curry. The children would look at my meals in bemusement.

"What is that?" they would ask. I would tell them. I would point out the different ingredients and tell them why they were good for you. I never told the pupils they should eat what I was eating. I never told them why their meals were unhealthy. I focused on the positive benefits of what I was doing. I told them how I got up at five in the morning to meditate and go to the gym before coming to school.

This was a bit of a culture shock to some of the pupils, who had never seen a piece of spinach before (I'm not exaggerating here!). They would return to their burgers and chips with ponderous frowns.

As time went on, however, a funny thing began to happen. The pupils began to recognise the ingredients in my food. They could remember why they were good for you. One day, one of them asked if they could try a bit of spinach. A couple of the children then started to make their own packed lunches. No longer did they have sandwiches, crisps and biscuits. I was now seeing potatoes, lightly seasoned chicken and green beans.

Those children had been fed lectures and pie charts for over half a decade and had it got them to change? No. I managed to create that change in just a couple of months. What did I do differently? Nothing.

The children didn't do as they were told, they did as they were shown. This is why as everyday leaders, we have a huge responsibility to monitor our actions. How can a parent tell their children not to smoke with any credibility when they have a cigarette in their mouth? How can you tell a friend that they are drinking too much when you are sharing a bottle of wine with them? How can a manager tell you to work harder when you see them idling about in their office?

If you cannot lead yourself, how can you hope to lead others? We've covered leading yourself in huge depth through the sections on Consciousness and Calling but I feel it is worth reiterating here. In my industry, I see a number of coaches and speakers who are not credible leaders. Not because they are not nice people. Not because they lack any genuine desire to help people. But because they are not practicing what they preach; they are not teaching from a deep foundation of integrity. If you don't fully embody and believe in a message, why should the people you are delivering that message to?

I hear a speaker talk about confidence but their voice cracks and their hand shakes. I hear a consultant talk about organisation yet they are late when meeting me for coffee. I read a coach's book and they write about not seeking social validation but their Instagram is a string of carefully polished and filtered selfies.

I don't intend for these observations to be unkind. What I am saying is that if we want to lead people, then we need to step our game up. As Gandhi said, we have to be the change we want to see in the world. This is something I have had to work hard on too. When I first started my business, I could be too preachy and forceful with my message, rather than embracing my values of love and compassion. I could focus too much on myself, my story, and my accolades rather than embracing my values of giving and service. I had to work on living from my values more and leading by example, rather than by lip-service.

As an everyday leader, this is your responsibility too. Are you the role model you want to be for your children, your colleagues, your romantic partner? If you want to inspire them to be better people, then you must first take responsibility.

Persuasion

We rounded off talking about responsibility by saying that you lead by what you do, not what you say. This is true, but that is not to imply that what we say has no bearing at all. The power of a leader's words can send shivers down our spine. We have all had leaders who moved and inspired us through the power of their words.

Most of us had that teacher at school who seemed to know how to awaken enthusiasm in us. Most of us had a caregiver who knew how to stop us feeling upset. Most have been with a partner who encouraged us to stick at something.

Leaders convince us to take a path we weren't planning on travelling or to go further down that path than we thought was possible. This is not, as many would believe, a matter of "charisma". It is not some voodoo magic. It is not psychological mind tricks (although this is the closest explanation).

Leaders simply understand, whether innately or through learning, what motivates people. They understand how to speak to a person's needs and desires. If someone stimulates these core components for you, you will follow them.

This is all persuasion is. It can sometimes have darker connotations of tricking someone or making them act against their morals or intentions. What persuasion really is, is activating someone's needs. Now of course you can do this with noble intentions or less than noble intentions.

You can use it to get a woman to sleep with you by targeting her insecurities or you can help her overcome those insecurities. You can win an election by targeting people's fears or you can address those fears. You can threaten your employees to get work done or you can make them better workers. You can be a Taker or you can be a Giver.

To introduce persuasion, I'd like to recount an Aesop's fable. In this fable, the Sun and the Wind have an argument about who is most powerful. Unable to settle the argument with words, they agree to a contest. They see a man below them walking with his jacket on. They decide that whoever can get the man to take his jacket off will be the most powerful.

The Wind takes the first turn. He begins with a strong breeze that whips and snaps the man's jacket. The man grabs the jacket and pulls it into his body. The Wind, frustrated, blows harder and sends a gale towards the man. The man struggles against this and fastens his jacket up, closing every clasp and tightening every strap. The Wind perseveres for as long as he can but he is unable to remove the man's coat from his body. Finally the Wind forfeits his effort.

Now the Sun takes her turn and sends some gentle rays towards the man. The man, feeling this warmth, begins to undo his jacket. The Sun generates stronger rays and the man removes the jacket and folds it under his arm. The Sun amplifies this heat until eventually the man removes the rest of his clothes and jumps in a nearby river to cool off.

The moral of the story is that we are more likely to get someone to do something with warmth rather than force. Now we nod and agree with the moral of the fable but that does not seem to extend often into our everyday leadership. The manager rollicks the employee. The parent scolds the child. One spouse nags the other.

We think we can force people into doing things and sometimes in the short-term we can. But as a long-term strategy it doesn't have great success and certainly doesn't win you the respect of those you lead. Excellent persuaders, and thus leaders, use warmth, just like the sun.

There are two ways leaders do this. Before someone acts, they give encouragement. After someone acts, they give praise.

Encouragement

Encouragement is another important lesson I've learned from working with children and my time in the education system. In the classroom I've see a lot of negative motivation strategies: shouting, extra work, exam pressure. Certain children get labelled as "troublemakers" and automatically receive extra scrutiny as well as faster and more severe reprimands. What I've seen is that this simply doesn't work. A shout, a visit to the headteacher or an exclusion temporarily glosses over the problem but it never solves it. The children continue to misbehave; continue to fall behind; continue to resent the education system.

Why do teachers continue with this method even though it clearly doesn't work? Well, because it's easier. In a class of 20-30 children, it is easier to shout to restore order than to build the respect of the students. It is easier to remove someone from a class than to find out what's going on for them in their lives. It is easier to label than to understand.

It is much harder to take a positive, proactive approach to the child, but I've seen it work. In another of my school positions, I was placed with an incredibly difficult pupil. Their behaviour meant they were excluded from all classes and they were only allowed into the school for two hours a day, where they were kept in a special internal exclusion base (and the school was struggling for even those two hours).

This child had been labelled a "troublemaker", yet when I first met him, I saw an intelligent, polite, friendly and cheerful young man. This was despite horrible family history. He had been sexually abused as a child and placed in the foster care system. All his behaviour stemmed from that history. I looked past that conditioned behaviour and focused on his true character.

What I quickly observed as I went into classes with him was that some of the teachers had a prejudice against him because of his reputation. Because of this, the young man would get angry and was most likely to act up in these classes. They were also clearly unaware of his family history and how they were triggering defence patterns in him. They were treating him like a normal pupil, when he really needed a specialised approach.

I saw many great qualities in this young man and I was really fond of him. It frustrated me that the school was unaware to fully adapt to his needs and provide for him. During the time that I worked with him, I decided to focus on his good qualities and draw focus away from his bad qualities.

The school had a system of awarding "positive" and "negative" points for behaviour. When I first started with this child, he had 80 positive points, and a 120 negative points. By the end of my time with him, he had 200 positive points, and 170 negative points. He had moved from a -40 deficit to a +30 lead.

In class I noticed there were a number of behaviours that got him into trouble but there were also behaviours that were worthy of merit. He was keen to put up his hand and answer a question. He enjoyed being involved in a practical demonstration the teacher was doing. He was eager to run errands for the teachers. Rather than reprimand him for the negative behaviours, I aimed to gently steer him towards the positive behaviours. I would encourage him to put his hand up; I would do practical demonstrations with him at the front of the class; I would accompany him on errands for the teacher.

Through that process of encouragement, we started to make progress. He went from being in school two hours a day to being accepted back into the full timetable. He was allowed into all his classes again. That positive to negative ratio shifted. There was still a lot of work to be done — and sadly I think I left him long before he was ready — but I learned the importance of encouraging people who have been given up on.

It is through this process of encouragement that leaders inspire great action. Leaders convince others that something is possible. In 2008, when Barak Obama became the first black president of the USA, he did so with the campaign slogan "Yes We Can." (44)

As you know well, people often don't believe in themselves. They don't recognise their own capabilities. It doesn't help that there are plenty of other people who will say the same to them. People who will tell them how hard it is or that they haven't got what it takes. People will tell them that it's okay to fail and at least they gave it "a good shot".

Will you be the person who tells them they can? Will you be the person who makes them believe it's possible?

To encourage someone, focus on the positive. Don't tell your child they don't have the height to make the basketball team, focus on their speed and manoeuvrability that will allow them to avoid the clumsy, lanky players. On our high school basketball team, our captain and star player was about 5' 6" and played at the national level. His parents didn't tell him he wasn't "tall enough" for basketball.

Point out the positive traits that someone has. Unlike some of us who have been doing personal development for a while, many people haven't done all the personality tests, strengths finders and character assessments that make them self-aware of their strengths. Often people are not aware of their abilities. Tell them what you think they are good at. Tell them why those aspects of their character can help them succeed.

Whenever you see someone you lead engaging in a new pursuit or activity, be sure to remark on this. Show an interest in their new pastime. Offer them support or advice with this new endeavour.

For example, whenever I noticed my young pupil asking questions about something in class, I would try to tell him more about it. I would provide extra information. I would show him something on Google Images or Maps to give him extra visual representations of what we were talking about. I would speak about it enthusiastically to raise his own energy and engagement.

Now, sometimes we do offer encouragement, yet we taper it with a horrible word: "but". The word "but" automatically disqualifies everything you said before it. Look at these examples:

"I love you, but…"
"I'm not racist, but…"
"I'm happy, but…"

Look what that word "but" does. It completely destroys positive sentiment. If you put it in your encouragement, you might as well not have bothered. How do these encouraging statements sound?

"I believe you can start your own business but how about applying to a few jobs just in case?" (Implicit message: I think you might fail)

"You are a great communicator but you sometimes speak too fast." (Implicit message: don't be so enthusiastic)

"I think you look great honey but didn't you say you wanted to lose some weight?" (Implicit message: I don't love you as you are)

Not the encouragement we're looking for. However, we can save these motivational disasters with a simple change in syntax. Rather than make additions with the word "but", make additions with the word "and". Let's try that encouragement again.

"I believe you can start your own business and how about applying to a few jobs to keep you going in the meantime?" (Implicit message: I think you will eventually succeed)

"You are a great communicator and I think you can be even better by varying your pace." (Implicit message: you have more to offer)

"I think you look great honey and is there anything you'd still like to improve?" (Implicit message: you're going in a great direction)

A lot of well-meaning encouragement goes astray with the "but". However, with the "and", we encourage those we are leading to do more. We simultaneously encourage them where they are right now and also point them towards a better future. It's a simple, implicit way to help someone move forward.

Praise

Good persuaders give praise frequently. I'm not talking about the superficial praise that is often used: awarding prizes for participation and ticking a box on someone's evaluation sheet. I'm talking about genuine, specific, meaningful praise.

Praise is simply not done well in our culture. According to the American Psychological Association's 2016 Work and Well-Being survey, only about half of employed adults in the United States feel valued by their employer and sufficiently rewarded and recognised for their efforts. (45) The number one reason people leave a job is because they don't feel appreciated in that role, with an astonishing 79% of people citing this as the reason for their resignation. (46) I am one of those statistics.

When my dad died, I was working in a restaurant. Obviously I wasn't in the best place emotionally at the time but this was not helped by the conditions of the restaurant. It was fast-paced, exerting work which was tiring. I was working shifts, sometimes starting work at seven am, sometimes finishing at one or two in the morning. What compounded these problems was the leadership we received. I remember one Saturday night (the busiest night in hospitality) we were understaffed. There should have been four people in my position, but there were only two of us. Unsurprisingly, we were struggling to keep up, so our manager decided to lead us.

There was not enough cutlery for the tables and we were scrubbing furiously in the sink to try and get them cleaned and replaced. Our manager came into the kitchen and snarled at us: "You need to work harder. You're just not good enough."

Wow. How inspiring. We were two people trying to do the job of four. The manager thought that the best way to help us in this situation was to criticise us and attack our character. That helped me finalise a decision I had been contemplating for a while to resign. Shortly afterwards, I gave my week's notice.

I remember my final shift and one of the other managers approached me at the end of the shift and said: "Well done David, you were such a grafter". Sounds nice doesn't it? However, I had never been told this before during my employment, by her or the other managers. I had never been praised for my work, only chased up, cajoled and flat out criticised. If I had received that type of feedback every shift, instead of my last, I might have stayed in that job longer or at least left with much less hard feeling.

That is what happens when you don't praise. You create resentment. You get begrudging compliance rather than enthusiastic agreement. You disempower rather than empower.

One of our core needs is the need for acceptance. At the end of the day, we all just want people to like us and value us. If you meet this need for people, they will follow you. Sometimes, all people need to hear is "well done".

Do you remember our chemical serotonin? When we praise someone, we give them a burst of serotonin. (47) It actually encourages people to "serve" us again or do something worthy of our recognition. As leaders we receive serotonin from earning the respect of those we lead and we activate serotonin in others through our empowering efforts.

To feel and earn pride is a powerful motivator. It is why I write books and step onto stage...and not for the reason you think. Yes, receiving recognition from students or people I respect or look up to is nice but there's only one person's recognition that matters. I want to live a life that would make my dad proud.

When I step off stage and I've inspired people by talking about Dad, I know I've done him proud. In fact, I am writing this after just delivering one such talk. Thinking right now about how I've done him proud again is bringing a tear to my eye. Now that might seem crazy. I will never receive that recognition. I can only imagine those words "I'm really proud of you son" (admittedly he has said them before). However, that is providing me with an intense fuel that is spurring me on. That is the power of praise. It only needs to be imagined and it can push people into a life of growth and contribution.

<u>Vision</u>

When we examine what makes a leader a leader, another standout quality is that they seem to see things differently from those around them. They have a vision for what they and those they lead can be and achieve. Remember we created a vision for you in the Calling section? Well leaders take this one step further, and create a vision for others. Moreover, they don't just build others into it, they empower others to contribute to it themselves.

An outstanding example of this is Martin Luther King with his "I have a Dream" speech. Why is that speech so famous? There were plenty of other campaigners in the Civil Rights movement. There were other preachers and charismatic speakers apart from King.

That speech resonates because we see ourselves in it. In his speech Dr. King talks about black children and white children holding hands. We see ourselves as children or see our children and imagine how the world can be better for them. It is not a speech for black people, it is a speech for all people. It is why 25% of the audience that day in Washington were white. It's why I, a white man born long after the events of this time, watch the video of that speech when I'm looking for inspiration. I know I'm not the only young white person who does. I want to shape part of King's vision even after he has gone.

Leaders create a vision that inspires others. However, they don't do this in an autocratic, lecturing way. They invite others into that vision. They invite the people they are leading into this vision. They ask them to craft it with them. The vision might begin with the leader's perspective but it grows beyond that. Dr. King wanted to secure the right for African Americans to vote but it was the people who came after him who decided to use that vote to put an African American in the White House.

So how do you create a vision for you and those you lead? In Brendon Burchard's E6 framework for leadership, the very first of his six Es is Envision. (48) From Burchard's description of the principle, three steps are apparent to me.

Step one is to identify the problem you are addressing, and the solution you desire. Burchard states this as "If we do this (vision) we will stop that (problem with the status quo)". This is what Martin Luther King did. He said: if we grant civil rights to all Americans, we will create a country free of conflict and separation. If Black Americans have the same rights as White Americans, then America will be a greater country; a land of more opportunity, prosperity and harmony. At its foundational level, that is all a vision is. It offers a solution to the problem.

Stage two is to provide a road map. As Simon Sinek reminds us: "It's called vision because we need to be able to see it." (49) This is what Martin Luther King gives us in "I Have a Dream". In the speech Dr. King tells us:

"I have a dream that one day on the red hills of Georgia the sons of former slaves and the sons of former slave owners will be able to sit down together at the table of brotherhood." He tells us that the history of slavery will no longer matter, and we see the result of this in our mind's eye.

"...one day right there in Alabama, little black boys and black girls will be able to join hands with little white boys and white girls as sisters

and brothers." He tells us that white and black children will start off as equals, and we see this possibility in our mind's eye.

How King proposed to accomplish this was through non-violent means. His very presence at the Lincoln Memorial in 1963 was as part of a peaceful protest. In his speech, he reminded those who were listening:

"In the process of gaining our rightful place we must not be guilty of wrongful deeds. Let us not seek to satisfy our thirst for freedom by drinking from the cup of bitterness and hatred. We must forever conduct our struggle on the high plane of dignity and discipline. We must not allow our creative protest to degenerate into physical violence."

This was a reminder from Dr King of the road map. The militancy of other activists like Malcolm X was not the answer. The path to freedom was through non-violent protest.

Stage three is to attach emotional appeal. No one is inspired by a strategy. Managers provide strategy, leaders provide vision. What makes the difference is the emotion behind the plan, the heart behind the head. Burchard notes that visions often contain a sense of pride, a desire for greatness, a competitive spirit, service to others, doing the right things and overcoming odds. (50)

It is the emotional component of "I Have a Dream" that makes it such a great speech and such a great example of vision. In this speech, Martin Luther King hits upon a number of the markers that Burchard identifies:

"I have a dream that one day this nation will rise up and live out the true meaning of its creed: "We hold these truths to be self-evident: that all men are created equal." (Fairness)

"With this faith we will be able to hew out of the mountain of despair a stone of hope." (Overcoming Odds)

"And if America is to be a great nation this must become true." (Desire for Greatness)

Simon Sinek wittingly remarks "It was the 'I Have a Dream' speech, not the 'I Have a Plan' speech". (51) If we want to inspire others as Martin Luther King did, then we need to convey the emotional aspect of the vision. It's not enough to talk about what you're going to do, or how you're going to do it, you have to talk about *why* you're doing it. Sinek notes that people don't buy what you do, they buy why you do it. (52) If you want those you lead to buy into a vision, you have to tell them why to buy into it.

So how does this all translate into being an everyday leader? As an everyday leader I don't expect you to stand on top of the Lincoln Memorial and address the world (even though we had fun imagining that earlier in the book). But what you can do is communicate a vision as if you were.

When you want your children to do something, work through these three steps. Have a conversation with them where you identify the problem and the solution; then give them the road map; then connect with them emotionally. When you want your employees to do something, work through the three steps in a meeting, or even just in the emails you send out to them. When a friend comes to you for help, take them through the process.

When you introduce the framework to those you lead, allow their feedback to inform and evolve the vision. The Civil Rights movement didn't die with Martin Luther King. Why? Because others took on his vision. Politicians addressed discriminative legislature. Journalists exposed institutional racism. Judges punished hate crimes. Today thousands of people will protest and make a stand when they believe that someone, whether due to the colour of their skin or any other factor, has been discriminated against. They don't need Dr. King to tell them to because they have already engrained the vision for themselves.

That is what you are looking to create in those you lead. You don't want to have to tell your children every time you want them to do the dishes; you want them to recognise the importance of doing the dishes. You don't want to have to tell you employees to sell more products; you want them to recognise the value the product brings to their customers. You don't want to have to tell your friend to stop smoking; you want them to recognise the increased energy and harmony they feel when they do.

There are many ways that leaders inspire and create change. The concepts we have covered will allow you to step into your role as an everyday leader and inspire some of your own change in the world. Rather than summarise this chapter myself, I will allow a great leader, Sir Alex Ferguson, to do that for me.

"I slowly came to understand my job was different. It was to set very high standards. It was to help everyone else believe they could do things that they didn't think they were capable of. It was to chart a course that had not been pursued before. It was to make everyone understand that the impossible was possible. That's the difference between leadership and management." (53).

__Impact__

You can enjoy your deepest levels of Connection when you Impact those around you. The people around you need you, and you can serve them to a greater degree than you thought possible. Through this service, you will truly start to become the hero of your story. That is the final and most important stage of the the Author Your Life journey.

In this chapter you have learned:

- Why Givers rise to the top, but can also languish at the bottom
- How to protect yourself as a Giver
- That kindness makes you happier
- How to practice and even train your kindness
- That you are an Everyday Leader
- How to improve your leadership by embracing three key principles of Responsibility, Persuasion and Vision

My biggest takeaway from this chapter is

_____.

Section 5: The Story From Here

"Live a good, honourable life. Then when you're older, you'll be able to look back and enjoy it a second time"- **The Dalai Lama**

You are reaching the end of this book. There are not many pages left. Your story, however, is just beginning. Blank pages are ahead of you. What are you going to write on those pages?

The journey ahead may not be simple or clear to you. You may not have read one section of this book and said "aha, that's the missing piece." Throughout this book, I'm sure you've spotted aspects in each of the three sections, Consciousness, Calling and Connection, that you would like to improve and expand. Life after all is a holistic experience and I've written this as a holistic book.

In these sections, I hope you've realised the power and autonomy you have over your life. You can decide from this moment on what person you want to be and what type of life you want to lead. This book is here to help you on that journey. This book is not a program, to be done and discarded, it is a companion that you can refer back to at any time.

In the section on Consciousness, we examined the fear you might be experiencing: the fear of change, failure, and perhaps even the fear of success. Remember that we don't admire the hero because they don't feel fear. We admire them because they feel the fear and act regardless. They don't let the fear stop them from doing what they believe is right. Don't let your fear stop you from becoming the hero you are capable of being.

We delved deep into your mind to understand how it works and how you can push through that fear. There is huge untapped potential in your mind and in this section you have learned techniques to access more of your potential. You learned the habits and mechanisms that lead to happiness and ultimately, if you implement and embed these practices, you will be a happier person.

In the section on Calling, we addressed the confusion you might be stuck in: confusion about your why, your how, and your what. Don't worry if you're not quite sure what your Calling in life is or how you are going to accomplish it. All heroes start from humble beginnings but they keep persevering until they have fulfilled the quest that is presented to them. Don't let your confusion stop you from fulfilling your quest.

We explored purpose to help you connect to your "why" so that you can identify your personal mission. In this section you also learned the key principles that unite all successful people and, if you apply them, will bring about your success too. You learned key skills and techniques that will allow you to carry out your mission and achieve success in whatever endeavour you pursue.

In the section on Connection, we addressed the isolation you might feel: isolation from mentors, peers and people you serve. Know that on this journey you are never alone, the hero always has support around them.

Every story has a wide array of characters who educate, support and motivate the hero; your story is no different.

We explored how to interact with each of the characters in your story. You examined how to find growth and learning from the mentors and teachers around you. You learned how to interact with confidence and build rapport with your peers. You learned how to truly serve those who look up to you. With these skills, you will find love in all your relationships.

The easy mistake to make when you've read a book like this is to feel more positive and inspired and have ideas and aspirations for how you can make changes in your life...then not do anything.

The key factor in change is not how much you've learned, it's how much you implement. So don't put this book back on the shelf and forget about it for another couple of years. I want you to think right now of something that stood out to you from this book — a concept or a technique that you think will make a difference in your life — and spend the next seven days implementing it. Just one thing, for just seven days. It is a small commitment, but as the Chinese proverb goes: "The journey of a thousand miles begins with a single step.".

In addition to this, I recommend re-reading this book in the next couple of months. As I near the conclusion of this book, I can't remember everything that's in it and I'm the one who's written it! How can you hope to remember everything? Even if you did remember it all, how could you hope to implement it all at once? This is why I've told you to implement one thing now and come back later and identify what you're going to implement next.

It's time to decide how you want to live your life. Who do you want to be? How do you want to contribute? What impact do you want to make? It's time to get serious about your life, because I was reminded once again during the writing of this book that life can be snatched from us at any time.

From the start of 2017, my stepdad Andrew was having constant respiratory problems. In 2014 he had two-thirds of a cancerous lung removed. We all thought that these problems were arising as a result of his lungs having to work harder to shake off infection. As the problems persisted for months, further medical advice was sought. In June 2017, we found out the answer. Andrew's cancer had returned and the doctors gave him 9-12 months to live.

Andrew started chemotherapy over that summer to try and extend his quality of life but he reacted poorly to it. In September he was taken into hospital for a couple of weeks. He was released but left the hospital a different man to how he entered. He had deteriorated dramatically and continued to do so. On October 19th he was given a new prognosis. He no longer had months, he had weeks.

In October, Andrew, my mum, and my half-brother were booked in for a holiday, their last as a family. They had to cancel that holiday. Mum had planned to take leave from work at the end of the year so that her and Andrew could have a few months of quality time together before the end. Now she had to take that leave to be his full time carer. It was tragic news at the best of times but doubly so that what time they had left with him was being cut shorter.

I was running a seminar the day after I found out the news and my head was a mess. I was shocked at the injustice of it; sad to be losing Andrew so quickly; and angry because I was an eight-hour train journey away from them. I wasn't able to just up sticks and be there to support them during this difficult time. There I was speaking to an audience about the experience of losing my dad and now it seemed history was repeating itself. I was not as close to Andrew as I was to my own dad but I had a deep respect and fondness for him. I felt the loss on a personal level for me and for how it would affect my mum.

It was two weeks before myself and my partner managed to find the time to make the journey. I knew that this was going to be the last time I would see Andrew. I had made this type of journey before.

We arrived late in the evening and were leaving the following afternoon. There was a short window to get some meaningful time with Andrew. The evening we arrived we were able to see him briefly but he was tired and spent the night in his room, the downstairs office that had a bed placed in it so he didn't have to climb the stairs.

The following morning, I sat down with Mum and Andrew and we were able to carve out some time together. Andrew was using an oxygen tank to breathe and found it difficult to talk, so he was writing down small phrases and getting Mum to interpret and expand for him. Andrew wanted me to be master of ceremony for the funeral and we discussed his preferences for it. I also revealed to Andrew my intentions to propose to my partner and expressed regret that he wasn't going to be able to make it to the wedding. Andrew said, not wrote, "Congratulations". Our whole discussion lasted about an hour. Just like with Dad, I got the last sixty minutes with Andrew too.

This discussion tired Andrew and he went back to his room. Already my partner and I had to get ready to go home. We got our stuff ready and went through to see Andrew one last time. I shook his hand, looked him in the eye and said "goodbye Andrew", knowing that it really was goodbye. We made our way out to the car and I looked through the window into the office. I saw Andrew again and waved, he waved back. That was the last time I saw him.

Andrew died ten days later, on Remembrance Sunday. I honoured my promise to help organise and deliver his funeral a couple of weeks later. Andrew was a lovely gentleman and we miss him dearly. Mum lost her husband of fifteen years, a man who had treated her brilliantly and made her happy. They never got to enjoy a retirement together, to enjoy life without the obligations of work and family. My half-brother lost his dad at the age of fourteen. His dad will never see him finish school; never see him working on his calling; never see him start a family.

On those eight-hour train journeys, I wrote parts of this book. During this time, the fragile line between life and death was made clear to me again. We never know when our time is up. We never know how much time we've got on this Earth. We've got to make the most of it. We have to live life on our terms, because we only get one shot at this. We have to decide what story we want to create for ourselves.

The following year, I continued to write my story. I continued to work on everything I hope my life can be. On the 2nd of June, 2018, I proposed to my partner. She said yes. We came together at the most difficult time in my life, when my dad was in the last weeks of his life. She went through that experience with me and has been there for me ever since. I want to create a magical life together. I want to share joy and fun with her. I want to pursue our callings and make an impact on the world together. I want to raise a family and bring more love into the world together with her.

I share these two stories to illustrate that life is all about contrasts. Funerals and Weddings; Injustice and Fortune; Loss and Love; they come together as a package. Just like a coin, life is made up of two sides. However, we get to choose which side of the coin we want to live on. We get to choose if we want our life to be happy or unhappy, prosperous or scarce, meaningful or meaningless. That is what Author Your Life is all about. If you don't like a particular narrative, you have the power to rewrite that.

Your life is under your control. It doesn't matter what has happened in your past. It doesn't matter where you start from. It doesn't matter about what odds you face.

You are a hero. You have wonderful qualities that make you a re-markable human being.

You are a champion. You have an important mission to carry out in the world.

You are a leader. You have people who need your help and guidance.

When you embrace these three principles of Consciousness, Calling and Connection, then you can have it all. You can live a life of fulfilment. When that final day comes and you sit on your deathbed and look back at it all, you can say "Wow, what an incredible life I've lived." You are the author of your life. You hold the pen and you can write whatever script you want for yourself. So go out today, and the rest of your days, and write yourself a beautiful story.

Pick Up The Pen

Your new story starts here. It's an exciting journey and I would love to continue to help you along it. With this in mind, there are a few directions I would like to point you in.

Rate and Review

If you have enjoyed this book and think it would be valuable to others, I would love to hear more about your experience. Head to Amazon and leave a rating and review to not only communicate to me what you've taken from the book, but also to other people who want to read the book and would benefit from its contents.

Digital Contact

You can stay in contact with my work through:

- Website: www.authoryourlife.org
- Facebook: David McCrae: Author Your Life
- Instagram: @authoryourlife
- Youtube: David McCrae: Author Your Life

Author Your Life Book Resources

I love the power of the written word, but like everything, it has its limits. There are some exercises and techniques discussed in this book that are better to present in a different medium. For this reason, I have created a free portal of online resources attached to this book. There you can download PDFs, audio files and instructional videos related to concepts discussed in this book. I have provided the link multiple times throughout, but once again, for your convenience, it is:

http://davidmccrae.thinkific.com/courses/author-your-life-book-resources

Author Your Life Community

Join the free Facebook Group to engage and connect with other readers of the book. When you join the group, you can access a free online course "Become The Hero of Your Story" I created that will help you ingrain and implement the concepts and strategies of Author Your Life.

Author Your Life Podcast

This podcast delivers weekly episodes where I have either interviewed someone inspiring or created a tailored piece of training to help you change your narrative and become the hero of your story. Subscribe for free on iTunes.

Author Your Life Monthly

Join the Author Your Life membership to access additional learning, mentorship and community. As a member you get a new 60-90 minute training video every month delivered by myself, the opportunity for Q+A with me in exclusive live videos and the opportunity to share your journey with other members in a secret Facebook Group. Subscription is just £19.97 ($27) a month. Find out more by following the link below:

http://davidmccrae.thinkific.com/courses/authoryourlife

Author Your Life Summit

This is a multi-day live event I run to give you a deep-dive into the principles and practices of Author Your Life. Over a weekend you will find inspiration, motivation and connection that will kickstart exciting new changes in your life. To learn more, visit:

http://www.authoryourlife.org/speaking.

Acknowledgements

Behind every successful man is his woman. I disagree with this entirely. The woman can be found standing next to him, actively supporting and encouraging a joint effort. My woman is Kerrie, who has now agreed to stand next to me as my future wife. The changes I have aspired to make in my life and the lives of others would not have happened without Kerrie in my life. She has a level of integrity, courage, passion and kindness that I have not observed in any other individual and I count myself lucky to get to share every day with her. I look forward to creating our future vision and family together.

I would also like to thank my mum, Sarah, for her contributions in my life. Mum is role model of determination for me. As I have shared in this book, Mum has had a tough time during the two years I have been writing this book, but what amazes me is how she just keeps moving forward and getting on with things. She has had a lot of challenging times in her life but she has constantly persevered. I would like to thank my mum for the inspiration and perspective she gives me.

I would like to express my appreciation for my role models: Nelson Mandela, Arnold Schwarzenegger, Brendon Burchard, Wayne Dyer, Tim Ferriss and Tony Robbins. Each of you in your different ways have show me the possibilities and potential that exists in life, and I hope to emulate each of your achievements in any small way I can.

Of these, Brendon Burchard deserves particular attention for his direct influence. In 2016, I attended Brendon's four-day seminar *Experts Academy* and it changed my life. When I attended this event, for the first time in my life I actually believed I was capable of something. By this I don't mean capable of getting good grades at school, capable of attending a good university, or capable of succeeding in a respectable job. For the first time I realised that I was actually capable of making a real, meaningful difference in the world, and that this was my duty to fulfil in my lifetime. For awakening my potential, I thank you Brendon.

I would also like to thank the other people who I have met in my life who have been generous with their time and knowledge to mentor me. These include Lauren Robertson, Ehab Hamarneh, Bob Train, Carolyn George, Jo Richings, Dan Gregory, Ash Phillips, Francis Ghiloni and Karen Yates. Each of you has believed in me and helped me find a missing piece of the puzzle.

I would like to show appreciation to my oldest and dearest friends Josh, Andy (x2), Owen, Jamie (x2), Ruairidh and David for the many great memories we've made and the exciting adventures that are to come.

I would like to thank John and Katrina and the rest of the Morton family who have welcomed and accepted me as their future in-law and a new part of the family.

I would like to thank the proofreaders of this book: Megan (x2), Fiona, Jemma, Allison, Jamie (x2), Hau-Yin, Andy, Jason, Julie, Anita, Tom, Viktor, Jenni, John and Kit for helping me improve the original version and make this a more valuable book to the reader.

As well as the role models and mentors I have listed above, I would like to thank the psychologists, teachers and authors who's work has heavily influenced and shaped the content of this book. These include Sonja Lyubomirsky, Daniel Amen, Richard Davidson, Carol Dweck, Angela Duckworth, Stephen Covey, Loretta Breuning, Martin Seligman, Dan Pink, Brian Johnson, Cal Newport, Vanessa Van Edwards, Adam Grant and Simon Sinek.

I would like to thank Paulo Duelli for the great cover design. I had an idea in my head of how I wanted the cover to look but Paulo you have created something beyond my imagination.

Finally I'd like to thank *you,* the reader. I'd like to thank you for reading this book that I have invested a lot of time and energy into. I'd like to thank you for supporting my work through buying this book. I'd like to thank you for believing in me.

About The Author

David was born in Aberdeen, Scotland, to an English mum and a Scottish dad. He jokes that this makes him a Half-Blood, just like Harry Potter. He was raised in the village of Banchory just outside Aberdeen. Arguably the village's biggest claim to fame is that the Queen of the United Kingdom drives through it every time she stays in her Balmoral Estate in the Cairngorm National Park.

David was a nerd long before it was cool to be one. David has watched the Lord of the Rings films over 100 times and used to own a replica sword from the movies, which will naturally be replaced with a lightsaber when they get invented. David knows, as any intelligent person does, that Han shot first.

David is a long-suffering fan of Scottish Rugby. Every year he sits down eagerly to watch the Six Nations Championship and hopes this year will be the year that Scotland win their first title (they're getting closer!).

David also has a minor obsession with cats. He speaks to the cats in his neighbourhood and has assigned them all names and personalities. Some of the cats reciprocate his attention. All of his neighbours give him a wide berth.

David likes to consider himself a "Pun Master". He knows the double-meaning of far too many words and will jump upon any opportunity to showcase that knowledge. His personal favourite is when he went to a restaurant and a waiter greeted him with a tray of drinks.

"Aperitif?" the waiter asked.

"No thanks," David said, pointing to his teeth, "I've already got a set."

Endnotes

Section 1: The Story So Far

1. https://www.mind.org.uk/information-support/types-of-mental-health-problems/statistics-and-facts-about-mental-health/how-common-are-mental-health-problems/#.W3iC_9hKg1g
2. https://inews.co.uk/news/business/half-uk-workers-unhappy-jobs/
3. https://www.ons.gov.uk/peoplepopulationandcommunity/birthsdeathsandmarriages/divorce/bulletins/divorcesinenglandandwales/2015#what-percentage-of-marriages-end-in-divorce

Chapter 1: Your Story So Far

1. http://bigthink.com/ideafeed/expensive-weddings-result-in-shorter-marriages
2. https://www.iamselfpublishing.com/90-americans-want-to-write-a-book/
3. http://smallbusiness.co.uk/working-brits-consider-starting-business-2017-2536327/
4. https://www.statisticbrain.com/new-years-resolution-statistics/

Chapter 2: My Story So Far

1. http://www.cancerresearchuk.org/health-professional/cancer-statistics-for-the-uk#heading-Three

Chapter 3: Becoming The Author

1. Lyubomirsky, S. (2007). *The How of Happiness*. London: Piatkus.
2. Mandela, N. (1994). *Long Walk to Freedom*. London: Abacus.

Section 2: Elevate Your Consciousness

1. https://www.verywellmind.com/how-many-neurons-are-in-the-brain-2794889
2. Amen, D. (2016). *Change Your Brain Change Your Life*. London: Piatkus.

Chapter 4: Understand

1. Ben-Shahar, T. (2008). *Happier*. McGraw Hill.
2. Lyubomirsky, S. (2007). *The How of Happiness*. London: Piatkus.
3. Davidson, R. (2012). *The Emotional Life of Your Brain*. London: Hodder & Stoughton.
4. Ibid.

5. Davidson, R. and Fox, N. (1982). Asymmetrical Brain Activity Discriminates Between Positive Versus Negative Affective Stimuli in Human Infants. *Science*. 218: 1235-37.

6. Cartensen, L. and Mikels, J. (2005). At The Intersection Of Emotion And Cognition: Aging And The Positivity Effect. *Current Directions in Psychological Science*. 14.3: 117-121.

7. Dweck, C. (2006). *Mindset: How You Can Fulfil Your Potential*. London: Robinson.

8. Sadato, N., Pascual-Leone, A., Grafman, J., Ibañez, V., Deiber, M. P., Dold, G., and Hallet, M. (1996). Activation of the Primary Visual Cortex by Braille Reading in Blind Subjects. *Nature*. 380: 526-28.

9. Bavelier, D., Tomann, A., Hutton, C., Mitchell, T., Corina, D., Liu, G., and Neville, H. (2000). Visual Attention to the Periphery is Enhanced in Congenitally Deaf Individuals. *Journal of Neuroscience*.20:1-6.

10. Taub, E., Uswatte, G., King, D. K., Morris, D., Crago, J. E. and Chatterjee, A. (2006). A Placebo-Controlled Trial of Constraint-Induced Movement Therapy for Upper Extremity After Stroke. *Stroke*. 37: 1045-49.

11. Burchard, B. (2017). *High Performance Habits*. London: Hay House.

12. Duckworth, A. (2016). *Grit*. London: Penguin Random House.

13. Dweck, C., Blackwell, L.S., and Trzesniewski. Referenced in Dweck, C. (2006). *Mindset: How You Can Fulfil Your Potential*. London: Robinson.

14. Dweck, C. (2006). *Mindset: How You Can Fulfil Your Potential*. London: Robinson.

15. Dweck, C., Baer, A., Grant, H. Referenced in Dweck, C. (2006). *Mindset: How You Can Fulfil Your Potential*. London: Robinson.

16. Rydall, D. (2015). *Emergence*. New York: Simon & Schuster.

17. Randy Pausch Last Lecture: *Achieving Your Childhood Dreams*: https://www.youtube.com/watch?v=ji5_MqicxSo

18. Mangels J. A., Butterfield, B., Lamb, J., Good, C., and Dweck, C. (2006). Why Do Beliefs About Intelligence Influence Learning Success? A Social Cognitive Neuroscience Model. *Social Cognitive and Affective Neuroscience*. 1: 75-86

19. Burchard, B. (2017). *High Performance Habits*. London: Hay House.

20. Covey, S. R. (1989). *The 7 Habits of Highly Effective People: Powerful Lessons in Personal Change*. London: Simon & Schuster.

21. Brooks, D., (2015). *The Road to Character*. London: Allen Lane

22. Burchard, B. (2017). *High Performance Habits*. London: Hay House.

23. Ibid.

24. Ibid.

25. Burchard, B. (2012). *The Charge: Activating the 10 Human Drives That Make You Feel Alive*. London: Simon & Schuster.

26. Covey, S. R. (1989). *The 7 Habits of Highly Effective People: Powerful Lessons in Personal Change*. London: Simon & Schuster.

27. Burchard, B. (2017). *High Performance Habits*. London: Hay House.

Chapter 5: Unlock

1. Credit for much of this section goes to Breuning, L. G. (2016). Habits of a Happy Brain. Avon: Adams Media.

2. Ibid.

3. Olds, J., and Milner, P., (1954). Positive reinforcement produced by electrical stimulation of septal area and other regions of rat brain. *Journal of Comparative and Physiological Psychology*. 47: 419-27.

4. https://www.huffingtonpost.com/david-j-linden/compass-pleasure_b_890342.html

5. http://content.time.com/time/magazine/article/ 0,9171,1015863-1,00.html

6. Amen, D. (2016). *Change Your Brain Change Your Life*. London: Piatkus.

7. Blumenthal, J. A., Babyak, M. A,, Moore, K. A., Craighead, E., Herman, S., Khatri, P., Waugh, R., Napolitano, M. A., Forman, L. M., Appelbaum, M., Doraiswamy, P. M., and Krishnan, K. R. (1999). Effects of Exercise Training on Older Patients with Major Depression. *Archives of Internal Medicine*. 159: 2349-2356.

8. Thayer, R. E., Newman, J. R., and McClain, T. M. (1994). Self Regulation of Mood: Strategies for Changing a Bad Mood, Raising Energy, and Reducing Tension. *Journal of Personality and Social Psychology*. 67: 910-925.

9. Young, S. N., (2007). How to Increase Serotonin in the Human Brain Without Drugs. *Journal of Psychiatry & Neuroscience*. 32: 394–399.

10. Foley, T. E. and Fleshner, M. (2008). Neuroplasticity of Dopamine Circuits After Exercise: Implications for Central Fatigue. *Neuromolecular Medicine*. 10: 67-80.

11. Breuning, L. G. (2016). Habits of a Happy Brain. Avon: Adams Media.

12. Labuschagne, I., Phan, K. L., Wood, A.., Angstadt, M., Chua, P., Heinrichs, M., Stout, J. C., and Nathan, P. J. (2010). Oxytocin Attenuates Amygdala Reactivity to Fear in Generalised Social Anxiety Disorder. Neuropsychopharmacology. 35: 2403-13.

13. Davidson, R. (2012). *The Emotional Life of Your Brain*. London: Hodder & Stoughton.

14. https://www.washingtonpost.com/national/health-science/ecstasy-could-be-breakthrough-therapy-for-soldiers-others-suffering-from-ptsd/ 2017/08/26/009314ca-842f-11e7-b359-15a3617c767b_story.html? noredirect=on&utm_term=.4b67be4d2b9c

15. Clipman, J. M. (1999). *A hug a day keeps the blues away: the effect of daily hugs on subjective well-being in college students.* Paper presented at the Seventieth Annual Meeting of the Eastern Psychological Association, Boston, MA.

16. Fiske, S. T. (1980). Attention and Weight in Person Perception: The Impact of Negative and Extreme Behaviour. *Journal of Personality and Social Psychology.* 38: 889–906.

17. Rozin, P. and Royzman, E. B. (2001). Negativity Bias, Negativity Dominance, and Contagion. *Personality and Social Psychology Review.* 5: 296–320

18. Nolen-Hoeksema, S., Wisco, B. E., and Lyubomirsky, S. (2008). Rethinking Rumination. *Perspectives on Psychological Science.* 3: 400-424.

19. Credit to Gabrielle Bernstein for this technique: https://www.youtube.com/watch?v=eiLWO9jOTao

20. O'Connor, J., and McDermott, I., (1996). *Way of NLP.* London: Thorsons.

21. Amen, D. (2016). *Change Your Brain Change Your Life.* London: Piatkus.

22. Byron, K., and Mitchell, S. (2002). Loving What Is: Four Questions That Can Change Your Life. New York: Three Rivers Press.

23. ORZEŁ-GRYGLEWSKA, J. (2010). CONSEQUENCES of SLEEP DEPRIVATION. *International Journal of Occupational Medicine and Environmental Health.* 23: 95–114.

24. Oztürk, L., Pelin, Z., Karadeniz, D., Kaynak, H., Cakar, L., Gözükirmizi, E. (1999). Effects of 48 Hours Sleep Deprivation on Human Immune Profile. *Sleep Research Online.* 2: 107-11.

25. http://serendipstudio.org/exchange/node/1690

26. Nir, Y., Andrillon, T., Marmelshtein, A., Suthana, N., Cirelli, C., Tononi, G., and Fried, I. (2017). Selective Neuronal Lapses Precede

Human Cognitive Lapses Following Sleep Deprivation. *Nature Medicine*. 23: 1474–1480

27. Zhang, J., Zhu, Y., Zhan, G., Fenik, P., Panossian, L., Wang, M. M.,Reid, S., Lai, D., Davis, J. G., Baur, J. A., and Veasey, S. (2014). Extended Wakefulness: Compromised Metabolics in and Degeneration of Locus Ceruleus Neurons. *Journal of Neuroscience*. 34: 4418-4431.

28. https://www.health.harvard.edu/newsletter_article/sleep-and-mental-health

29. http://www.sleepeducation.org/news/2013/08/01/sleep-and-caffeine

30. https://sleepfoundation.org/sleep-topics/how-alcohol-affects-sleep

31. Murphy P. J., and Campbell S. S. (1997). Nighttime Drop in Body Temperature: a Physiological Trigger for Sleep Onset? *Sleep*. 20: 505-11.

32. Black, D. S., O'Reilly, G. A., Olmstead, R., Breen, E. C., and Irwin, M. R. (2015). Mindfulness Meditation and Improvement in Sleep Quality and Daytime Impairment Among Older Adults With Sleep Disturbances. *JAMA Internal Medicine*. 175: 494-501.

33. https://eocinstitute.org/meditation/meditation-for-insomnia-and-better-sleep/

34. Digdon, N., and Koble, A.,(2011). Effects of Constructive Worry, Imagery Distraction, and Gratitude Interventions on Sleep Quality: A Pilot Trial.

Chapter 6: Unleash

1. Peterson, C., (1988). Explanatory Style As a Risk Factor for Illness. *Cognitive Therapy and Research*. 12: 117-30.

2. Greer, S., Morris, T., and Pettingale, K. W. (1979). Psychological Response to Breast Cancer: Effect on Outcome. *The Lancet*. II: 785-7.

3. Gillham, J. E., and Reivich, K. J. (1999). Prevention of Depressive Symptoms in School Children: A Research Update. *Psychological Science*. 10: 461-462.

4. Maruta, T., Colligan, R. C., Malinchoc, M., and Offord, K. P. (2000). Optimists vs Pessimists: Survival Rate Among Medical Patients Over a 30-Year Period. *Mayo Clinic Proceedings*. 75: 140-143.

5. Lyubomirsky, S. (2007). *The How of Happiness*. London: Piatkus.

6. Frankl, V. E. (1959). *Man's Search for Meaning*. St Ives: Random House.

7. Seligman, M. (2006). *Learned Optimism: How to Change Your Mind and Life*. New York: Random House.

8. King, L. A. (2001). The Heath Benefits of Writing About Life Goals. *Personality and Social Psychology Bulletin*. 27: 798-807.

9. Lyubomirsky, S. (2007). *The How of Happiness*. London: Piatkus.

10. https://www.statista.com/statistics/269918/daily-tv-viewing-time-in-the-uk-by-age/

11. Seligman, M. (2002). *Authentic Happiness: Using the New Positive Psychology to Realise Your Potential for Lasting Fulfilment*. New York: Simon and Schuster.

12. Wood, J. V., Perunovie, W. Q. E. and Lee J. W. (2009). Positive Self-Statements: Power For Some, Peril For Others. *Psychological Science*. 20: 860-66

13. Strack, F., Martin, L. L., and Stepper, S. (1988). Inhibiting and Facilitating Conditions of a Human Smile: a Nonobtrusive Test of the Facial Feedback Hypothesis. *Journal of Personality and Social Psychology*. 54: 768-777.

14. Ekman, P., Davidson, R. J., and W. V. Friesen (1990). The Duchenne Smile: Emotional Expression and Brain Physiology II. *Journal of Personality and Social Psychology*. 58: 342-53.

15. Finzi, E. and Wasserman, E. (2006). Treatment of Depression with Botulinum Toxin A: A Case Series. *Dermatologic Surgery.* 32: 645-650.

16. Haidt, J. (2007). *The Happiness Hypothesis: Putting Ancient Wisdom to the Test of Modern Science.* Arrow.

17. Lazar, S. W., Kerr, C. E., Wasserman, R. H., Gray, J. R., Greve, D. N., Treadway, M. T., McGarvey, M., Quinn, B. T., Dusek, J. A., Benson, H., Rauch, S. L., Moore, C. I., and Fischld, B. (2005). Meditation Experience is Associated With Increased Cortical Thickness. *Neuroreport.* 16: 1893–1897.

18. Hölzel, B. K., Carmody, J., Vangel, M., Congleton, C., Yerramsetti, S. M., Gard, T., and Lazara, S. W. (2011). Mindfulness Practice Leads to Increases in Regional Brain Gray Matter Density. *Psychiatry Research.* 191: 36–43.

19. Desbordes, G., Negi, L. T., Pace, T. W. W., Wallace, B. A., Raison, C. L., and Schwartz, E. L. (2012). Effects of Mindful-Attention and Compassion Meditation Training on Amygdala Response to Emotional Stimuli in an Ordinary, Non-Meditative State. *Human Neuroscience.*

20. Davidson, R. J., Kabat-Zinn, J., Schumacher, J., Rosenkranz, M. A., Muller, D., Santorelli, S. F., Urbanowski, F., Harrington, A., Bonus, K. and Sheridan, J. F. (2003). Alterations in Brain and Immune Function Produced by Mindfulness Meditation. *Psychosomatic Medicine.* 65: 564-70

21. Miller, J. J., Fletcher, K., and Kabat-Zinn, J. (1995). Three-Year Follow-Up and Clinical Implications of a Mindfulness Meditation-Based Stress Reduction Intervention in the Treatment of Anxiety Disorders. *General Hospital Psychiatry.* 17: 192-200

22. https://www.independent.co.uk/news/uk/this-britain/the-happiest-man-in-the-world-433063.html

23. Lutz, A. Greischar, L. L., Rawlings, N. B., Ricard, M. and Davidson, R. J. (2004). Long-Term Meditators Self-Induce High-Amplitude Synchrony During Mental Practice. *Proceedings of the National Academy of Sciences*. 101: 16369-73

24. Davidson, R. (2012). *The Emotional Life of Your Brain*. London: Hodder & Stoughton.

25. Lyubomirsky, S. (2007). *The How of Happiness*. London: Piatkus.

26. Ibid

27. Ibid

28. Algoe, S. B., and Way, B. M. (2014). Evidence for a role of the oxytocin system, indexed by genetic variation in CD38, in the social bonding effects of expressed gratitude. *Social Cognitive and Affective Neuroscience*. 9: 1855–1861.

29. McCullough, M. E., Emmons, R. A., and Tsang, J. (2002). "The Grateful Disposition: A Conceptual and Empirical Topography". *Journal of Personality and Social Psychology*. 82: 112-127.

30. Watkins, P. C., Grimm, D. L., and Kolts, R. (2004). Counting Your Blessings: Positive Memories Among Grateful Persons. *Current Psychology: Developmental, Learning, Personality, Social*. 23: 52-67.

31. Lyubomirsky, S. (2007). *The How of Happiness*. London: Piatkus.

32. Lyubomirsky, S., King, L., and Diener, E. (2005). The Benefits of Frequent Positive Affect: Does Happiness Lead to Success? *Psychological Bulletin*. 131: 803-855.

33. Seligman, M. P., Steen, T. A., Park, N., and Peterson, C. (2005). Positive Psychology Progress. *American Psychologist*. 60: 410-421

34. McCraty, R., Atkinson, M., Tomasino, D., and Bradley, R. T. (2009). The Coherent Heart, Heart–Brain Interactions, Psychophysiological Coherence, and the Emergence of System-Wide Order. *INTEGRAL REVIEW*. 5.

35. https://tim.blog/2016/09/18/how-to-resolve-internal-conflict/

Section 3: Pursue Your Calling

1. https://news.gallup.com/opinion/chairman/212045/world-broken-work-place.aspx?
   g_source=position1&g_medium=related&g_campaign=tiles
2. https://www.iamselfpublishing.com/90-americans-want-to-write-a-book/
3. https://www.statista.com/statistics/572476/number-writers-authors-usa/

Chapter 7: Purpose

1. https://www.fastcompany.com/3032126/how-to-find-meaning-during-your-pursuit-of-happiness-at-work
2. https://news.gallup.com/poll/165269/worldwide-employees-engaged-work.aspx
3. https://www.samaritans.org/about-us/our-research/facts-and-figures-about-suicide
4. Buettner, Dan (2012). *The Blue Zones, Second Edition: 9 Lessons for Living Longer From the People Who've Lived the Longest.* Washington, D.C.: National Geographic.
5. https://en.wikipedia.org/wiki/List_of_countries_by_life_expectancy
6. Santrock, J. W. A (2002). *Topical Approach to Life-Span Development (4 ed.).* New York: McGraw-Hill.
7. Buettner, Dan (2012). *The Blue Zones, Second Edition: 9 Lessons for Living Longer From the People Who've Lived the Longest.* Washington, D.C.: National Geographic.

8. https://www.forbes.com/sites/chrismyers/2018/02/23/how-to-find-your-ikigai-and-transform-your-outlook-on-life-and-business/#6864eca22ed4

9. Duckworth, A. (2016). *Grit*. London: Penguin Random House.

10. Shortz, W., (2001). How to Solve the New York Times Crossword Puzzle. *New York Times Magazine*.

11. Pink, D. H. (2009). *Drive: The Surprising Truth About What Motivates Us*. New York: Riverhead.

12. Ibid.

13. This anecdote is shared in Pink, D. H. (2009). *Drive: The Surprising Truth About What Motivates Us*. New York: Riverhead.

14. Karim, R. L., and Wolf, R. G. (2005). "Why Hackers Do What They Do: Understanding Motivation and Effort in Free/Open Source Software Projects" in *Perspectives on Free and Open Software*, edited by Feller, J., Fitzgerald, B., Hissam, S. and Lakhani, K. Cambridge: MIT Press.

15. Blitzer, J., Schrettl, W., and Schroeder, P. J. H. (2007). Intrinsic Motivation in Open Source Software Development. *Journal of Comparative Economics*. 35: 160-169.

16. Mandela, N. (1994). *Long Walk to Freedom*. London: Abacus.

17. *What Oprah Learned from Jim Carrey* | Oprah's Life Class | Oprah Winfrey Network: https://www.youtube.com/watch?v=nPU5bjzLZX0

18. https://www.statisticbrain.com/jim-carrey-movie-film-career-earnings/

19. https://www.breakthroughbasketball.com/mental/visualization.html

20. Pascual-Leone, A., Amedi, F., Fregni, F., and Merabet, L. B. (2005). The Plastic Human Brain Cortex. *Annual Review of Neuroscience*. 28: 377-401.

Chapter 8: Proficiency

1. Duckworth, A. (2016). *Grit*. London: Penguin Random House.

2. https://www.collegefactual.com/colleges/united-states-military-academy/academic-life/graduation-and-retention/

3. Duckworth, A. L., Peterson, C., Matthews, M. D., and Kelly, D. R. (2007). Grit: Perseverance and Passion for Long-term Goals. *Journal of Personality and Social Psychology*. 92: 1087-1101.

4. Willingham, W. H. (1985). *Success in College: The Role of Personal Qualities and Academic Ability*. New York: College Entrance Examination Board.

5. Ibid.

6. Burchard, B. (2017). *High Performance Habits*. London: Hay House.

7. Ibid.

8. Ibid.

9. Ferguson, A. and Moritz, M. (2015). *Leading*. London: Hodder & Stoughton.

10. https://www.cnbc.com/2017/11/15/warren-buffett-and-mark-cuban-agree-reading-is-key-to-success.html

11. https://www.lionsroar.com/a-day-in-the-life-of-the-dalai-lama/

12. Brian Johnson | *Consistency on the Fundamentals*: https://www.youtube.com/watch?v=qb6rfknkS3g

13. Burchard, B. (2012). *The Charge: Activating the 10 Human Drives That Make You Feel Alive*. London: Simon & Schuster.

14. Dunn, E. W., Aknin, L. B., and Norton, M. I. (2008). Spending Money on Others Promotes Happiness. *Science*. 319: 1687-88.

15. Schwarzenegger, A. (2012). *Total Recall: My Unbelievably True Life Story*. London: Simon & Schuster.

16. Newport, C. (2016). *Deep Work*. London: Piatkus.

17. https://www.businessinsider.com/kobe-bryant-work-ethic-2013-2?
    IR=T#he-counts-all-of-his-made-shots-in-practice-and-stops-when-he-
    gets-to-400-5

18. https://seths.blog/

19. Ericsson, K. A., Krampe, R. T., and Tesch-Romer, C. (1993). The Role
    of Deliberate Practice in the Acquisition of Expert Performance. *Psy-
    chological Review*. 100: 363-406.

20. Ericsson, K. A. and Pool, R. (2016). *Peak: Secrets from the New Sci-
    ence of Expertise*. New York: Houghton Mifflin Harcourt)

21. Credit to Angela Duckworth for this summary in Duckworth, A.
    (2016). *Grit*. London: Penguin Random House.

22. Burchard, B. (2017). *High Performance Habits*. London: Hay House.

23. Credit to Dan Pink for this analogy in Pink, D. H. (2009). *Drive: The
    Surprising Truth About What Motivates Us*. New York: Riverhead.

24. Kreps, D. (2010). "Beyonce, Taylor Swift Dominate 2010 Grammy
    Awards". *Rolling Stone*.

25. https://web.archive.org/web20170203095703/http://www.thewrap.com/
    oscar-nominations-jennifer-lawrence-youngest-ever-3-time-oscar-act-
    ing-nominee/

26. 12th IAAF World Championships in Athletics: IAAF Statistics Hand-
    book. (2009). *Monte Carlo: IAAF Media & Public Relations Depart-
    ment*. 410.

27. Smith, A., Segal, L., and Cowley, S., (2012). "Facebook Reaches One
    Billion Users". *CNN*.

28. Cooper, B. J. (2012). Taylor Swift Opens Up About a Future in Acting
    and Admiration for Emma Stone. *Taste of Country*.

29. (2008) News : CMT Insider Interview: Taylor Swift (Part 1 of 2). *CMT*.

30. Eells, J. (2012). Jennifer Lawrence: America's Kick-Ass Sweetheart.
    Rolling Stone.

31. Windolf, J., and Diehl, J. (2013). Girl, Uninterruptible. *Vanity Fair*.

32. Frater, A. (2008). Bolt's Sherwood on 'gold alert'. *Jamaica Gleaner.*

33. Carifta Games (Under 17 boys). *GBR Athletics.*

34. http://www.letsintern.com/blog/4-thing-mark-zuckerberg/

35. November 2010 – Gold & Platinum Certifications. *Canadian Recording Industry Association.*

36. Bieber's 'Baby' YouTube's most-watched video. *Today.*

37. Herrera, M. (2009). 'Time' is right for teen singer Justin Bieber. *Reuters.*

38. Hoffman, J. (2009). Justin Bieber is Living the Tween Idol Dream. *The New York Times.*

39. Brian Johnson I +1 or -1: https://www.youtube.com/watch?v=PtJW9o-IhMpY

40. Csíkszentmihályi, M., and Larson, R. (1983). The Experience Sampling Method. New Directions for Methodology of Social and Behavioural Science. 15: 41-56

41. Csikszentmihályi, M. (1990). *Flow: The Psychology of Optimal Experience.* Harper & Row.

42. Nakamura, J., and Csikszentmihályi, M. (2002). "The Concept of Flow" in Snyder C. R., and Lopez, S. J. (Eds). *Handbook of Positive Psychology* (pp. 89-105). Oxford: Oxford University Press.

43. Csíkszentmihályi, M. (1975). *Beyond Boredom and Anxiety.* Jossey-Bass Publishers

44. Diagnostic and Statistical Manual of Mental Disorders, 5th Edition: DSM-5. (2013) *American Psychological Association.*

45. Brian Johnson I Optimize Interview: The Rise of Superman with Steven Kotler: https://www.youtube.com/watch?v=U0fphfbVU1A

46. Csikszentmihályi, M. (1990). *Flow: The Psychology of Optimal Experience.* Harper & Row.

47. Kotler, S. (2014). *The Rise of Superman: Decoding the Science of Ultimate Human Performance.* Houghton Mifflin Harcourt.

Chapter 9: Performance

1. Covey, S. R. (1989). *The 7 Habits of Highly Effective People: Powerful Lessons in Personal Change*. London: Simon & Schuster.
2. Schwarzenegger, A. (2012). *Total Recall: My Unbelievably True Life Story*. London: Simon & Schuster.
3. Mandela, N. (1994). *Long Walk to Freedom*. London: Abacus.
4. Kennedy, J. F. (1962). *President John F. Kennedy: The Space Effort*. Rice University.
5. Covey, S. R. (1989). *The 7 Habits of Highly Effective People: Powerful Lessons in Personal Change*. London: Simon & Schuster.
6. https://nypost.com/2017/11/08/americans-check-their-phones-80-times-a-day-study/
7. https://www.mckinsey.com/industries/high-tech/our-insights/the-social-economy
8. https://www.ft.com/content/7686ea3e-e0dd-11e7-a0d4-0944c5f49e46
9. Newport, C. (2016). *Deep Work*. London: Piatkus.
10. Ibid.
11. Ibid.
12. Csikszentmihályi, M. (2004). *Flow, The Secret to Happiness*. https://www.youtube.com/watch?v=fXIeFJCqsPs
13. Sanbonmatsu, D.M., Strayer, D.L., Medeiros-Ward, N., Watson, J.M. (2013). Who Multi-Tasks and Why? Multi-Tasking Ability, Perceived Multi-Tasking Ability, Impulsivity, and Sensation Seeking. *PLOS ONE*. 8: e54402
14. Leroy, S. (2009). Why is it so Hard to do my Work? The Challenge of Attention Residue When Switching Between Work Tasks. *Organizational Behavior and Human Decision Processes*. 109: 168-181.
15. Morris, E. (2001). *The Rise of Theodore Roosevelt*. New York: Random House.

16. Newport, C. (2016). *Deep Work*. London: Piatkus.

17. Burchard, B. (2017). *High Performance Habits*. London: Hay House.

Section 4: Deepen Your Connection

1. https://www.theguardian.com/lifeandstyle/2014/aug/12/one-in-ten-people-have-no-close-friends-relate

Chapter 10: Integrate

1. Asch, S.E. (1951). Effects of Group Pressure on the Modification and Distortion of Judgments. In Guetzkow, H. (Ed.), *Groups, leadership and men* (pp. 177–190). Pittsburgh: Carnegie Press.

2. Milgram, S. (1963). Behavioral Study of Obedience. *Journal of Abnormal and Social Psychology*. 67: 371–8.

3. Milgram, S. (1965). Some Conditions of Obedience and Disobedience to Authority. *Human Relations*. 18: 57–76.

4. Bandura, A., Ross, D., and Ross, S. A. (1961). Transmission of Aggression Through the Imitation of Aggressive Models. *Journal of Abnormal and Social Psychology*. 63: 575–582.

5. https://www.youtube.com/watch?v=dmBqwWlJg8U

6. Mednick, S. C., Christakis, N. A. and Fowler J. H. (2010). The Spread of Sleep Loss Influences Drug Use in Adolescent Social Networks. *Public Library of Science One*, 5: e9775.

7. Pachucki, M. A., Jacques, P. F. and Christakis, N. A. (2011). Social Network Concordance in Food Choice Among Spouses, Friends and Siblings. *American Journal of Public Health*. 101: 2170-2177.

8. O' Boyle, E. (2016). Does Culture Matter in Economic Behaviour? *Social and Education History*. 5: 52-82.

9. Christakis, N. A., and Fowler, J. H. (2008). The Collective Dynamics of Smoking in a Large Social Network. *New England Journal of Medicine*. 358: 2249-2258.

10. Christakis, N. A., and Fowler, J. H. (2007). The Spread of Obesity in a Large Social Network over 32 years. New England Journal of Medicine. 357: 370-379.

11. Rosenquist, J. N., Fowler, J. H. and Christakis, N. A. (2011). Social Network Determinants of Depression. Molecular Psychiatry. 16: 273-281.

12. McDermott, R., Fowler, J. H. and Christakis, N. A. (2013). Breaking Up is Hard To Do, Unless Everyone Else is Doing it Too: Social Network Effects on Divorce in a Longitudinal Sample. Social Forces. 92: 491.

13. Mednick, S. C., Christakis, N. A., and Fowler, J. H. (2010). The Spread of Sleep Loss Influences Drug Use in Adolescent Social Networks. Public Library of Science One, 5: e9775

14. Christakis, N. A., and Fowler, J. H. (2009). *Connected: The Surprising Power of our Social Networks and How They Shape Our Lives*. New York: Little, Brown and Company.

15. Christakis, N. A., and Fowler, J. H. (2008). Dynamic Spread of Happiness in a Large Social Network: Longitudinal Analysis over 20 years in the Framingham Heart Study. *British Medical Journal*. 337: 1-9.

16. Coyle, D. (2009). *The Talent Code: Greatness Isn't Born. It's Grown. Here's How*. New York: Bantam.

17. Rowling, J. K. (1997). *Harry Potter and the Philosopher's Stone*. London: Bloomsbury.

18. https://www.encyclopedia.com/social-sciences/applied-and-social-sciences-magazines/similarityattraction-theory

19. O'Connor, J., and McDermott, I., (1996). *Way of NLP*. London: Thorsons.

20. Christian, K. (2010). Mirror Neurons. *Current Biology*. 19: 971–973.

21. Amen, D. (2016). *Change Your Brain Change Your Life*. London: Piatkus.

22. Williamson, M. (1992). *A Return to Love: Reflections on the Principles of A Course in Miracles*. London: Harper Collins.

23. Burchard, B. (2012). *The Charge: Activating the 10 Human Drives That Make You Feel Alive*. London: Simon & Schuster.

24. Ibid.

25. Van Edwards, V. (2016). *Captivate: The Science of Succeeding With People*. St Ives: Penguin Random House.

Chapter 11: Influence

1. https://www.silentcommunication.org/single-post/2016/03/20/17-Nonverbal-communication-percentage

2. http://www.nonverbalgroup.com/research

3. https://www.spring.org.uk/2007/05/busting-myth-93-of-communication-is.php

4. https://www.youtube.com/watch?v=3QdnCRWATZ8

5. Argyle, M., and Dean, J. (1965). Eye-Contact, Distance and Affiliation. *Sociometry*. 28: 239-304.

6. Dalton, K. M., Nacewicz, B. M., Johnstone, T., Shaefer, H. S., Gernsbacher, M. A., Goldsmith, H. H., Alexander, A. L., and Davidson, R. J. (2005). Gaze Fixation and the Neural Circuitry of Face Processing in Autism. *Nature Neuroscience*. 8: 519-26.

7. Van Edwards, V. (2016). *Captivate: The Science of Succeeding With People*. St Ives: Penguin Random House.

8. Ibid.

9. Simon Sinek | TED | Start With Why: How Great Leaders Inspire Action: https://www.youtube.com/watch?v=qp0HIF3SfI4

10. , J. M. (1999). *A Hug a Day Keeps the Blues Away: The Effect of Daily Hugs on Subjective Wellbeing in College Students*. Paper presented at the Seventieth Annual Meeting of the Eastern Psychological Association, Boston, USA.

11. Harari, Y. N. (2014). *Sapiens*. London: Penguin Random House.

12. Tracy, J. L., and Matusumoto, D. (2008). The Spontaneous Expression of Pride and Shame: Evidence for Biologically Innate Nonverbal Displays. *Proceedings of the National Academy of Sciences*. 105: 11655-660.

13. Amy Cuddy | TED | Your Body Language May Shape Who You Are: https://www.youtube.com/watch?v=Ks-_Mh1QhMc

14. Ibid.

15. Ibid.

16. Ibid.

17. https://www.nytimes.com/2015/12/13/opinion/sunday/your-iphone-is-ruining-your-posture-and-your-mood.html

18. Tamir, D. I., and Mitchell, J. P. (2012). Disclosing Information About The Self is Intrinsically Rewarding. *Proceedings of the National Academy of Sciences*. 109: 8038-43.

19. Van Edwards, V. (2016). *Captivate: The Science of Succeeding With People*. St Ives: Penguin Random House.

20. Harari, Y. N. (2014). *Sapiens*. London: Penguin Random House.

21. Stephens, G. J., Silbert, L. J., and Hasson, U. (2010). Speaker-Listener Neural Coupling Underlies Successful Communication. *Proceedings of the National Academy of Sciences*. 107: 14425-430.

22. Van Edwards, V. (2016). *Captivate: The Science of Succeeding With People*. St Ives: Penguin Random House.

23. quoted in Carnegie, D. (1936). *How to Win Friends and Influence People*. Vermillion.

24. Kross, E., and Ayduk, O. (2008). Facilitating Adaptive Emotional Analysis: Distinguishing Distanced-Analysis of Depressive Experiences from Immersed-Analysis and Distraction. Personality and Social Psychology Bulletin. 34: 924-38.

25. Gottman, J. and Silver, N. (1999). The Seven Principles for Making Marriage Work. London: Orion.

26. Amen, D. (2016). *Change Your Brain Change Your Life*. London: Piatkus.

Chapter 12: Impact

1. Tony Robbins I Unleash The Power Within I 22/7/17: https://www.youtube.com/watch?v=yJ8TTMfhIfo

2. https://www.youtube.com/watch?v=sLKUvi8xR34

3. Grant, A. (2013). *Give and Take: Why Helping Others Drives Our Success*. London: Weidenfeld & Nicolson.

4. Flynn, F. J. (2003). How Much Should I Give and How Often? The Effects of Generosity and Frequency of Favour Exchange on Social Status and Productivity. *Academy of Management Journal*. 46: 539-553.

5. Grant, A. M., and Barnes, D. (2011). Predicting Sales Revenue. (working paper).

6. Grant, A. (2013). *Give and Take: Why Helping Others Drives Our Success*. London: Weidenfeld & Nicolson.

7. Oakley, B., Knafo, A., and McGrath, M. (2011). *Pathological Altruism.* New York: Oxford University Press.

8. Frimer, J. A., Walker, L. J., Dunlop, W. L., Lee, B. H. and Riches, A. (2011). The Integration of Agency and Communication in Moral Personality: Evidence of Enlightened Self-Interest. *Journal of Personality and Social Psychology.* 101: 149-163.

9. Mclean, B., and Elkind, P. (2004). *The Smartest Guys in the Room: The Amazing Rise and Scandalous Fall of Enron.* New York: Portfolio.

10. Keen, J. (2002). Bush, Lay Kept Emotional Distance. *USA Today.*

11. https://www.theguardian.com/us-news/2018/jan/18/us-leadership-world-confidence-poll

12. https://fivethirtyeight.com/features/the-year-in-trumps-approval-rating/

13. Maslach, C., Schaufeli, W., and Leiter, M. (2001). Job Burnout. *Annual Review of Psychology.* 52: 397-422.

14. van Dierendonck, D., Schaufeli, W. B., and Buunk, B. P. (2001). Burnout and Inequality Among Human Service Professionals: A Longitudinal Study. *Journal of Occupational Health Psychology.* 6: 43-52.

15. Turner, Y., Silberman, S., Joffe, S., and Hadas-Halpern, I. (2008). The Effect of Adding a Patient's Photograph to the Radiographic Examination. *Annual Meeting of the Radiological Society of North America.*

16. Grant, A. M., Campbell, E. M., Chen, G., Cottone, K., Lapedis, D. and Lee, K. (2007). Impact and the Art of Motivation Maintenance: The Effects of Contact with Beneficiaries on Persistence Behaviour. *Organisational Behaviour and Human Decision Processes.* 103: 53-67.

17. Grant, A. (2013). *Give and Take: Why Helping Others Drives Our Success.* London: Weidenfeld & Nicolson.

18. Newport, C. (2016). *Deep Work.* London: Piatkus.

19. Chatterjee, A., and Hambrick, D. C. (2007). It's All about Me: Narcissistic Chief Executive Officers and Their Effects on Company Strategy and Performance. *Administrative Science Quarterly.* 52: 351-386.

20. Grant, A. (2013). *Give and Take: Why Helping Others Drives Our Success.* London: Weidenfeld & Nicolson.

21. Lyubomirsky, S. (2007). *The How of Happiness.* London: Piatkus.

22. Ibid.

23. Lyubomirsky, S., Sheldon, K. M., and Schkade, D. (2005). Pursuing Happiness: The Architecture of Sustainable Change. *Review of General Psychology.* 9: 111-131.

24. Ibid.

25. Piliavin, J. A. (2003). "Doing Well By Doing Good: Benefits for the Benefactor" in C. L. M. Keyes, and J. Haidt (Eds.). *Flourishing: Positive Psychology and the Life Well-Lived* (pp. 227-247). Washington DC:APA.

26. US Department of Labor (2016): http://www.bls.gov/news.release/volun.nr0.htm

27. Windsor, T. D., Anstey, K. J., and Rodgers, B. (2008). Volunteering and Psychological Well-Being among Young-Old Adults: How Much Is Too Much?. *Gerontologist.* 48: 59-70.

28. Luoh, M-C., and Herzog, A. R. (2002). Individual Consequences of Volunteer and Paid Work in Old Age: Health and Mortality. *Journal of Health and Social Behaviour.* 43: 490-509.

29. Lum, T. Y. and Lightfoot, E. (2005). The Effects of Volunteering on the Physical and Mental Health of Older People. *Research on Ageing.* 27: 31-55.

30. http://drdavidhamilton.com/category/oxytocin/

31. https://drdavidhamilton.com/the-5-side-effects-of-kindness-2/

32. https://greatergood.berkeley.edu/article/item/how_our_bodies_react_human_goodness

33. Algoe, S., and Haidt, J. (2009). Witnessing Excellence in Action: The 'Other-Praising' Emotions of Elevation, Gratitude, and Admiration. *Journal of Positive Psychology.* 4: 105–127.

34. https://www.sciencedaily.com/releases/2010/03/100308151049.htm

35. Lutz, A., Brefczynski-Lewis, J. A., Johnstone, T., and Davidson, R. J. (2008). Voluntary Regulation of the Neural Circuitry of Emotion by Compassion Meditation: Effects of Expertise. *PLoS One.* 3:e1897.

36. Ferriss, T. (2016). *Tools Of Titans.* London: Vermillion.

37. Lyubomirsky, S. (2007). *The How of Happiness.* London: Piatkus.

38. Ferriss, T. (2016). *Tools Of Titans.* London: Vermillion.

39. Sharma, R. (2010). *The Leader Who Had No Title.* London: Simon & Schuster.

40. Willink, J., and Babin, L. (2017). *Extreme Ownership: How U.S. Navy SEALs Lead and Win.* New York: St. Martins.

41. Nelson Mandela On Oprah Winfrey Show: https://www.youtube.com/watch?v=cMl1lBPHp0o&t=139s

42. Sinek, S. (2017). *Leaders Eat Last: Why Some Teams Pull Together and Others Don't.* London: Penguin.

43. Ibid.

44. https://www.youtube.com/watch?v=V2ZlYy99QX4

45. http://www.apaexcellence.org/assets/general/2016-work-and-wellbeing-survey-results.pdf.

46. https://www.forbes.com/sites/davidsturt/2018/03/08/10-shocking-workplace-stats-you-need-to-know/#78a447d3f3af.

47. Breuning, L. G. (2016). *Habits of a Happy Brain.* Avon: Adams Media.

48. Burchard, B. (2009). *The Student Leadership Guide.* New York: Morgan James.

49. Sinek, S. (2017). *Leaders Eat Last: Why Some Teams Pull Together and Others Don't.* London: Penguin.

50. Burchard, B. (2009). *The Student Leadership Guide.* New York: Morgan James.

51. Simon Sinek | TED | Start With Why: How Great Leaders Inspire Action: https://www.youtube.com/watch?v=qp0HIF3SfI4

52. Ibid.

53. Ferguson, A. and Moritz, M. (2015). *Leading.* London: Hodder & Stoughton.

35595796R00240

Printed in Poland
by Amazon Fulfillment
Poland Sp. z o.o., Wrocław